P9-CFZ-140

Microsoft® Publisher 2007:
Essentials

Sharon Milanos
Electronic Medical Records Corporate Trainer,
Tamarack Management, Inc. (Western Montana Clinic)

LABYRINTH
L E A R N I N G ™

Microsoft Publisher 2007: Essentials
by Sharon Milanos

Copyright © 2008 by Labyrinth Learning

LABYRINTH
L E A R N I N G ™

Labyrinth Learning
PO Box 20820
El Sobrante, California 94803
800.522.9746
On the Web at labpub.com

President:
Brian Favro

Chief Operating Officer:
Ted Ricks

Acquisitions Editor:
Jason Favro

Series Editor:
Russel Stolins

Managing Editor:
Laura A. Lionello

Production Manager:
Rad Proctor

Editorial/Production Team:
Amy Berk, Karen Henry, Jill Murphy,
and Kevin Schweitzer

Indexing: Joanne Sprott

Cover Design:
Seventeenth Street Studios

All rights reserved. Printed in the United States of America. No part of this material protected by this copyright notice may be reproduced or utilized in any form or by any means, electronic or mechanical, including photocopying, recording, scanning, or by information storage and retrieval systems without written permission from the copyright owner.

No part of this publication may be reproduced or transmitted in any form or by any means without the prior written permission from the publisher.

Labyrinth Learning™ and the Labyrinth Learning logo are registered trademarks of Labyrinth Publications. Microsoft®, Outlook®, PowerPoint®, and Windows® are registered trademarks of Microsoft Corporation. Other product and company names mentioned herein may be the trademarks of their respective owners.

The example companies, organizations, products, people, and events depicted herein are fictitious.

No association with any real company, organization, product, person, or event is intended or should be inferred.

Screen shots reprinted with permission from Microsoft Corporation.

ITEM: 1-59136-126-5
ISBN-13: 978-1-59136-126-8

Manufactured in the United States of America.

10 9 8 7 6 5 4 3

Microsoft Publisher 2007:
Essentials

Contents in Brief

Table of Contents

Summary of Quick Reference Tables

Web Site Tasks

Keyboard Shortcut Summary

Document Commands

Check spelling	F7
Close	Ctrl + F4
Print	Ctrl + P
Save	Ctrl + S
Select all	Ctrl + A
Toggle object borders on and off	Ctrl + Shift + O
Exit	Alt + F4

Editing Commands

Bold	Ctrl + B
Copy	Ctrl + C
Cut	Ctrl + X
Italic	Ctrl + I
Paste	Ctrl + V
Underline	Ctrl + U
Undo	Ctrl + Z
Redo	Ctrl + Y

Preface

What Is Covered: *Microsoft® Publisher 2007: Essentials* is a complete survey of Microsoft Publisher. In Unit 1, students deal with basic skills. Topics covered include an introduction to Publisher, creating and editing text boxes, inserting and manipulating graphics, drawing objects, and creating e-mail publications. In Unit 2, students expand on the knowledge they gained in the previous unit as they deal with more complex Publisher tasks. Topics introduced include creating Business Information Sets, using the Format Painter, creating newsletters, using autoflow, creating mail merges, creating and formatting tables and calendars, and designing and creating web sites.

This book is also available in two Briefcase editions. *Microsoft Publisher 2007: Level 1* is composed of Lessons 1–5 and *Microsoft Publisher 2007: Level 2* is composed of Lessons 6–10.

What Is Different: For more than a decade, Labyrinth has been working to perfect our unique instructional design. The benefit of our approach is that learning is faster and easier for students. Instructors have found that our approach works well in self-paced, instructor-led, and "blended" learning environments. The Labyrinth approach has many key features, including the following:

■ *Concise concept discussions* followed by Hands-On exercises that give students experience with those concepts right away.

■ *Figures are always* in close context with the text so no figure numbers are necessary.

■ *Quick Reference* sections summarize key tasks with generic steps that will work without repeating an exercise. These can be particularly useful during open-book tests.

■ *Hands-On exercises* are carefully written and repeatedly tested to be absolutely reliable. Many exercise steps are illustrated with figures to make them easier to follow.

■ *Skill Builder exercises* provide additional practice on key skills using less detailed exercise steps as the student progresses through the lesson.

We are now expanding our book list by adapting this approach to teaching other application programs, including Intuit® QuickBooks®, Adobe Photoshop Elements®, Macromedia® Dreamweaver®, digital photography, and more.

Comprehensive Support: This course is also supported on the Labyrinth website with a comprehensive instructor support package that includes detailed lesson plans, PowerPoint presentations, a course syllabus, extensive test banks, and more. Our unique WebSims allow students to perform realistic exercises with the web, email, and application program tasks that be difficult to set up in a computer lab.

We are grateful to the many teachers who have used Labyrinth titles and suggested improvements to us during the 10 years we have been writing and publishing books. *Microsoft Publisher 2007: Essentials* has benefited greatly from the reviewing and suggestions of Deborah Call, Lane CC (Eugene, OR); Kathy Krueger, Fox Valley Technical College (Oshkosh, WI); Harriett Pollock, Clovis Adult Education (Clovis, CA); Pamela Thomas, Urbana Adult Education (Urbana, IL); Patty Wells, Mt. Hood CC (Portland, OR); and Diane Wilson, Fairfield-Suisun Adult Education (Fairfield, CA).

How This Book Is Organized

The information in this book is presented so that you master the fundamental skills first, and then build on those skills as you work with the more comprehensive topics.

Visual Conventions

This book uses many visual and typographic cues to guide you through the lessons. This page provides examples and describes the function of each cue.

Type this text
Anything you should type at the keyboard is printed in this typeface.

 TIP!
Tips, Notes, and Warnings are used throughout the text to draw attention to certain topics.

Command→
Command
This convention indicates multiple selections to be made from the menu bar. For example, File→Save means to select File, and then to select Save.

FROM THE KEYBOARD
Ctrl+S to save
These margin notes indicate shortcut keys for executing a task described in the text.

 QR >
Quick Reference tables provide generic instructions for key tasks. Only perform these tasks if you are instructed to do so in an exercise.

 On the Web
This icon indicates the availability of a web-based simulation for an exercise or other online content. You many need to use a WebSim if your computer lab is not set up to support particular exercises.

Hands-On exercises are introduced immediately after concept discussions. They provide detailed, step-by-step tutorials so you can master the skills presented.

The Concepts Review section includes both true/false and multiple choice questions designed to gauge your understanding of concepts.

Skill Builder exercises provide additional hands-on practice with moderate assistance.

Assessment exercises test your skills by describing the correct results without providing specific instructions on how to achieve them.

Critical Thinking exercises are the most challenging. They provide generic instructions, allowing you to use your skills and creativity to achieve the result you envision.

About the Author

Sharon Milanos (BS, Business Information and Computer Systems) has a wealth of experience in teaching, training management, technical support, curricula development, and training trainers in a corporate environment. She spent the first 16 years of her career working at the IBM Corporation in technical support, systems engineering, and computer sales. Sharon now has more than 15 years of experience teaching computer software in training centers, California government agencies, and a number of large corporations and law firms. She has written many courseware training manuals for corporations and law firms. Currently, Sharon is employed at a large medical clinic in Missoula, Montana, where she writes electronic medical records courseware training manuals as well as teaches doctors and staff how to use this software. Sharon has two lovely daughters and enjoys the country life in Montana with her partner, Ben.

Microsoft Publisher 2007:
Essentials

Unit 1

Basic Skills

In this unit, you will begin your exploration of Microsoft Office Publisher 2007, which allows you to create invitations, flyers, holiday newsletters, greeting cards, web sites, and much more. You will begin by creating a Quick Publication flyer. As you create additional publications, you will learn how to create, move, delete, and resize text boxes. You will also cut, copy, and paste text; add bullets; change font types, sizes, and colors; apply borders and fills; and use Publisher's proofreading tools. You will also insert clip art and pictures, create and format WordArt, add BorderArt objects, and insert drop caps. Next you will work with Publisher's Drawing tools by creating lines, rectangles, and ovals. You will also create complex AutoShapes and add 3-D effects and shadows. Finally, in this unit you will create an e-mail letter complete with a heading, a greeting, a closing, a signature box, and hyperlinks.

Lesson 1: Creating a Flyer

Lesson 2: Creating an Invitation Using Text Boxes

Lesson 3: Adding Interest with Graphics

Lesson 4: Drawing Directions in a Flyer

Lesson 5: Creating an E-mail Letter

Creating a Flyer

Microsoft Office Publisher 2007 is an easy-to-use publishing program that you can use to create business as well as personal publications. You don't need any prior desktop publishing experience to easily create professional-looking marketing and communication publications. For home use, you can create invitations, flyers, holiday newsletters, cards, signs, and so much more. At work you can create publications such as business cards, stationery, brochures, catalogs, newsletters, gift certificates, and more. You can even create your own web site. In this lesson, you will create a Quick Publication flyer and learn related skills.

LESSON OBJECTIVES

After studying this lesson, you will be able to:

- Navigate in Publisher
- Create a simple Quick Publication flyer
- Edit a simple flyer
- Save a publication
- Print a publication

Case Study: Fundraising with Publisher 2007

Andie Milanos has just volunteered to create a flyer for her good friend's school fundraiser. This fundraiser is a hugely successful community bake sale held each year, and it attracts many local businesses and families. Proceeds from the school fundraiser help finance college scholarships for the students. Andie would like to create flyers for the bake sale that will be distributed and posted in many downtown businesses on Laurel Street.

Andie recently retired from her career as school principal at an elementary school in San Francisco. She has wanted to start creating publications since her daughter introduced her to Publisher 2007 several months ago. Andie is pleasantly surprised at the many Publisher 2007 design choices she has to create her flyer.

Publisher offers numerous choices of quick publication flyer formats.

Introducing Publisher 2007

Microsoft Office Publisher 2007 is one of the easiest publishing programs to use and master. In no time at all, you can create, design, and publish professional-looking marketing and communication publications for home and for work. Publisher offers many design templates to help you quickly begin your publications. The templates also provide innovative design ideas.

Why Use Publisher?

The advantage of using Microsoft Publisher over other programs is that you don't need prior experience with publishing programs to quickly create professional publications either for your organization or for personal use. Publisher provides a number of important benefits and features that make it a good choice.

- **Ease of Use:** Publisher offers a wide variety of easy-to-use design templates that allow you to quickly create, design, and publish your professional-looking publications for business or commercial print, web, and e-mail.

- **Extensive Choice of Publications:** Select from an extensive collection of both business and home publications including professionally designed greeting and invitation cards, personal stationery sets, newsletters, flyers, brochures, business cards, programs, gift certificates, labels, and so many more.

- **Web Integration:** Publisher 2007 lets you easily publish your publications to the World Wide Web or to your company intranet. You can quickly create a polished, professional web site using one of Publisher's Web Sites wizards.

- **E-mail Publications:** You can create professional-looking, company-branded e-mail messages that have the same high-quality look and design as your print publications. Your e-mail messages can include your newsletter, featured product, flyer, event, etc.

- **Integration with Other Office Programs:** Publisher 2007 is part of the Microsoft Office 2007 suite of programs, which includes Outlook, PowerPoint, Excel, and Word. The ability to exchange data with these programs is one of the most powerful features of Publisher.

- **Publisher Compared with Word:** You can create publications using Word, but it can take much longer. Unlike Word, Publisher has an extensive catalog of publication templates to help you get a quick start creating your publications. These templates also provide design ideas that you may not have thought of on your own.

Starting Publisher

There are several techniques you can use to start Publisher:

- **Win XP:** Choose Start→All Programs→Microsoft Office→Microsoft Office Publisher 2007.

- **Win Vista:** Choose Start→All Programs→Microsoft Office→Microsoft Office Publisher 2007.

- **Publisher Desktop Icon:** This button many not appear on all computers.

- **Quick Launch Toolbar Publisher Icon:** This button may not appear on all computers.

Hands-On 1.1   **Start Publisher**

In this exercise, you will launch Publisher and become familiar with Publisher's window.

1. Click the ![start] button and choose (Win XP) All Programs or (Win Vista) Programs.

2. Launch the program according to either of the following bulleted steps:
   - ■ **Win XP:** Choose Microsoft Office Publisher 2007 from the All Programs menu.
   - ■ **Win Vista:** Choose Microsoft Office Publisher 2007 from the All Programs menu.

   The Microsoft Office Publisher window appears. Publisher displays the Publication Types list to help you get started with common publications such as Greeting Cards.

My Templates is a catalog of favorite template publications that are saved in a template folder.

You can also start a publication by choosing from many categories of publication design templates in the Publication Types list.

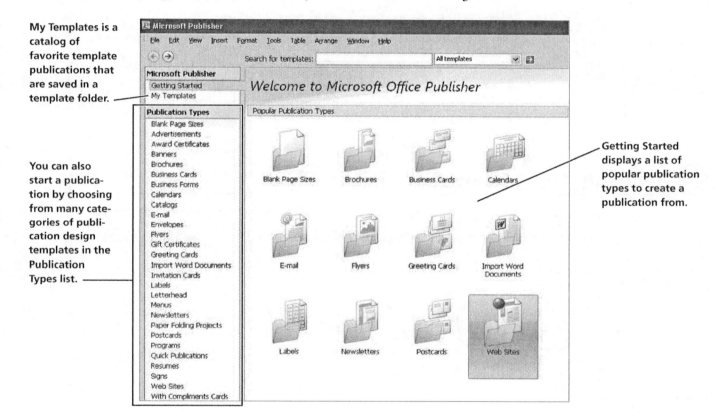

Getting Started displays a list of popular publication types to create a publication from.

Navigating the Publication Types List

Navigating to a publication from the Publication Types list is easy. The list displays categories of many publications with designs for the chosen publication displayed to the right. Choose a category, such as Greeting Cards, then choose a type of card such as Birthday or Holiday, and then choose a specific card design. You can also start a new blank publication or open an existing publication.

A publication type such as Greeting Cards...

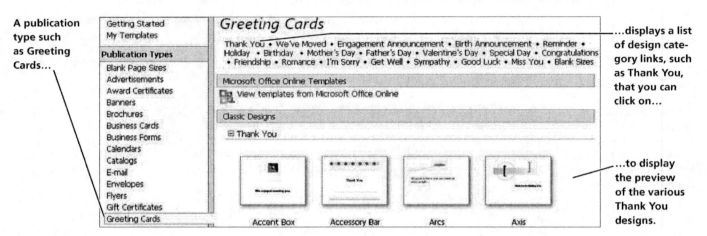

...displays a list of design category links, such as Thank You, that you can click on...

...to display the preview of the various Thank You designs.

Hands-On 1.2   Navigate to Publications

In this exercise, you will practice navigating to various publications in the Publication Types list.

1. Follow these steps to practice displaying the various publication design format choices:

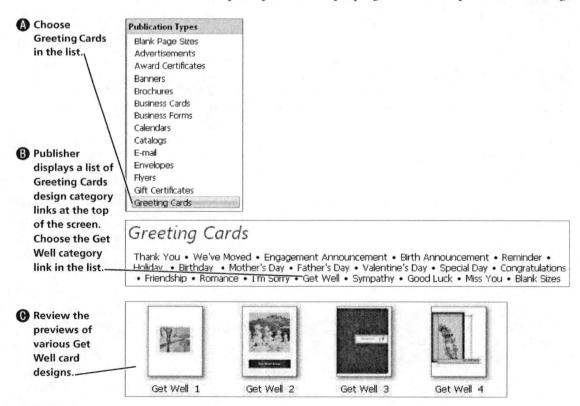

A Choose Greeting Cards in the list.

B Publisher displays a list of Greeting Cards design category links at the top of the screen. Choose the Get Well category link in the list.

C Review the previews of various Get Well card designs.

You will create your first new publication shortly.

Creating a Flyer

The Publication Types list offers many publication categories with which you can start a publication. The Quick Publications category is one of the quickest ways to begin a publication.

Choosing a Quick Publication

The Quick Publications category displays single-sheet, easy-to-create generic publications that can be used to get a quick start creating flyers, posters, invitations, etc. They are ideal for the novice and they offer design ideas that you may not have thought of on your own.

If you like, you can start a publication with a blank design.

When the Quick Publications category is chosen, it displays different designs to the right of the Publication Types list.

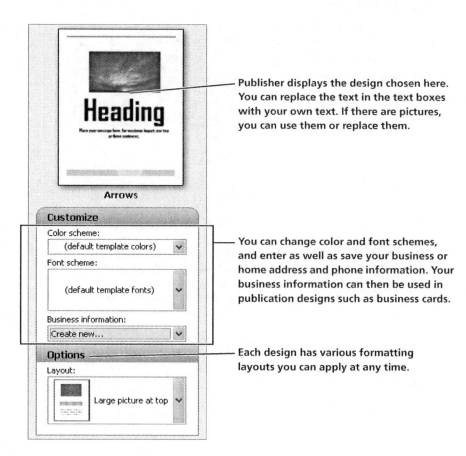

Publisher displays the design chosen here. You can replace the text in the text boxes with your own text. If there are pictures, you can use them or replace them.

You can change color and font schemes, and enter as well as save your business or home address and phone information. Your business information can then be used in publication designs such as business cards.

Each design has various formatting layouts you can apply at any time.

⚠ **NOTE!** *You will learn more about business information in Lesson 6, Creating Business Publications.*

Choosing a Different Layout

Each flyer design comes with a default layout that includes size and position of text, pictures, and color borders. You can change this layout at any time if you like.

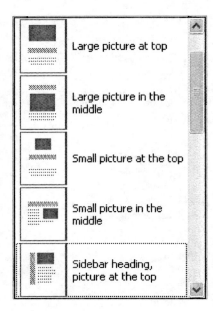

Large picture at top

Large picture in the middle

Small picture at the top

Small picture in the middle

Sidebar heading, picture at the top

Publisher has a variety of design layouts. A different design layout can be applied at any time to your publication.

Choosing a Color Scheme

A color scheme is a collection of colors designed to work well together. When you create a publication, a default collection of colors are chosen for you. You can, however, change to a different color scheme at any time.

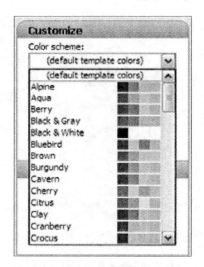

Publisher displays many color schemes to choose from. A different color scheme can be applied at any time when creating your publication.

Choosing a Font Scheme

A font scheme is a collection of fonts that work well together. When you create a publication, a default font scheme is chosen for you. You can, however, change to a different font scheme at any time.

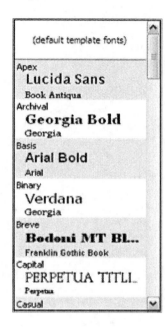

Publisher has many font schemes. A different font scheme can be applied at any time to the text in your publication.

QUICK REFERENCE: CREATING A QUICK PUBLICATION

Task	Procedure
Create a new quick publication	<ul><li>Choose Getting Started in the Microsoft Publisher task pane.</li><li>Choose Quick Publications under Publication Types.</li><li>Choose the New Designs or Classic Designs link at the top of the screen.</li><li>Choose one of the design layouts or choose a different layout under Options.</li><li>Choose a different color or font scheme under Customize.</li><li>Click the Create button to display the text editing window.</li></ul>

In this exercise, you will create a flyer based on the Pansies Quick Publication format.

1. Click Quick Publications in the Publication Types list.
   The Quick Publications design formats are displayed in the center pane.

2. Click the Classic Designs category link at the top of the screen.
   This scrolls the center pane down to the list of Classic Design thumbnail images.

3. Follow these steps to scroll down and open the Pansies publication design:

Ⓐ Drag the elevator bar down until the Pansies Quick Publication appears. (They are listed in alphabetical order.)

Ⓑ Click once on the Pansies Quick Publication design.

The Pansies Quick Publication design appears in the right pane along with its color scheme, font scheme, and layout designs.

Change the Layout

Each flyer design comes with a default layout that includes size and position of text, pictures, and color borders. You can change this layout at any time if you like.

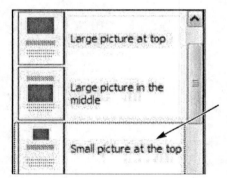

4. Click the drop down arrow in layout options to display a list of layout designs.

5. Choose the Small Picture at the Top layout, as shown at right.
   Publisher immediately applies the new layout setting to the Pansies design in the right pane. Notice that the large picture has changed to a small picture.

Change the Color and Font Schemes

Each flyer design comes with a default color and font scheme that you can change at any time.

6. Follow these steps to change the color scheme:

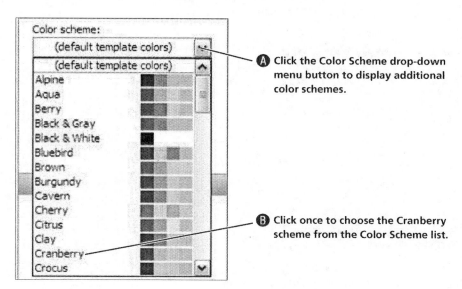

A Click the Color Scheme drop-down menu button to display additional color schemes.

B Click once to choose the Cranberry scheme from the Color Scheme list.

Publisher immediately applies the new color scheme to the borders of your publication.

7. Follow these steps to change the font scheme:

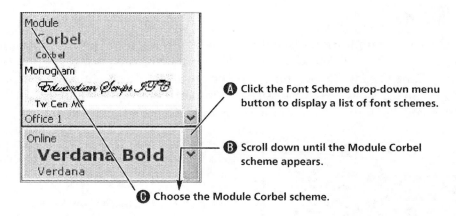

A Click the Font Scheme drop-down menu button to display a list of font schemes.

B Scroll down until the Module Corbel scheme appears.

C Choose the Module Corbel scheme.

Publisher immediately applies the new font scheme to your publication.

Create the Flyer

You are now ready to create the flyer.

8. Click the Create button located below the Layout design options.
Publisher opens the flyer into a text editing window.

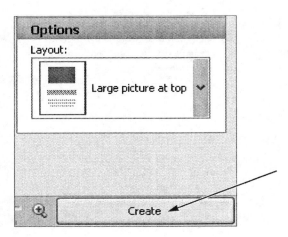

You are now ready to enter your text for the flyer.

Entering Text

When you create a publication (except for a blank one), sample text appears showing where you should type your text. These text samples are called *text objects,* or more commonly, *text boxes.* To replace the contents of a text box, click to select the text and then type over it. Selected text appears in reverse colors (for example, white on black instead of black on white). As you type your text, it will automatically wrap to fit into the text box.

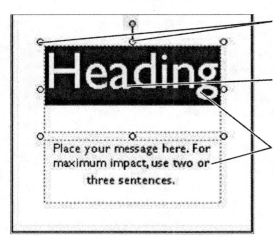

Notice the little circles around the perimeter of the box, called handles. They indicate that the text box is selected, and allow you to alter its shape and location.

This sample Heading text box is selected and is ready to be replaced with your text. The selected text appears in reverse colors (for example, white on black instead of black on white).

These are samples of two text objects, or text boxes. They show you where you should type your text. Notice the dotted lines around the perimeter of the boxes. You can keep or delete the text boxes and you can add new text boxes where needed.

QUICK REFERENCE: ENTERING TEXT IN A PUBLICATION

Task	Procedure
Enter text	■ Click anywhere on the text in a text box to select it.
	■ Type the new text to replace the sample text.
	■ Notice that the text will wrap automatically to fit into the text box.

 Hands-On 1.4   **Enter Text in a Flyer**

In this exercise, you will enter text in several text boxes in the publication.

1. Click anywhere on the Heading text box.
   Publisher selects the heading text box. Notice the handles around the edges of the text box, indicating your selection.

2. Type **Annual Bake Sale for Chocolate Lovers.**
   Your text replaces the sample text. Notice that as you type your text changes to fit into the text box.

3. Click the "Place your message…" text in the text box.

NOTE! *If a tip appears about using* Ctrl + A *to select all, click on the tip to dismiss it.*

Publisher selects the text box. Notice that the text is selected and that there are handles around the box.

4. Type the text shown in the message box in the following illustration, tapping Enter at the end of each line except the last one.

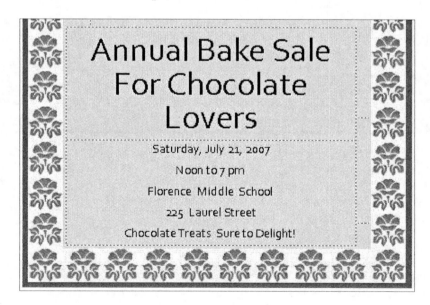

5. Click anywhere outside of the text box to deselect the text box.
   In just a few simple steps, you have a nicely laid out flyer!

Saving Publications

FROM THE KEYBOARD

Ctrl + S to save

It is important to save your publications frequently due to possible accidents or power outages resulting in lost data. It is a good idea to save your publications every 10 minutes or so after making changes. Documents are saved to various storage locations such as hard disks, USB flash drives, floppy disks, or the Internet.

The Save Command

If the publication has been saved previously, then Publisher replaces the previous version with the new, edited version. If the publication has never been saved, then Publisher displays the Save As dialog box. The Save As dialog box lets you pick the name and storage location of the new publication. You can also use the Save As dialog box to make a copy of a document by saving it with a new name or to a different location. You can use filenames with a maximum of 255 characters. The following illustration describes the Save As dialog box.

You can quickly choose a storage location from the Save In drop-down list.

The Create New Folder button allows you to create new folders from within Publisher.

The Views button allows you to change the file display.

This bar displays frequently used storage locations.

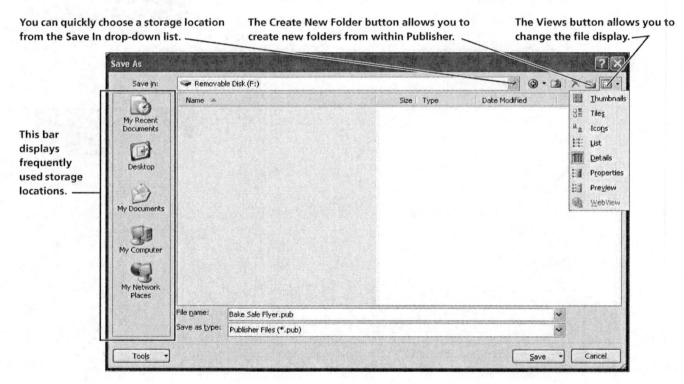

Publisher's AutoRecover Feature

When you enable the Save AutoRecover Info Every option, Publisher creates a temporary AutoRecover file that includes the latest changes in your document. This file is updated at the end of each preset period.

Publisher creates this AutoRecover file so that the file will be available when you restart Publisher in the event your computer shuts down unexpectedly. Each time you start Publisher, the program searches your computer for these temporary AutoRecover files and automatically opens them. Then, you can permanently preserve your work by saving the publication with a new name.

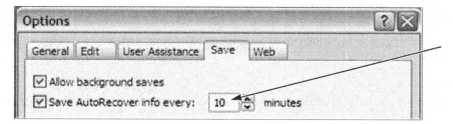

The default time that is set to save changes to the AutoRecover file is every 10 minutes. You can either increase or decrease this time interval.

QUICK REFERENCE: USING AUTORECOVER

Task	Procedure
Turn on AutoRecover	■ Choose Tools→Options from the menu bar.
	■ Choose the Save tab.
	■ Check the Save AutoRecover Info Every box.
	■ If desired, change the minutes in the Save AutoRecover Info Every box.
Recover a publication	■ Open Publisher. Publisher displays the file and the document title bar displays the filename of the publication as [filename] (Recovered).
	■ Choose the file to recover from the task pane.
	■ Choose File→Save As to save the recovered publication with a new filename.

Storing Your Exercise Files

Throughout this book you will be referred to files in a folder that corresponds to the lesson number you are studying (for example, the "Lesson 02 folder"). You can store your exercise files on various media such as a USB flash drive, the My Documents folder, or a network drive at a school or company. While some figures may display files on a USB flash drive, it is assumed that you will substitute your own location for that shown in the figure. See Appendix A, Storing Your Exercise Files for additional information on alternative file storage media.

QUICK REFERENCE: SAVING A PUBLICATION

Task	Procedure
Save a publication	■ Click the Save button on the Standard (top) toolbar or choose the File→Save command.

Hands-On 1.5   Save Your Flyer

In this exercise, you will save your flyer.

Before You Begin: *If you have not done so already, please turn to Downloading the Student Exercise Files section of Appendix A, Storing Your Exercise Files for instructions on how to retrieve the student exercise files for this book from the Labyrinth web site and for copying the files to your file storage location for use in this and future lessons.*

1. Click the Save button.
   Publisher displays the Save As dialog box since this is the first time you are saving this publication.

2. Follow these steps to save your flyer:

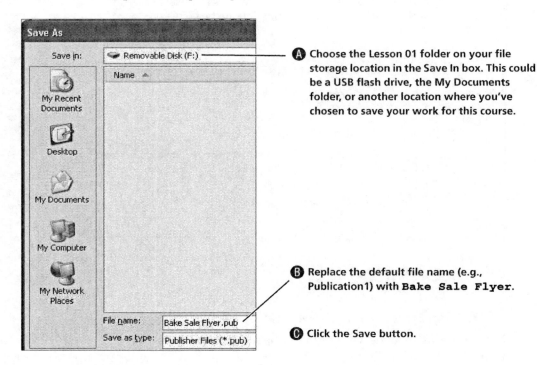

Ⓐ Choose the Lesson 01 folder on your file storage location in the Save In box. This could be a USB flash drive, the My Documents folder, or another location where you've chosen to save your work for this course.

Ⓑ Replace the default file name (e.g., Publication1) with **Bake Sale Flyer**.

Ⓒ Click the Save button.

Publisher saves your publication to your file storage location and leaves it displayed on the screen. You will continue working on the flyer throughout this lesson.

Printing Your Publication

When a publication is complete, you can print it to have a paper copy as a reference. You can also print specific pages from a publication that are not complete so that you can review them or work on them when you are not at a computer, such as one page of a 10-page newsletter. Before you print a publication, you should use Print Preview to make sure that it looks the way you would like it to.

Print Preview

You can save time and paper by viewing a publication in Print Preview prior to printing.

 TIP! *It is always a good idea to preview your publication before sending it to the printer.*

When you display the Print Preview window, the normal toolbars are replaced by the Print Preview toolbar. The following illustration describes two of the buttons on the Print Preview toolbar.

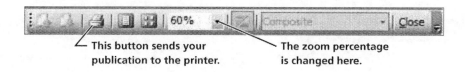

This button sends your publication to the printer.

The zoom percentage is changed here.

The Print Dialog Box

FROM THE KEYBOARD

Ctrl + P to print

When you print a publication, a printer icon appears in the system tray at the right end of the taskbar. The Printer icon indicates that Publisher is processing the print job and is preparing to send the job to the printer. The following illustration explains two useful options on the Print dialog box.

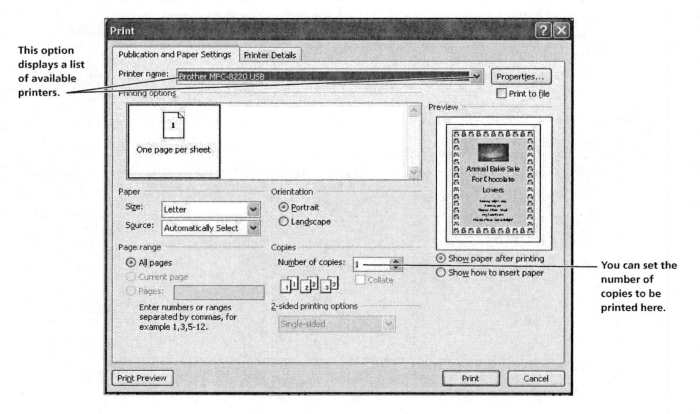

This option displays a list of available printers.

You can set the number of copies to be printed here.

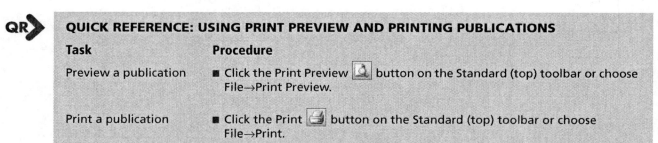

QUICK REFERENCE: USING PRINT PREVIEW AND PRINTING PUBLICATIONS

Task	Procedure
Preview a publication	■ Click the Print Preview 🔍 button on the Standard (top) toolbar or choose File→Print Preview.
Print a publication	■ Click the Print 🖨 button on the Standard (top) toolbar or choose File→Print.

Hands-On 1.6   Use Print Preview and Print a Publication

In this exercise, you will examine the Print Preview command and print your publication.

Use Print Preview

1. Click the Print Preview 🔍 button on the toolbar.

2. Position the mouse pointer over the flyer, and the pointer will look like a magnifying 🔍 glass.

3. Click once to zoom the flyer to 100 percent zoom.
   On most computer screens, only part of the flyer will be visible at this zoom level.

4. Click once again to zoom the flyer back to display the whole page.

5. Click the Close button on the Print Preview toolbar to exit Print Preview.

Publisher returns you to the normal view of the publication.

Print the Flyer

6. Choose File→Print from the menu bar to display the Print dialog box.
   Notice the various dialog box options.

7. Click the Print button to send your publication to your printer.

8. Retrieve your publication from the printer.
   Congratulations! You've just created and printed your first Publisher publication.

Closing a Publication and Exiting Publisher

When you close a publication, Publisher prompts you to save the changes. If you choose Yes at the prompt and the publication has previously been saved, then Publisher saves the changes. If the publication has not yet been saved, Publisher displays the Save As dialog box, where you can name your publication and specify a storage location.

FROM THE KEYBOARD
Ctrl+F4 to close a publication

You should exit Publisher and other programs when you are finished using them. This frees up memory for other programs.

Exiting from Publisher

You can use the File→Exit command or the Close ☒ button to exit Publisher. You should exit Publisher and other programs when you are finished using them. This frees up memory for other programs. When you close Publisher, it will prompt you to save any publications that were modified since they were last saved.

FROM THE KEYBOARD
Alt+F4 to exit Publisher

QUICK REFERENCE: CLOSING A PUBLICATION AND EXITING PUBLISHER

Task	Procedure
Close a publication	■ Choose File→Close.
Exit Publisher	■ Click the Close ☒ button on the Standard (top) toolbar or choose File→Exit.

Hands-On 1.7   Close a Flyer and Exit Publisher

In this exercise, you will close your publication, saving your changes. Then you will exit from Publisher.

Close the Flyer

1. Choose File→Close from the menu bar.
   You may see a prompt if you've made any changes to the publication since your most recent Save command.

2. Choose Yes if Publisher asks you to save the changes.
   You can close without saving the changes to eliminate changes that you have made since the last save.

Exit from Publisher

3. Click the Close ☒ button on the Publisher window.
   Publisher will close and the Windows Desktop will appear. Continue with the end-of-lesson exercises on the following pages.

Concepts Review

Key these hand in printout

True/False Questions

1. One of the categories on the Publication Types list is Greeting Cards. TRUE FALSE

2. You can apply a different design layout any time after creating a publication. TRUE FALSE

3. When you create a publication, a default font scheme is chosen for you. TRUE FALSE

4. Selected text in a text box appears in reverse colors (i.e., black text appears white). TRUE FALSE

5. When typing text in a text box, the text automatically wraps to the width of the text box. TRUE FALSE

6. You can tell if a text box is selected when you see small circles around the perimeter of the box. TRUE FALSE

7. AutoRecover is set to save every 10 minutes and cannot be changed. TRUE FALSE

8. You cannot print specific pages in a publication. TRUE FALSE

9. It is a good idea to view a publication with the Print Preview command prior to printing. TRUE FALSE

10. It is a good idea to exit Publisher when you are finished creating your publication. TRUE FALSE

Multiple Choice Questions

1. Which of the following is not true about Publisher?
   a. Easy to use
   b. Integrates with Word and Outlook
   c. Can create a web site
   d. Cannot create e-mail messages

2. Which publication below cannot be created in Publisher?
   a. Business cards
   b. Flyers
   c. Banners
   d. Financial reports

3. How many times can you change the color scheme for a publication?
   a. One
   b. Two
   c. Three
   d. Unlimited

4. What are handles?
   a. I-beams that appear when you move the mouse pointer over text
   b. Circles that appear around the edge of a selected object
   c. Circles that mark the margins of the publication page
   d. Circles that appear before and after text

Skill Builders

Skill Builder 1.1   Create a Quick Publication Birthday Party Flyer

It's time to create another publication! In this exercise, you will create a flyer based on the Party Time publication.

Before You Begin: *If you did not exit Publisher at the end of the last exercise, then exit and restart Publisher.*

1. Choose Quick Publications in the Publication Types list and choose the Classic Designs link at the top of the screen.

2. Scroll down and choose the Party Time design.

3. In the Layout Options in the right-hand pane, click the drop-down arrow and choose Sidebar Heading, Picture at the Bottom.
   Publisher rearranges the content of the flyer according to the new layout.

4. In the Color Scheme area of the right-hand pane, click the drop-down arrow and choose the Meadow scheme from the list.

5. In the Font Scheme list, scroll to the bottom of the list, and then choose the Virtual Trebuchet MS scheme.

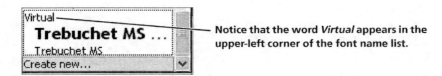

Notice that the word *Virtual* appears in the upper-left corner of the font name list.

6. Click the Create button at the bottom of the right-hand pane.
   You are now ready to add text to the flyer. The text will automatically resize to fit the space as more text is added.

!**TIP!** *Use Undo* 🔄 *if you make a mistake.*

7. Follow these steps to enter text in the flyer:

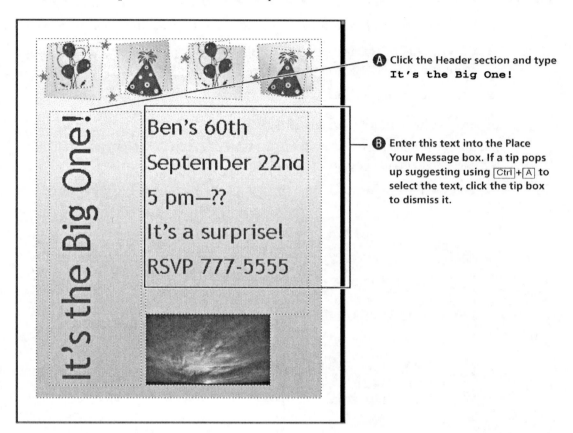

Ⓐ Click the Header section and type
It's the Big One!

Ⓑ Enter this text into the Place Your Message box. If a tip pops up suggesting using Ctrl+A to select the text, click the tip box to dismiss it.

8. Click Print Preview on the Standard toolbar.

9. Position the mouse pointer over the flyer so that the magnifying glass is visible, and then click to enlarge the flyer. Click again to zoom it back.

10. Close the Print Preview window.

11. Choose File→Print from the menu bar.

12. Click the Print button, and then retrieve the flyer from the printer.

13. Save the file as **Sb-Birthday Flyer** in your Lesson 01 folder, and then close it.

Skill Builder 1.2   Create a Business Card

In this exercise, you will create a business card that you can use in your new home-catering business.

1. Choose Business Cards from the Publication Types list, and then choose the Tabs design from the Newer Designs category in the center pane.

2. Click the Create button.

Change the Color and Font Schemes

You can use the Color Schemes option in the Format Publication task pane to change colors and the Font Schemes option to change to a different font.

3. Follow these steps to change the color scheme for the business card:

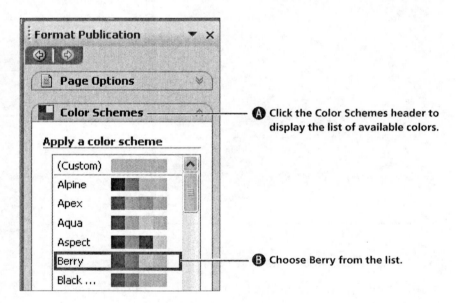

Ⓐ Click the Color Schemes header to display the list of available colors.

Ⓑ Choose Berry from the list.

4. Follow these steps to change the font:

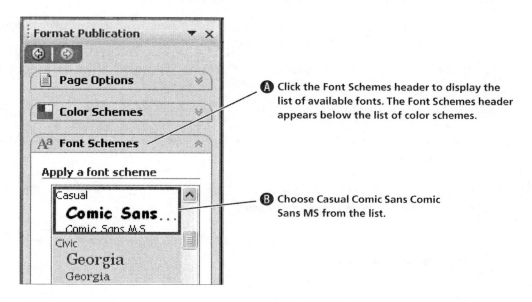

A Click the Font Schemes header to display the list of available fonts. The Font Schemes header appears below the list of color schemes.

B Choose Casual Comic Sans Comic Sans MS from the list.

Modify the Sample Text

5. Follow these steps to enter text in your business card:

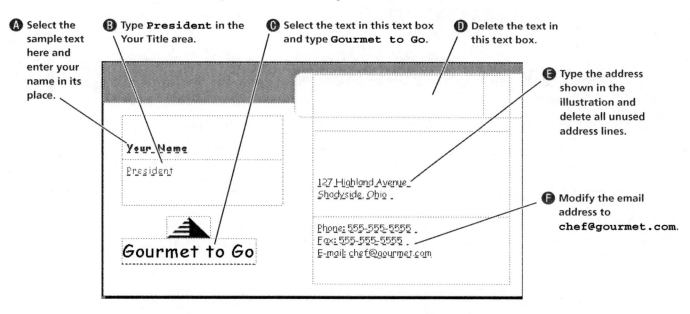

A Select the sample text here and enter your name in its place.

B Type **President** in the Your Title area.

C Select the text in this text box and type **Gourmet to Go**.

D Delete the text in this text box.

E Type the address shown in the illustration and delete all unused address lines.

F Modify the email address to **chef@gourmet.com**.

6. Click the Print Preview button on the toolbar, and then close Print Preview after observing the publication.

7. Save the file as **sb-Gourmet Business Card** in your Lesson 01 folder, and then close the file.

Skill Builder 1.3   Create an Award Certificate

In this exercise, you will create an award certificate to distribute to the students who complete your etiquette class. You will modify the text to meet your needs.

1. Choose Award Certificates from the Publication Types list on the left side of the screen, and then scroll down to Celtic Knotwork.

2. Double-click the Celtic Knotwork icon to open the certificate in the text editing window.

3. Select the Certificate of Appreciation heading and replace it with **Certificate of Completion.**

 TIP! *If you find the print in the sample text too small to read, use the zoom* *buttons on the toolbar to increase (plus sign) and decrease (minus sign) the magnification.*

4. Select the text shown in the following illustration and replace it with **To certify that they have completed.**

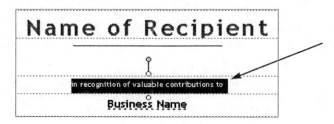

5. Select the Business Name text and replace it with **Etiquette for the 21st Century.**

6. Select the text below the pyramid graphic and type **December 4, 2007.**

7. Save the file as **sb-Award Certificate** in your Lesson 01 folder, and then close the file.

Assessments

Assessment 1.1 Create a Gift Certificate

In this exercise, you will create a gift certificate. You've decided to teach yoga classes in your home and you will use the gift certificates to entice new students.

1. Choose the Gift Certificates category and the Borders design.

2. In the right-hand pane, choose the Rain Forest color scheme and the Basis Arial Bold Arial font scheme.

3. Click the Create button.

4. Follow these steps to complete the certificate:

Ⓐ Type **The Yoga Studio** in both of these text boxes.

Ⓑ Add **the bearer** to the end of this text.

Ⓒ Type the following text after the word to: **2 FREE regularly-scheduled yoga classes.**

Ⓓ Type your name at the end of the text in this box.

Ⓔ Enter the following for the address: **311 Miller Avenue, Forest Grove, CA** on two lines as shown in the example. Delete any unneeded address lines.

Ⓕ Enter **December 31, 2007** as the expiration date.

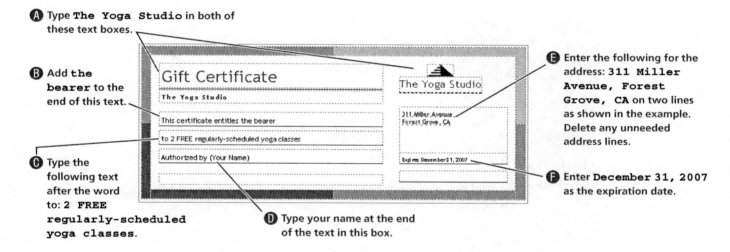

5. Save the file as **as-Yoga Certificate** in your Lesson 01 folder, and then close the file.

Assessment 1.2   Edit a Letterhead Publication

In this exercise, you will create a letterhead publication for the Arlington Senior Center. The center wants to spiff up its communications with its members by using nicely designed letterhead.

1. Choose the Letterhead category and the Brocade design.

2. Complete the letterhead as shown in the following illustration, deleting any unnecessary text boxes.

 TIP! *Remember that you can use the* *buttons or the* F9 *key to increase and decrease the magnification of the publication.*

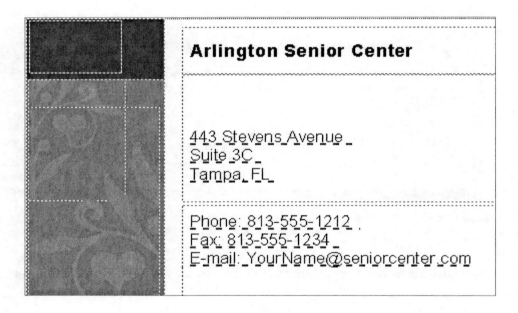

3. Save the letterhead as **as-Arlington Letterhead** in your Lesson 01 folder, and then close the file.

# Critical Thinking

Critical Thinking 1.1   Create an Opening Day Flyer

Sarah Katherine is helping out this week at the new Gardener's Delight nursery, which was started by her neighbor Jane. It is home to every gardening tool imaginable. Sarah would like to use Publisher to create a flyer announcing the grand opening. She will post the flyer in the various storefronts in town. In this exercise, you will help Sarah create her flyer.

1. Follow these guidelines to prepare a flyer announcing opening day:
   - Choose a flyer design from Quick Publications.
   - Choose a layout that best fits the announcement.
   - Choose your font and color scheme.
   - Choose a header that will catch people's attention.
   - Include the date, time, and location of the opening.
   - Add any other information that you feel enhances the flyer, and delete any unwanted text.

2. Save your completed flyer as **ct-Gardener's Delight** in your Lesson 01 folder, and then close it.

Critical Thinking 1.2   Create a Gift Certificate

Ben Hillicoss is President of the Civic Club, which is sponsoring a local dinner and dance fundraiser to pay off the loan for the new bike paths in and around Florence. Several local restaurants will provide Dinner for Two as door prizes. In this exercise, you will help Ben publish gift certificates for the door prize drawings.

1. Choose a gift certificate design you think will be best for the drawing.

2. Experiment with different font and color schemes.

3. Specify that the certificate entitles the bearer to Dinner for Two.

4. Include any other information you deem appropriate, and delete any text you do not want to use.

5. Save your publication as **ct-Restaurant Certificate** in your Lesson 01 folder, and then close it.

Creating an Invitation Using Text Boxes

In this lesson, you will expand upon the basic skills that you developed in the previous lesson. You will create a graduation invitation publication, where you will learn to create text boxes and enter text. You will also move, delete, and resize a text box. You will find that working with text inside text boxes is important and is very similar to working with text in Word. You will select, cut, copy, and paste text from one text box to another. You will add bullets; change fonts, font sizes, and font colors; and apply a border and fill color to your text box. And finally, you will work with Publisher's proofreading tools, spelling checker, and AutoCorrect.

LESSON OBJECTIVES

After studying this lesson, you will be able to:

- Create a text box and enter text
- Select, cut, copy, and delete text in a text box
- Add bullets and change the bullet style
- Format the text in the text box
- Apply a border, border color, and fill color
- Move and delete a text box
- Check spelling and use AutoCorrect

Case Study: Making Invitations Easy with Publisher

Sarah Hillicoss is eager to complete a graduation invitation for her daughter, who is graduating from college this year. Sarah knows that she has time to order invitations from a local stationery store, but she is confident that with Publisher, she can create a beautiful graduation invitation for her daughter and print them on her printer at home.

Sarah is somewhat familiar with Publisher. A few years back, she helped a friend create basic publications for her startup business. So she has some very basic Publisher skills, but she wants to enhance them. One area she would like to learn more about is creating and working with text boxes. She would also like to know how to use Publisher's proofreading tools.

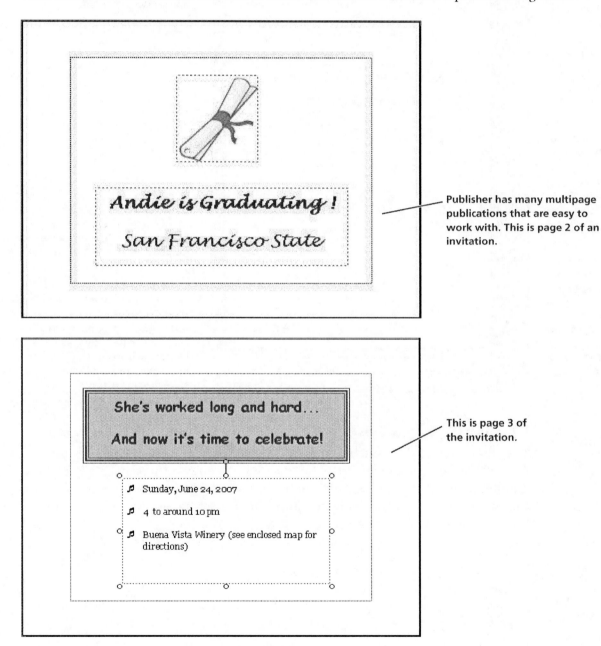

Publisher has many multipage publications that are easy to work with. This is page 2 of an invitation.

This is page 3 of the invitation.

Adding a Text Box

Many Publisher templates, such as invitations, consist of $8^1/_2 \times 11$ multiple pages that will be folded into a card. On these pages are text boxes already created with text inserted into them, as well as other objects such as pictures. At times you may want to create a new text box when you want to place a block of text in a spot where there is not already a text box.

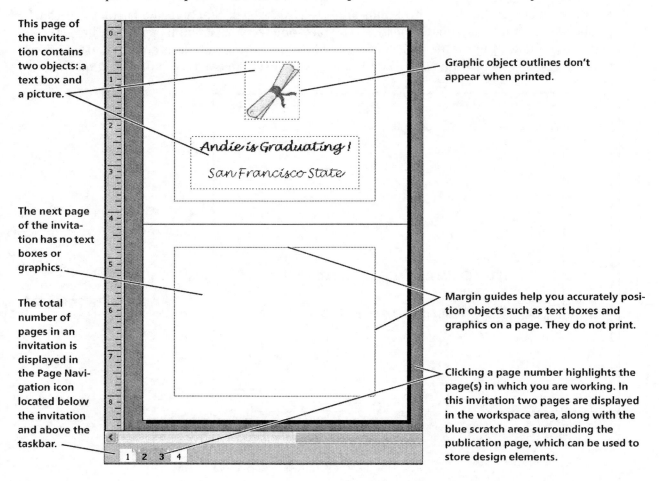

This page of the invitation contains two objects: a text box and a picture.

Graphic object outlines don't appear when printed.

Andie is Graduating !

San Francisco State

The next page of the invitation has no text boxes or graphics.

The total number of pages in an invitation is displayed in the Page Navigation icon located below the invitation and above the taskbar.

Margin guides help you accurately position objects such as text boxes and graphics on a page. They do not print.

Clicking a page number highlights the page(s) in which you are working. In this invitation two pages are displayed in the workspace area, along with the blue scratch area surrounding the publication page, which can be used to store design elements.

Creating a Text Box

A text box can hold as much text as you want, so there is no need to create a separate text box for each paragraph. Create a new text box when you want to separate one block of text from another. The following illustration points out the tool for creating text boxes, some features that help you work with text boxes, and a brief introduction to the task pane and the Formatting toolbar.

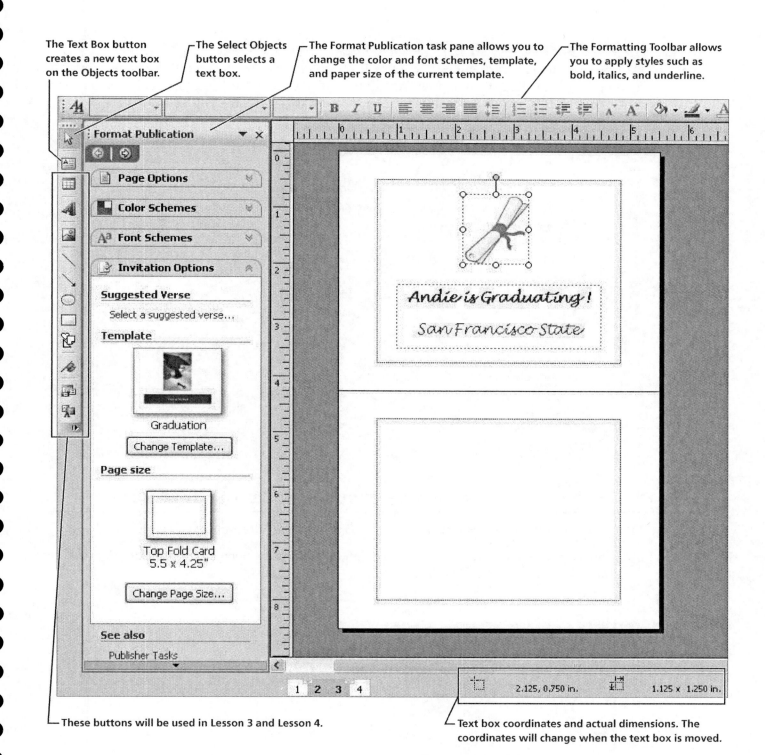

The Text Box button creates a new text box on the Objects toolbar.

The Select Objects button selects a text box.

The Format Publication task pane allows you to change the color and font schemes, template, and paper size of the current template.

The Formatting Toolbar allows you to apply styles such as bold, italics, and underline.

These buttons will be used in Lesson 3 and Lesson 4.

Text box coordinates and actual dimensions. The coordinates will change when the text box is moved.

Moving, Resizing, and Deleting a Text Box

At times you may want to move a text box if it's not in its right location. You can also resize a text box if it's too large or not large enough to hold your text. And you can easily delete a text box, whether it is built into the template or is one that you created yourself.

QUICK REFERENCE: CREATING A TEXT BOX

Task	Procedure
Create a text box	■ Click the Text Box button on the Objects toolbar. ■ Drag across the page, holding down the left mouse button, to create the text box. ■ Release the mouse button.
Move a text box	■ Position the mouse pointer over the text box border so that the Move pointer appears. ■ Click the Move pointer, and drag the text box to a new location.
Resize a text box	■ Click on the text box to select. ■ Position the mouse pointer over a selection handle, so the pointer turns into a double-headed arrow ←→ . ■ Hold down the left mouse button. ■ Drag the handle down and to the right to resize the clip.
Delete a text box	■ Click on the text box to select. ■ Press the Delete key.

 Hands-On 2.1   Create, Resize, Move, and Delete Text Boxes

In this exercise, you will open a Graduation Invitation, create two text boxes, and enter text into them.

1. Choose File→Open, navigate to the Lesson 02 folder, and open Graduation Invitation.
   The invitation opens to the first page.

2. Click 3 on the Page Navigation icon at the bottom of the screen.
Both pages 2 and 3 of the invitation are displayed. Notice that pages 2 and 3 are highlighted in the Page Navigation icon.

3. Click the Text Box button on the Objects toolbar on the left side of the screen.

4. Move your mouse pointer to page 3 at approximately the location shown in the following picture.
Notice that your mouse pointer turns into a ⊞ button as you move it into the invitation.

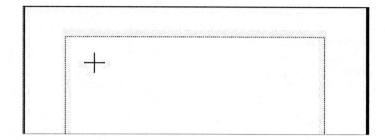

Next you will use the dimensions indicator on the status bar to draw a text box of a particular size.

5. Holding down the left mouse button, drag your mouse pointer down and to the right to approximately 3.6 or 3.7 × 1 inch, as shown in the following figure, and release the mouse button.
Notice that when you release the mouse button the new text box is selected (circular handles appear in the perimeter of the object) and the cursor appears in the upper-left corner. Also, notice the text box's dimensions on the status bar as you create the box.

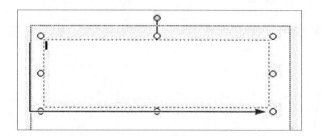 

6. Click the Text Box button on the Objects toolbar on the left side of the screen.

7. Holding down the left mouse button again, drag your mouse pointer down and to the right to draw a second text box approximately 3 or 3.1 × $1\frac{1}{2}$ inches below the other text box.

8. Before beginning to type, press F9 to enlarge the selected text box to 100% magnification. Pressing F9 a second time returns the layout to its previous magnification.

9. If necessary, click in the second text box as shown in the following illustration and enter the text, tapping ⎡Enter⎤ at the end of the first line.

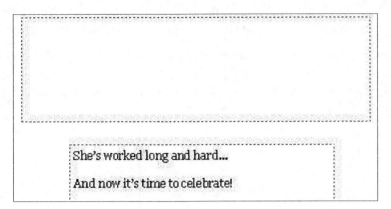

Resize a Text Box

Sometimes the text box may be too large or not large enough to display your text as you would like.

10. Position the mouse pointer over the right bottom corner selection handle, so the pointer turns into a double-headed arrow ↔.

11. Hold down the left mouse button and drag the handle up and to the left.

12. Position the mouse pointer over the right bottom corner selection handle again until the pointer turns into a double-headed arrow ↔.

13. Hold down the left mouse button and drag the handle down and to the right to approximately the original text box size.

Move Text Boxes

Sometimes the text box may not be in the exact location you would like, but you can easily move the box to your desired location.

14. Position the mouse pointer over the dotted line border of the second text box until the Move pointer ✛ appears.

15. Practice dragging the text box and then position it centered and below the first text box.

Delete a Text Box

16. Click the 4 on the Page Navigation icon on the status bar to go to page 4 of the invitation.

17. Click to select the text box and press ⌈Delete⌉.

Selecting, Moving, and Copying Text

Publisher allows you to select and move or copy any amount of text you wish and work with it as a whole. For example, you can select one character or the entire contents of a text box and move or copy it to a different text box.

FROM THE KEYBOARD
⌈Ctrl⌉+⌈A⌉ to select all text
⌈Ctrl⌉+⌈X⌉ to cut
⌈Ctrl⌉+⌈C⌉ to copy
⌈Ctrl⌉+⌈V⌉ to paste

QUICK REFERENCE: SELECTING TEXT IN A TEXT BOX

Select	Procedure
Character	Drag through character or press ⌈Shift⌉+⌈→⌉.
Word	Drag through word or double-click word.
Line	Press ⌈Shift⌉+⌈End⌉ or ⌈Shift⌉+⌈↓⌉.
Paragraph	Drag through paragraph or triple-click paragraph.
All text in a text box	Press ⌈Ctrl⌉+⌈A⌉.

All of the text in the second text box...

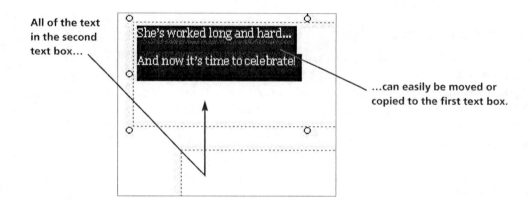

...can easily be moved or copied to the first text box.

QUICK REFERENCE: MOVING AND COPYING TEXT

Task	Procedure
Move text by dragging	■ Position the mouse pointer over the selected text. ■ Hold down the left mouse button and drag the text to a new location. ■ Release the mouse button.
Move text with cut and paste	■ Select the text to be moved. ■ Press Ctrl+X or click the Cut button. ■ Position the insertion point where you want to move the text. ■ Press Ctrl+V or click the Paste button.
Copy text by dragging	■ Position the mouse pointer over the selected text. ■ Hold down the Ctrl key. ■ Hold down the left mouse button and drag the copy to a new location. ■ Release the mouse button. ■ Release the Ctrl key.
Copy text with Copy and Paste	■ Select the text to be copied. ■ Press Ctrl+C or click the Copy button. ■ Position the insertion point where you want to place a copy of the text. ■ Press Ctrl+V or click the Paste button.

Deleting, Undoing, and Redoing Text

FROM THE KEYBOARD
Ctrl+Z to undo
Ctrl+Y to redo

Just like in Word, you can delete as well as undo and redo text when editing. You can delete individual characters or all the contents in a text box. Undo allows you to reverse the last action you took. For example, if your last action was to resize a text box, the command will be Undo Resize Object. The Redo command reverses an Undo action. You can redo as many actions as you have undone, as long as you have not done anything else in the interim. Redo is not available if you have not undone anything.

The Undo or Redo drop down arrows...

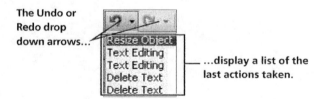

...display a list of the last actions taken.

QUICK REFERENCE: DELETING, UNDOING, AND REDOING TEXT

Task	Procedure
Delete text	■ Select the text to be deleted.
	■ Press the `Delete` key.
Undo an action	■ Press `Ctrl`+`Z`, or click the Undo `⤺` `▾` button.
Redo an action	■ Press `Ctrl`+`Y`, or click the Redo `⤻` `▾` button.

 ## Hands-On 2.2   Move, Copy, and Delete Text

In this exercise, you will practice selecting, moving, and deleting text in text boxes on page 3 of the invitation.

Select and Move Text

1. Click 3 on the Page Navigation icon at the bottom of the window to go to page 3.

2. Click anywhere in the text box containing text on page 3.
   Publisher selects the text box. Notice the handles around the edges of the text box, indicating your selection.

3. Press `Ctrl`+`A`.
   All of the text in this text box is selected.

4. Follow these steps to move the text to the top text box on page 3:

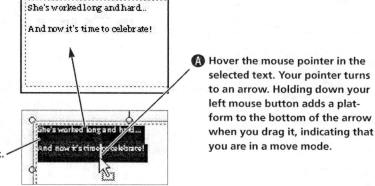

Ⓐ Hover the mouse pointer in the selected text. Your pointer turns to an arrow. Holding down your left mouse button adds a platform to the bottom of the arrow when you drag it, indicating that you are in a move mode.

Ⓑ Drag the text to the top-left corner of the blank text box.

Delete and Undo Text

5. Double-click *celebrate* and press the `Delete` key.

6. Press `Ctrl`+`Z` to undo the deletion.

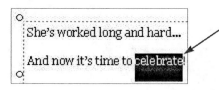

Adding Bullets in a Text Box

Bulleted lists help you emphasize key elements in your publication in a more interesting and readable format. A bullet is a dot or other symbol that is placed before the text to add emphasis. As in Word, bullets require a hanging indent for the first line, but the Bullets feature in Publisher sets up these indents for you automatically, so the process is easy.

Inserting Bullets

A bullet list format can be applied either before or after the text is typed. When editing a bulleted list, each time you press the Enter key, a bullet displays at the beginning of the next line or paragraph.

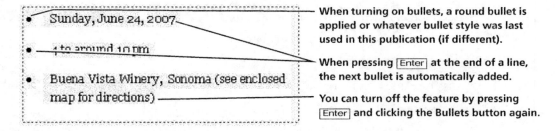

- Sunday, June 24, 2007

- 4 to around 10 pm

- Buena Vista Winery, Sonoma (see enclosed map for directions)

When turning on bullets, a round bullet is applied or whatever bullet style was last used in this publication (if different).

When pressing Enter at the end of a line, the next bullet is automatically added.

You can turn off the feature by pressing Enter and clicking the Bullets button again.

Changing Bulleted List Formatting

You can choose a different bullet character, change the size of the bullet, and change the indentation for bulleted paragraphs.

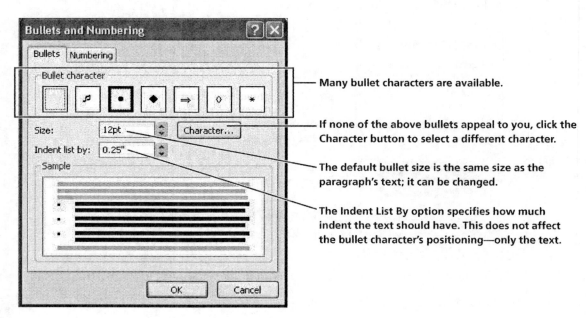

Many bullet characters are available.

If none of the above bullets appeal to you, click the Character button to select a different character.

The default bullet size is the same size as the paragraph's text; it can be changed.

The Indent List By option specifies how much indent the text should have. This does not affect the bullet character's positioning—only the text.

You can choose any font that is installed on your computer. Some useful fonts
for bullets include Wingdings, Webdings, Symbol, and Marlett.

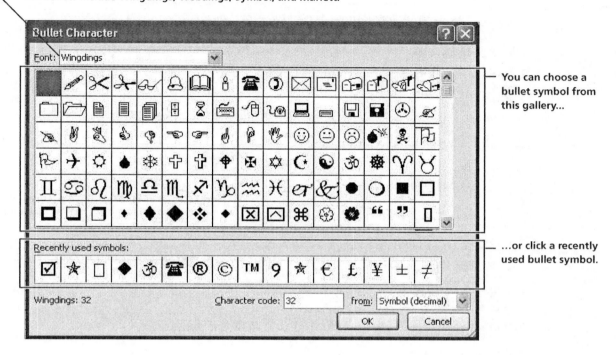

You can choose a bullet symbol from this gallery...

...or click a recently used bullet symbol.

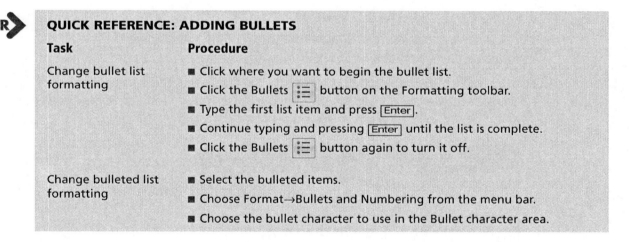

QUICK REFERENCE: ADDING BULLETS

Task	Procedure
Change bullet list formatting	■ Click where you want to begin the bullet list.
	■ Click the Bullets [≔] button on the Formatting toolbar.
	■ Type the first list item and press [Enter].
	■ Continue typing and pressing [Enter] until the list is complete.
	■ Click the Bullets [≔] button again to turn it off.
Change bulleted list formatting	■ Select the bulleted items.
	■ Choose Format→Bullets and Numbering from the menu bar.
	■ Choose the bullet character to use in the Bullet character area.

Hands-On 2.3   Add Bullets and Change Their Format

In this exercise, you will add bullets and text and then change the bullet format.

Add Bullets

1. Click anywhere in the blank text box.

2. Click the Bullets ⊞ button.
   A bullet is applied: either a plain, round bullet or the last bullet used.

3. Follow these steps to add bullets:

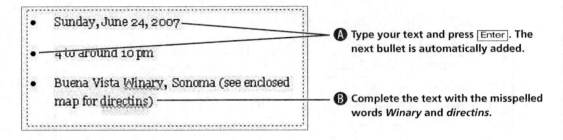

- Sunday, June 24, 2007

- 4 to around 10 pm

- Buena Vista Winary, Sonoma (see enclosed map for directins)

Ⓐ **Type your text and press** ⌐Enter⌐. **The next bullet is automatically added.**

Ⓑ **Complete the text with the misspelled words** *Winary* **and** *directins*.

Your text may wrap differently from what is shown in the figure.

Change Bullet Formatting

4. Click anywhere in the text box and press ⌐Ctrl⌐+⌐A⌐.

5. Choose Formats→Bullets and Numbering from the menu bar.
   Publisher displays the Bullets and Numbering dialog box.

6. Click the Character button, as shown in the following figure.
   The Bullet Character dialog box opens. You can choose one of the bullet characters shown or, if you prefer another bullet, you can click the Character button.

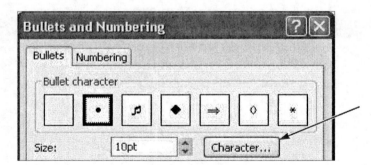

7. Follow these steps to change the bullet character:

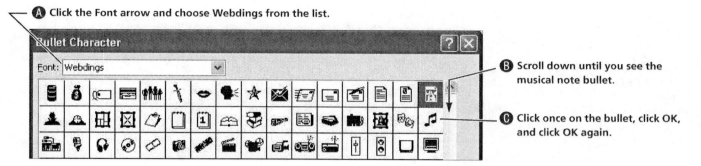

(A) Click the Font arrow and choose Webdings from the list.

(B) Scroll down until you see the musical note bullet.

(C) Click once on the bullet, click OK, and click OK again.

8. Click anywhere outside of the text box to deselect the text box.

Formatting Text Boxes

If you have created text boxes or are using text boxes automatically created for you in a publication, you may want to dress up the formatting by applying a different font, size, style, alignment, and color as well as adding a border and colored background.

FROM THE KEYBOARD
Ctrl + B for bold
Ctrl + I for italic
Ctrl + U for underline

Changing the Font, Size, Style, and Color

Just like in Word, you can choose a different font, font size, style, alignment, and color to apply to the text in text boxes. Each publication has a specific color scheme. When you apply a different font color, a selection of font colors within that color scheme will display. If you don't want to choose a color within the publication color scheme, you can choose a fixed color. A fixed color is a color not included in the current color scheme. You can also add font styles such as bold, italic, underline, and so forth. The following figures show toolbar options that allow you to change the font and the size of your font:

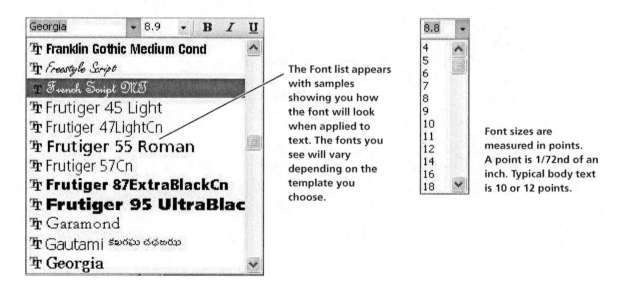

The Font list appears with samples showing you how the font will look when applied to text. The fonts you see will vary depending on the template you choose.

Font sizes are measured in points. A point is 1/72nd of an inch. Typical body text is 10 or 12 points.

The following illustration shows several options for working with font colors:

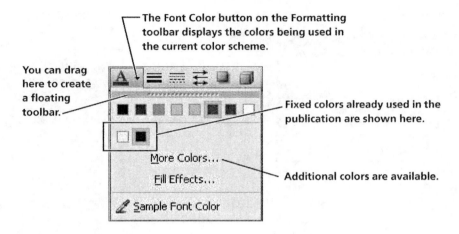

The Font Color button on the Formatting toolbar displays the colors being used in the current color scheme.

You can drag here to create a floating toolbar.

Fixed colors already used in the publication are shown here.

Additional colors are available.

QUICK REFERENCE: FORMATTING TEXT BOXES FROM THE TOOLBAR

Task	Procedure
Change the font	■ Select the text to be changed.
	■ Open the Font drop-down list `Arial`.
	■ Type the first letter of a font's name to jump quickly to that part of the list.
	or
	■ Scroll through the list and click the font you want.
Change the font size	■ Select the text to be changed.
	■ Open the Font Size drop-down list `10`.
	■ Scroll through the list and click the size you want.
Change the font color	■ Select the text to be formatted.
	■ Click the Font Color drop-down arrow `A`.
	■ Select the color you want to use.
Decrease font size by one size	■ Select the text to be changed.
	■ Click Decrease Font Size `A˅` button.
Increase font size by one size	■ Select the text to be changed.
	■ Click Increase Font Size `A˄` button.
Change font style	■ Select the text to be changed.
	■ To make the text italic (or turn italics off) click the Italic `I` button.
	■ To make the text bold (or turn bold off) click the Bold `B` button.
Align text	■ Select the text to be changed.
	■ Click the Center `≡` button.

Hands-On 2.4   Change the Font and Alignment

In this exercise, you will change your text to a different font and font size, make the text bold, and change the font color.

Change the Font and Font Size

1. If necessary, press `F9` to enlarge the invitation to 100% magnification.

2. Select both lines of text, as shown in the following text box.

3. Click the Font drop-down list [Georgia ▾].

4. Scroll and choose Comic Sans MS.

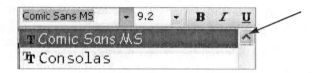

Your text has now changed to Comic Sans MS.

5. Click the Font Size drop-down list [9.2 ▾].

6. Scroll and click Font Size 14.

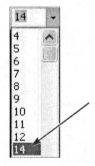

7. Click the Font Color drop-down arrow [A ▾].

8. Click Violet, the seventh option in this row.

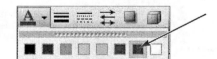

Change the Font Style and Alignment

9. Click the Bold **B** button to bold the text.

10. Click the Center button to center the text.
Your text box should look like this:

> ### She's worked long and hard...
>
> ### And now it's time to celebrate!

Applying Borders and Fill Color

FROM THE KEYBOARD
Ctrl+Shift+O to toggle object borders on and off

You can apply border formatting in a variety of thicknesses, line styles and colors to any text box or other objects such as pictures or drawings. The default border of any object in Publisher appears as a dotted line. This line does not print unless you apply border formatting to the object. You can choose border formatting for any object so that the boundaries are visible when printed. Text boxes are transparent by default, so the background on which they are placed shows through. Sometimes you may want to give a text box a colored background.

The following illustrations show Line/Border styles available on the Formatting toolbar and a variety of Line options that appear in the Format Text Box dialog box.

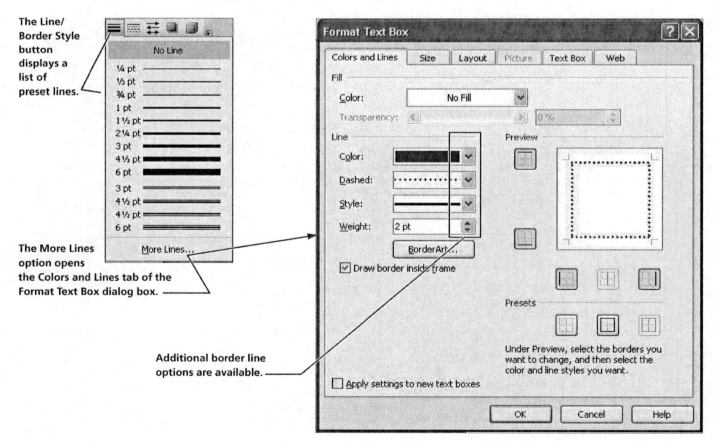

The Line/Border Style button displays a list of preset lines.

The More Lines option opens the Colors and Lines tab of the Format Text Box dialog box.

Additional border line options are available.

The following illustrations display line color and fill color options available on the Formatting toolbar.

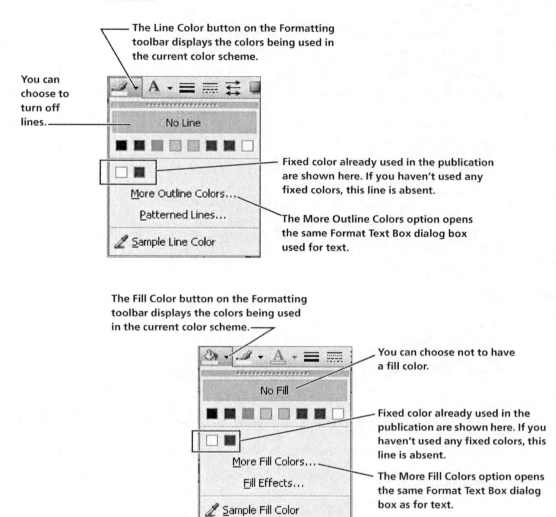

The Line Color button on the Formatting toolbar displays the colors being used in the current color scheme.

You can choose to turn off lines.

No Line

Fixed color already used in the publication are shown here. If you haven't used any fixed colors, this line is absent.

More Outline Colors...

Patterned Lines...

The More Outline Colors option opens the same Format Text Box dialog box used for text.

Sample Line Color

The Fill Color button on the Formatting toolbar displays the colors being used in the current color scheme.

You can choose not to have a fill color.

No Fill

Fixed color already used in the publication are shown here. If you haven't used any fixed colors, this line is absent.

More Fill Colors...

Fill Effects...

The More Fill Colors option opens the same Format Text Box dialog box as for text.

Sample Fill Color

QUICK REFERENCE: APPLYING BORDER AND FILL COLORS FROM THE FORMATTING TOOLBAR

Task	Procedure
Apply a border	■ Select the text box. ■ Click the Line/Border Style 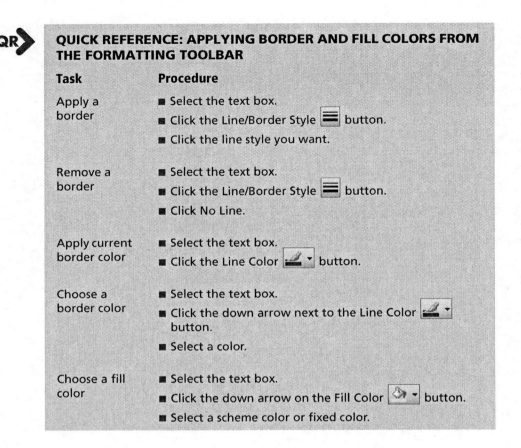 button. ■ Click the line style you want.
Remove a border	■ Select the text box. ■ Click the Line/Border Style button. ■ Click No Line.
Apply current border color	■ Select the text box. ■ Click the Line Color button.
Choose a border color	■ Select the text box. ■ Click the down arrow next to the Line Color button. ■ Select a color.
Choose a fill color	■ Select the text box. ■ Click the down arrow on the Fill Color button. ■ Select a scheme color or fixed color.

 Hands-On 2.5   Apply a Border and Change Fill Color

In this exercise, you will apply a border, line color, and fill color to a text box on page 3 of the invitation.

Apply a Border and Line Color

1. Click in the text box you just formatted.

2. Follow these steps to add a border and line color:

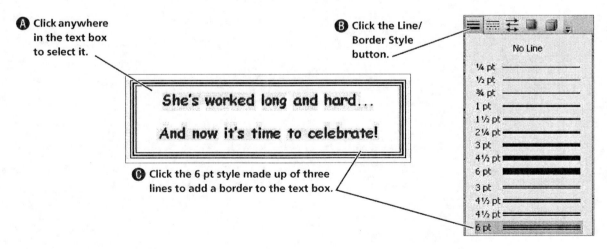

Ⓐ **Click anywhere in the text box to select it.**

Ⓑ **Click the Line/ Border Style button.**

She's worked long and hard...

And now it's time to celebrate!

No Line
¼ pt
½ pt
¾ pt
1 pt
1½ pt
2¼ pt
3 pt
4½ pt
6 pt
3 pt
4½ pt
4½ pt
6 pt

Ⓒ **Click the 6 pt style made up of three lines to add a border to the text box.**

3. Click the drop-down arrow on the Line Color 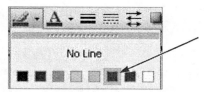 button and choose the sixth color as shown.
   The line color is added to the border.

Add Fill Color

4. Click the down arrow on the Fill Color 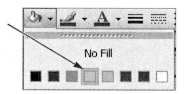 button and choose the fourth color option.

   Fill color is added inside the text box.

5. Click outside the invitation to deselect the text box.

Proofreading Your Publication

Just like in a Word document, you should always check your spelling to make sure you haven't made any mistakes. AutoCorrect is a popular feature in Word that has been included in Publisher. It maintains a list of commonly misspelled words. Whenever you make one of these misspellings, Publisher automatically fixes the error.

Checking Spelling

As in Word, Publisher automatically checks your spelling as you type and marks any words that are not in its dictionary with a wavy red underline. Not all red-underlined words are necessarily misspelled. Many proper names and brand names are erroneously marked as misspelled, because they are not in Publisher's dictionary.

You can check the spelling in your entire publication. The spelling checker looks for misspellings in each story. A story is the text in a text box. If a misspelled word is identified, you can choose to add it to the dictionary, ignore it, or correct it.

FROM THE KEYBOARD
[F7] to check spelling

The following illustration shows Publisher checking spelling as you type.

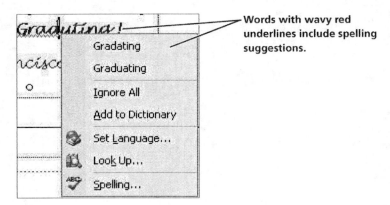

Words with wavy red underlines include spelling suggestions.

The following dialog box allows you to perform a spell check after you complete your publication.

The unrecognized word appears here.

Suggested spellings are shown here.

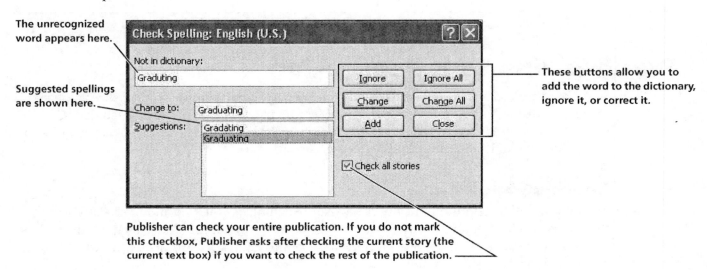

These buttons allow you to add the word to the dictionary, ignore it, or correct it.

Publisher can check your entire publication. If you do not mark this checkbox, Publisher asks after checking the current story (the current text box) if you want to check the rest of the publication.

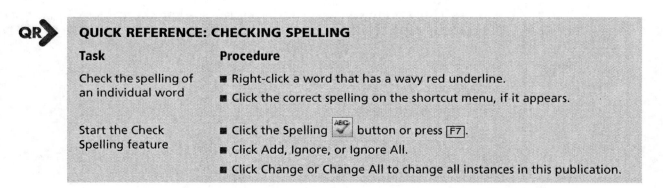

QUICK REFERENCE: CHECKING SPELLING

Task	Procedure
Check the spelling of an individual word	■ Right-click a word that has a wavy red underline.
	■ Click the correct spelling on the shortcut menu, if it appears.
Start the Check Spelling feature	■ Click the Spelling [icon] button or press F7.
	■ Click Add, Ignore, or Ignore All.
	■ Click Change or Change All to change all instances in this publication.

Hands-On 2.6 Check Spelling

In this exercise, you will correct a misspelling with a wavy red underline and finish spellchecking the invitation using the Spell Checker.

Correct a Misspelling

1. On page 2, right click on the misspelled word *Graduting*.
   A list of suggested words is displayed.

2. Click the correct spelling, *Graduating*.

3. Click anywhere outside the invitation to deselect the text box.

Spellcheck the Invitation

4. Click the Spelling button AEG or press F7.
   Check Spelling opens and the word Andie *displays as the unrecognized word. If* Andie *does not appear as an unrecognized word, move to step 5 to correct the word* Winary.

5. Click Ignore.
   The word Winary *displays as the unrecognized word.*

6. Click Change.
   The word directins *is shown as the next unrecognized word.*

7. Click Change and then OK when prompted that the Spelling is complete.
   If Publisher returns you to page 1 of the invitation, click 2 on the Navigation Page icon to return to page 2.

Using AutoCorrect

AutoCorrect has a long list of words that it automatically corrects for you if you type a word incorrectly. AutoCorrect works automatically. You do not need to do anything special to turn it on. You can also add or remove entries from the AutoCorrect list. For example, you might work for a company that uses a © in its documents to indicate a heading level. AutoCorrect automatically changes (C) to the Copyright symbol ©. You may want to remove this correction from the list.

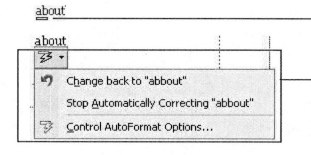

Publisher corrects some misspellings for you. A small blue minus sign appears below the corrected text when your mouse pointer is over it.

If you point to that minus sign, the AutoCorrect Options button appears. You can click that button to open a menu, from which you can choose how you want this and other similar situations to be handled.

The AutoCorrect dialog box provides a variety of options for controlling the feature.

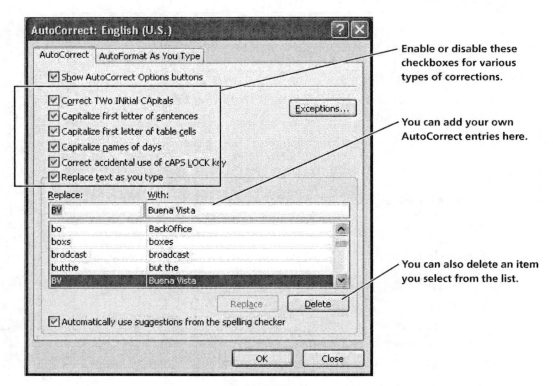

Enable or disable these checkboxes for various types of corrections.

You can add your own AutoCorrect entries here.

You can also delete an item you select from the list.

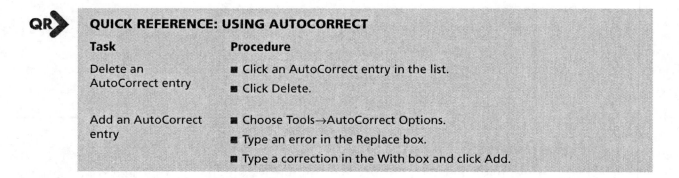

QUICK REFERENCE: USING AUTOCORRECT

Task	Procedure
Delete an AutoCorrect entry	■ Click an AutoCorrect entry in the list. ■ Click Delete.
Add an AutoCorrect entry	■ Choose Tools→AutoCorrect Options. ■ Type an error in the Replace box. ■ Type a correction in the With box and click Add.

Hands-On 2.7   Use AutoCorrect

In this exercise, you will type in an incorrect word and have it automatically corrected with AutoCorrect. You will then add an entry to the AutoCorrect list.

Use AutoCorrect to Correct a Misspelled Word

1. Go to page 3 of the invitation.

2. Select the correctly spelled word *around,* including the space after it, and type the misspelled word **arond** in the second bullet; tap the `Spacebar` and watch AutoCorrect make the correction. Arond *is corrected to the word* around.

• 4 to around 10 pm

Add an Entry to the AutoCorrect List

3. Click Tools→AutoCorrect Options from the menu bar. *The AutoCorrect dialog box opens.*

4. Type **bv** in the Replace box, press `Tab`, and type **Buena Vista** in the With box.

Replace:	With:
bv	Buena Vista

5. Click Add. *The* Buena Vista *entry is added to the AutoCorrect List.*

6. Click OK to close the AutoCorrect Option box.

7. In the second text box on page 2, select the words *Buena Vista,* type **bv** and tap the `Spacebar`, and watch AutoCorrect make the correction. *The abbreviation* bv *is replaced with* Buena Vista.

Remove an Entry from the AutoCorrect List

8. Click Tools→AutoCorrect Options from the menu bar.

9. Scroll to the *bv* entry if not already selected.

10. Click `Delete` and OK. *The* Buena Vista *entry is deleted from the AutoCorrect List.*

11. Click the Print Preview ⌂ button to view your invitation. *Your invitation displays in an invitational card format.*

12. Click the Close button on the Print Preview toolbar.

13. Choose File→Close to close the Graduation Invitation and Save if prompted for changes. *Publisher returns to the Getting Started with Microsoft Office Publisher 2007 window.*

 # Concepts Review

True/False Questions

1. Many Publisher publication templates such as invitations consist of multiple pages. TRUE FALSE

2. You should create a new text box when you want to separate one block of text from another. TRUE FALSE

3. You can redo as many actions as you have undone, as long as you have not done anything else in the interim. TRUE FALSE

4. A bullet is a dot or other symbol that is placed before the text to add emphasis. TRUE FALSE

5. A fixed color is a color that is part of a publication's color scheme. TRUE FALSE

6. Publications do not have default specific color schemes. TRUE FALSE

7. The default border of any object in Publisher appears as a dotted line. TRUE FALSE

8. You don't need to add border formatting to a text box in order for the border to print. TRUE FALSE

9. If a misspelled word is identified, you can choose to add it to the dictionary, ignore it, or correct it. TRUE FALSE

10. All words with a wavy red underline are misspellings and need to be corrected. TRUE FALSE

Multiple Choice Questions

1. What is a story?
   a. The I-beam that appears when you move the mouse pointer over text
   b. Text in a text box
   c. Circles that mark the margins of the publication page
   d. A type of bullet

2. Which of the following is not true about publications?
   a. You should create a new text box when you want to separate one block of text from another.
   b. A fixed color is not part of a publication's color scheme.
   c. All publications have chosen color schemes.
   d. You cannot check the spelling in a story.

3. Which key is pressed to zoom into a selected area?
   a. F8
   b. F9
   c. F7
   d. F2

4. To detect and correct misspellings, AutoCorrect uses _____.
   a. a list of AutoCorrect entries
   b. the main dictionary
   c. the custom dictionary
   d. a thesaurus

Skill Builders

Skill Builder 2.1   Create, Resize, Move, and Delete Text Boxes

It's time to create another invitation! In this exercise, you will create an invitation for a Halloween party, add several text boxes, and enter text.

1. Choose Invitation Cards from the Publication Types list, and then click the Holiday Party link at the top of the center pane.

2. Double-click the Halloween Party 1 design in the center pane to open the invitation in the text editing window.

3. Select the text in the text box at the bottom of page 1.

4. Click the drop-down arrow on the Font list on the Formatting toolbar and choose the Broadway font.

5. Click the drop-down arrow on the Font Size list on the Formatting toolbar and choose 18 pt.

6. Click the 2 on the Page Navigation icon at the bottom of the screen.
   Pages 2 and 3 are displayed side by side.

7. Select the Invitation Title text in the second text box on page 2 and type **Halloween Party** in its place.

8. Select the text you just typed and use the Formatting toolbar to change to the Broadway font, 16 pt.

Delete a Text Box

9. Select and delete the remaining text boxes on page 2.

10. Click the Text Box 🖼 button on the Objects toolbar on the left side of the screen.

11. Draw a text box of approximately the same size and in approximately the same location shown in the following illustration:

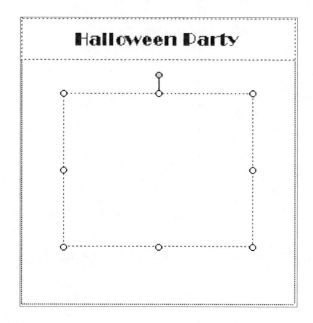

Move Text

12. On page 3, select the text in the top text box and drag the text into the text box you just created.
Notice that the text is automatically centered, since it was centered in the other text box.

13. Position the cursor at the end of the text you just moved and tap Enter.

14. Select the text in the second text box on page 3.

15. Drag the text below the other text in your new text box.

16. Select all of the text and format it with Script MT Bold, 16 pt.

17. Resize the text boxes in this exercise any time it is appropriate.

Delete Text Boxes

18. Delete both text boxes on page 3.

19. Draw a new text box of the approximate size and in the approximate position, as shown in the following illustration:

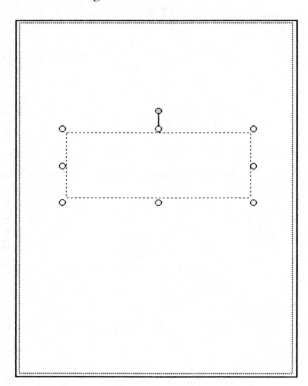

20. Position the cursor in the text box, and type **Don't Miss our 10th Annual Halloween Party!**

21. Select the text and format it with Broadway, 12 pt, and then Center ≡ the text.

Apply a Border and Fill Color

22. Select the text box, click the Line/Border  button, and choose $2^{1}/_{4}$ pt.

23. Click the drop-down arrow on the Line Color button and choose the sixth color option.

24. Click the drop-down arrow on the Fill Color button and choose the fifth color option.

Add a Text Box with Bullets

25. Draw another text box of approximately the size and in approximately the location shown in the following illustration:

26. Position the cursor in the text box and type the following lines, tapping ⌐Enter⌐ after the first two lines:

Sonia and Kent's: 777-8888

Date: October 31st

Time: 6 pm until midnight

27. Select all three lines and choose Format→Bullets and Numbering from the menu bar.

28. Choose any bullet you wish from the Bullet character row, and then click OK.

29. Save the file as **Sb-Halloween Invitation** in your Lesson 02 folder, and then close the file.

Skill Builder 2.2   Spell Check a Postcard Appointment Reminder

Yesterday, you created a postcard appointment reminder for your friend Dr. Vadgama but you didn't have time to spell check it at the time. In this exercise, you will open the publication and correct the spelling errors.

1. Open sb-Appointment Postcard from your Lesson 02 folder.

2. Click the Spelling and Grammar ABC button on the Standard toolbar.
   The Check Spelling dialog box appears indicating that Vadgama *is not in Publisher's dictionary.*

3. Click the Ignore All button.
   Spell check marks Bakry *as a possible misspelling and it proposes the incorrect word in the Change To box.*

4. Click *Bakery* in the Suggestions list and click the Change button.
   Spell check marks helth *as a possible misspelling and chooses the correct spelling in the Change To box.*

5. Click the Change button.

6. Click the Change button to replace *Yo* with *You*.
   A message appears indicating that spell check is complete.

7. Click OK to dismiss the message box.

8. Save 🖫 the file in your Lesson 02 folder, and then close it.

Skill Builder 2.3   Use AutoCorrect with a Menu Publication

You have been hired to print the daily specials menu for your local French restaurant and you've discovered that many of the French dishes are tricky to spell. In this exercise, you will create AutoCorrect shortcuts and use them to help type these difficult terms.

1. Choose Menus from the Publication Types list, and then double-click the Scallops design in the Daily Specials section of the center pane.
   The publication opens in the text editing window.

2. Select the text in the top text box, and replace it with **L'Orangerie**.

3. Delete the Organization text box toward the bottom of the menu and delete the last text box at the bottom.

4. Enter today's date in the Date text box.

Create AutoCorrect Shortcuts

5. Choose Tools→AutoCorrect Options from the menu bar.

6. Type **bd** in the Replace box, press ⬚Tab⬚, type **Bordelaise** in the With box, and then click the Add button.

7. Repeat the above technique to add three more shortcut terms in the AutoCorrect dialog box. (You can type right over the top of the terms in the Replace and With boxes.)

Shortcut Term	AutoCorrect Term
bb	Bouillabaisse
bg	Bourguignon
bq	Blanquette

8. Click OK to close the dialog box.

9. Click the term *Item* for the first menu entry and type **Baked Oysters bd**, and tap the Spacebar to print out the word *Bordelaise*.

10. Select the text *A brief description of the dish* and replace it with the description shown in the menu at the end of this exercise.

11. Complete the remaining menu items using *bb* for *Bouillabaisse,* *bg* for *Bourguignon,* and *bq* for *Blanquette.* Be sure to include the descriptions for each dish, and add the prices in the column on the right as shown in the illustration.

12. Save 💾 the menu as **sb-Specials Menu** in your Lesson 02 folder, and then close the file.

Assessments

Assessment 2.1   Create a Fax Cover

In this exercise, you will create a fax cover for your company, Medical Equipment Supplies. You will format, delete, and move text boxes.

1. Choose Business Forms from the Publication Types list, and then click the Fax Cover link at the top of the center pane.

2. Choose the Quadrant design, and then click the Create button.

3. Delete the top text box from the form.

4. Change the font of the Fax Transmittal Form text to Comic Sans MS, 14 pt.

5. Select the To text box and apply a 1 pt border and the fill color of your choice.

6. Enter your name in the text box below the From text box.

7. Change the area codes for the phone and fax to your own area code.

8. Delete the e-mail text below the fax number.

9. Delete the text box with the word Urgent at the top, and slide the Date and Time text box to the left to replace the deleted text box.

10. Type **Medical Equipment Supplies** in the text box below the pyramid graphic in the bottom-left corner of the publication.

11. Drag the text box you just completed to the top of the document just to the left of the Fax Transmittal Form text box.

12. Delete the remaining text boxes in the bottom-left corner of the publication.

13. Save 🖫 the file as **as-Fax Form** in your Lesson 02 folder, and then close the file.

Assessment 2.2   Create a Gift Certificate with Bullets

The Senior Center is holding a garage sale to raise funds for redecorating its kitchen. In this exercise, you will create a gift certificate that contains a bulleted list of free gifts participants can choose from.

1. Create a gift certificate using the Bars design.

2. In the upper-left corner text box, replace the sample text with **Senior Center Garage Sale**.

3. Delete the text box in the bottom-left corner of the publication.

4. Delete all of the text boxes below the Gift Certificate text box except the text box with the pyramid graphic.

5. Type **Senior Center** in the text box below the pyramid graphic.

6. Draw a text box below the Gift Certificate text box to contain the following text and bullet points. Resize and position the text box as needed. Use a bullet format of your choice.

> This certificate entitles the bearer to one item up to a $10 value from one of the following categories:
>
> ⇒   Antique jewelry
>
> ⇒   Woodworking tools
>
> ⇒   Pool toys

7. Save 🖫 the publication as **as-Senior Gift Certificate** in your Lesson 02 folder, and then close the file.

 # Critical Thinking

Critical Thinking 2.1   Create a Fun Fundraiser Invitation

Sarah Katherine is Vice President of her local Community Center. The Community Center has decided to throw a fundraiser to help raise money to build a hiking and biking trail. The trail will be six miles long running from the San Carlos Community Center to the San Carlos Park and Recreation Center.

Local artisans and craftsmen will sell their wares at the Community Center and donate 50 percent of their proceeds to the Center. In this exercise, you will help Sarah create a fundraiser invitation.

1. Follow these guidelines to prepare an invitation for the fundraiser:
   - Open the ct-Fundraiser Invitation from the Lesson 02 folder.
   - On page 2, create a fun heading text box with text that will catch people's attention. Add text formatting that is colorful.
   - On page 3, create a text box with the following text:
     Date: Sunday, August 12, 2007
     Time: Noon to 6 pm—local artisans and craftsmen will sell their crafts at the Community Center (50% proceeds will go to the trail)
     Where: San Carlos Community Center
   - Add bullets that reflect the mood of the invitation.
   - Add text formatting to the bulleted text.
   - If necessary, resize and move the bulleted text box to center it on page 3.

2. Check the spelling in your invitation.

3. Look at your invitation in Print Preview mode.

4. Save 🖫 your changes and close the invitation.

Critical Thinking 2.2   Create Matching Business Cards and Letterhead

Your granddaughter is starting her own image-consulting business called Personal Style, and it's important that she presents a good image to her prospective clients. Knowing that you have been using Publisher, she asks for your help! In this exercise, you will coordinate her designs and personalize the publications with her company's information.

1. Create a business card using the Bounce design.

2. Use the following illustration as a guide, but feel free to experiment with any Publisher features you have learned about so far:

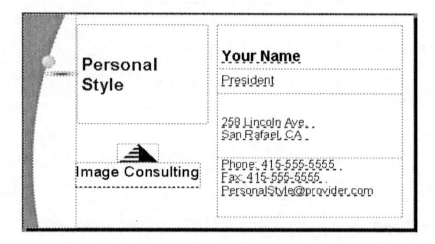

3. Save 🖫 the business card as **ct-Image Business Card** in your Lesson 02 folder.

4. Create a letterhead using the Bounce design.

5. Provide the same address, phone, fax, and e-mail information as it appears on the business card. Once again, feel free to experiment and be creative.

6. Save 🖫 the letterhead as **ct-Image Letterhead** in your Lesson 02 folder, and then close the file.

Adding Interest with Graphics

In this lesson, you will create a holiday greeting card. You will search for clip art images and pictures and add them to your card. You will also move and resize pictures and work with the cropping tool. Then you will create and format WordArt. You will also add interest to your card by adding a BorderArt object. And finally, you will add a polishing touch to a paragraph by inserting a drop cap.

LESSON OBJECTIVES

After studying this lesson, you will be able to:

■ Search for and add clip art images
■ Search for and add a picture from a file
■ Resize, move, and crop a picture
■ Create and format WordArt
■ Add a BorderArt object
■ Insert a drop cap

Case Study: Creating Happy Holidays with Publisher

The holidays are approaching and Sarah is eager to create a holiday greeting card. Some of her friends have created holiday cards using Publisher in the past and have shared that they are easy and fun to create. She knows that she has time and energy to create them at home.

Sarah is getting more comfortable working with Publisher. She created a few flyers for friends and recently enjoyed learning how to create and format text boxes. So, Sarah has some basic Publisher skills, but she wants to enhance them by learning how to work with graphic images.

WordArt can dress up any heading.

This is one of many clip art images that can enhance your publication.

Pictures can be added from a file.

Adding and Formatting Clip Art

Clip art can make your publication more appealing than text alone can. Clip art is ready-to-use electronic artwork. The name comes from the days when professional designers could buy books full of generic drawings with many on a page. The designers would then *clip* the desired drawing out of the book with scissors and paste the clip art image directly onto their page layout. Publisher comes with hundreds of clip art images, and you can download more clip art images from Microsoft's web site.

Finding and Inserting Clip Art

You can use the Clip Art task pane to search for clip art images that will enhance your publication. Each clip has one or more keywords associated with it. When typing in this keyword, all clip art images associated with the keyword will be displayed. Most of the clip art images that come with Publisher are in Windows Metafile, or WMF, format. This format allows you to scale (resize) without losing any image quality.

Media Collections

As in Word, Publisher has three collection areas where clip art images can be found:

- My Collections
- Office Collections: Included with Office 2007 software
- Web Collections: Clip art collections located on Microsoft Office Online

Media Types

When using the Clip Art task pane to search, you can search for different media types:

- Clip Art: Images drawn by graphic artists
- Photographs: Photographic images
- Movies: Simple animated pictures or brief video clips
- Sounds: Sound effects, such as the noise made by a car horn

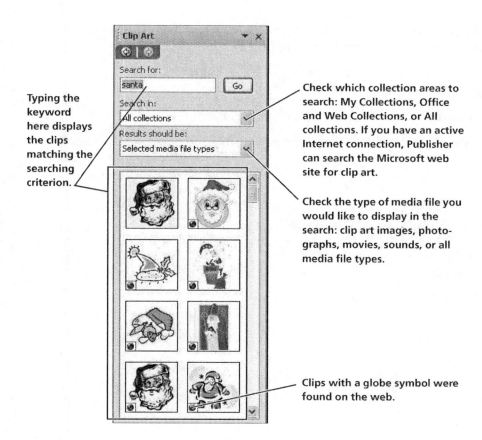

Typing the keyword here displays the clips matching the searching criterion.

Check which collection areas to search: My Collections, Office and Web Collections, or All collections. If you have an active Internet connection, Publisher can search the Microsoft web site for clip art.

Check the type of media file you would like to display in the search: clip art images, photographs, movies, sounds, or all media file types.

Clips with a globe symbol were found on the web.

QUICK REFERENCE: ADDING CLIP ART

Task	Procedure
Add clip art	■ Click the Picture Frame 🖼 button on the Objects toolbar.
	■ Choose Clip Art from the menu to display the Clip Art task pane.
	■ Display the page of the publication on which the clip art images should appear.
	■ Type the keyword to search for in the Search For text box.
	■ Click Go.
	■ Click the clip art image to insert it.

 Hands-On 3.1   Create Holiday Greeting Card and Add Clip Art

In this exercise, you will create a holiday greeting card and add a clip art image.

1. Start Publisher, if necessary.

2. Choose Greeting Cards from the Publication Type list on the left side of the screen.

3. Choose the Holiday design category at the top of the center pane, and choose the Christmas 1 design.

4. If necessary, under Customize, click the Color Scheme drop down arrow and choose Garnet.

5. Also if necessary, under Customize, click the Font Scheme drop down arrow and choose (default template fonts), and then click the Create button.

6. Click the Create button in the bottom-right corner of the window.
The Christmas 1 design holiday card opens to page 1.

7. Save the publication to the Lesson 03 folder as **Christmas Card**.

8. Use the Page Navigation icon at the bottom of the screen to go to page 2 of the Holiday Card.
Both pages 2 and 3 of the holiday card are displayed.

Insert Clip Art

9. Click the Picture Frame ![icon] button on the Objects toolbar at the left side of the screen.

10. Choose Clip Art from the menu.
The Clip Art task pane appears.

11. Click the Results Should Be drop down and check only Clip Art.

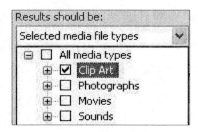

12. In Search For box, type **santa claus** and click Go.

⚠ **NOTE!** *If prompted to include thousands of additional clip art photos and pictures from Microsoft Office Online, click Yes.*

13. Click the clip shown in the following illustration if it is listed, or choose a clip of your choice.

The clip is placed in the middle of pages 2 and 3 in its own frame.

14. Click anywhere in the scratch area to deselect the clip art image.

Formatting Clip Art

You can move and resize a clip art picture just like a text box. When resizing clip art, you can maintain the aspect ratio. Aspect ratio is the ratio of width to height. If you resize one dimension more than another, the picture can become distorted.

As in Word, the Picture toolbar appears when the clip art image is selected in your publication. You can use its tools to change how the picture appears. Some of the tools give you the ability to change the color, contrast, and brightness of clip art images and pictures. These same tools appear for pictures inserted from a file or from a scanner or camera. You'll learn about inserting a picture from a file in the next section.

These five buttons enable you to change the coloring or shading of the clip art image.

These four buttons allow you to change the picture's area or border.

The last three buttons allow you to format a picture, set a transparent color, and return all settings back to their defaults.

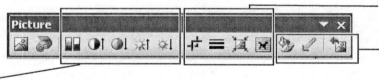

QUICK REFERENCE: FORMATTING CLIP ART

Task	Procedure
Move clip art	■ Click the clip frame to select it. ■ Position the mouse pointer over the clip art image (but not on a selection handle), so the pointer turns into a Move pointer. ■ Hold down the left mouse button. ■ Drag the clip to a new location. ■ Release the mouse button.
Resize clip art	■ Click the clip art frame to select. ■ Position the mouse pointer over a selection handle so the pointer turns into a double-headed arrow ←→. ■ Hold down the left mouse button. ■ Drag the handle to a new position, resizing the clip art image. ■ Release the mouse button.
Change clip art appearance	■ Click the clip art image to select. ■ Click the Color button. ■ Choose the Automatic, Grayscale, Black & White, or Washout option. ■ Click the More Contrast button. ■ Click the Less Contrast button. ■ Click the More Brightness button. ■ Click the Less Brightness button.
Reset clip art	■ Click the clip art image to select. ■ Click the Reset Picture button.

 Hands-On 3.2 **Move, Resize, and Format Clip Art**

In this exercise, you will practice moving, resizing, and formatting the holiday greeting card.

Move Clip Art

1. Click the clip art image to select it.

2. Position your mouse pointer over the clip art image (but not on a selection handle), so the pointer turns into a Move pointer.

3. Hold down the left mouse button.

4. Drag the clip art image to where it is approximately centered on page 2.
Notice that when the clip art image is selected, the Picture toolbar appears.

Resize Clip Art

5. If necessary, click the clip art frame to select the object.

6. Position the mouse pointer over the upper-left corner selection handle so the pointer turns into a double-headed arrow ↔.

7. Hold down the left mouse button.

8. Drag the handle down and to the right to resize the clip to approximately half its original size.

9. Drag the left side handle to the left about an inch.
Notice that the clip art image has become distorted.

10. Press Ctrl + Z to undo.

11. Move the clip art image back to the center of page 2.

Format Clip Art

12. If necessary, click the clip art frame to select the image.

13. Click the Color ▦ button.

14. Choose Grayscale.
    The clip art color displays in shades of gray. This might be helpful if you are printing on a black and white printer.

15. Click the Less Contrast 🔘 button three times.
    The clip art image's contrast decreases each time with each click.

16. Click the More Brightness ☒ button two times.
    The clip art image becomes brighter by increments with each click.

17. Click the Color ▦ button.

18. Choose Automatic.
    The clip art image's color returns.

19. Click anywhere in the scratch area to deselect the clip art image and close the picture toolbar.

Inserting and Cropping a Picture from a File

The clip art images that come with Publisher can be helpful, but you might want to use pictures also. For example, if you are creating a holiday greeting card, you might want to add a picture of your family or even your pets. You can download pictures from the Internet or receive pictures as e-mail attachments. If you use a picture you have acquired from a web page, make sure it is not copyrighted and that you have permission to use it. Otherwise you might be subject to legal penalties. You can also create pictures yourself with a digital camera, or convert a hard-copy photo to a picture file with a scanner. Sometimes you may want to focus on one part of a picture. You can do this with Publisher's cropping tool.

Inserting a Picture from a File

Inserted pictures are embedded graphics, which means they are stored inside the Publisher file. Publisher accepts a wide variety of graphic formats, so there should not be a problem with the format being compatible. Some of the formats Publisher accepts include PCS, BMP, JPG, GIF, PNG, TIF, CGM, Kodak Photo CD, CorelDraw, Postscript and Macintosh PICT. The Insert Picture dialog box displays the pictures you have saved to a file.

These are pictures saved to a file, displayed in Thumbnails view.

Thumbnails view is one way you can view your pictures.

Publisher displays the various types of picture formats that it accepts.

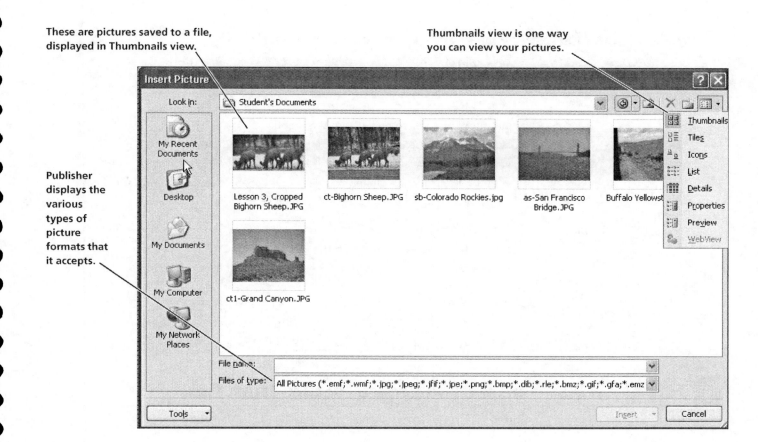

Cropping a Picture

You can crop any kind of image, including clip art images, but you will probably need to crop a picture more often. Cropping removes one or more edges of the picture, zooming in on the part you want to use.

This picture of the bighorn sheep is the original picture and not cropped.

This picture of the bighorn sheep has been cropped and enlarged.

QUICK REFERENCE: INSERTING A PICTURE FROM A FILE

Task	Procedure
Insert a picture from a file	■ Display the page on which picture should appear. ■ Click the Insert Picture ⊞ button on the Objects toolbar. ■ Choose Picture from File from the menu. ■ Drag the mouse on the page to draw the new picture frame. ■ Release the mouse button. ■ In the Insert Picture Dialog box, click the Look In drop-down box and navigate to the folder and picture file you want to insert.
Crop a picture	■ Click the picture to select it. ■ Click the Crop ⌗ button on the Picture toolbar. ■ Position the mouse pointer over a selection handle, which changes to a Crop icon. ■ Drag inward, holding down the left mouse button, to crop the picture. ■ Crop other parts of the picture as desired. ■ Click the Crop ⌗ button again to turn it off.

 Hands-On 3.3   **Insert and Crop a Picture from File**

In this exercise, you will insert and crop a picture on page 3 of your card.

Insert a Picture from File

1. Click the Picture Frame ⊞ button on the Objects toolbar.

2. Choose Picture from File.

3. Click 3 on the Navigation Bar to go to page 3.

4. Follow these steps to insert a picture from file:

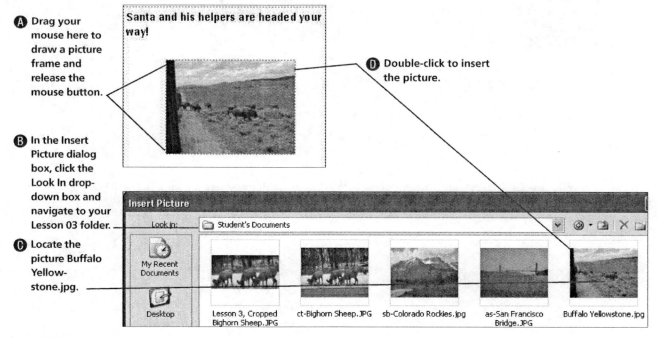

Ⓐ Drag your mouse here to draw a picture frame and release the mouse button.

Ⓑ In the Insert Picture dialog box, click the Look In drop-down box and navigate to your Lesson 03 folder.

Ⓒ Locate the picture Buffalo Yellowstone.jpg.

Ⓓ Double-click to insert the picture.

Santa and his helpers are headed your way!

Insert Picture

Look in: Student's Documents

My Recent Documents

Desktop

Lesson 3, Cropped Bighorn Sheep.JPG | ct-Bighorn Sheep.JPG | sb-Colorado Rockies.jpg | as-San Francisco Bridge.JPG | Buffalo Yellowstone.jpg

Crop a Picture

5. If necessary, click the picture to select.

6. Click the Crop  button on the Picture toolbar.

7. Position your mouse pointer over the lower-right cropping handle.

8. Drag up while holding down the left mouse button. Use the following illustration as a guide for how much of the picture to crop.

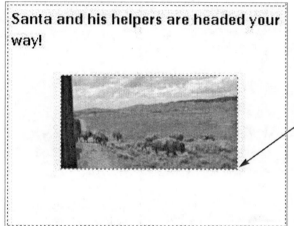

9. Position your mouse pointer over the left side middle cropping handle and drag to the right to remove the black line.

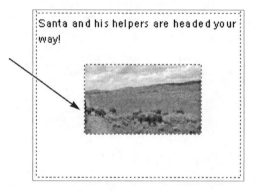

10. If necessary, move the picture to center it.

11. Click anywhere outside of the text box to deselect the text box.

Adding WordArt

WordArt helps you format your text with arches, fancy patterns, twists, 3-D effects, and other enhancements. WordArt is great for creating terrific headings and attention getters.

Creating WordArt

WordArt allows you to enter a few words of text and then manipulate that text in a variety of ways, as a graphic. You can create very interesting special effects using it.

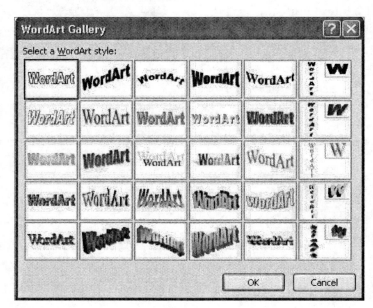

The WordArt Gallery contains many WordArt design styles to choose from.

Enter and edit the WordArt text.

Moving, Resizing, and Formatting WordArt

Once you create your WordArt graphic, you will probably need to move and resize it in your publication. You move and resize it the same way you move and resize a text box. You can also modify its appearance. When a piece of WordArt is selected a WordArt toolbar appears. It contains buttons you can use to modify the WordArt appearance. WordArt formatting applies to the entire piece of WordArt. You cannot format one part separate from another. You would need to create two separate pieces of WordArt to format separately.

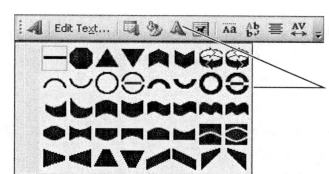

The WordArt Shapes button opens a palette of alternative shapes.

QUICK REFERENCE: CREATING AND FORMATTING WORDART

Task	Procedure
Create WordArt	■ Display the page on which you want to place the WordArt. ■ Click the Insert WordArt ◄ button on the Objects toolbar. ■ Choose a WordArt style and click OK. ■ Type the text for the WordArt.
Edit WordArt text	■ Double-click the WordArt to open the Edit WordArt Text dialog box. ■ Edit the text.
Change WordArt style	■ Click the WordArt to select it. ■ Click the WordArt Gallery button on the Objects toolbar. ■ Choose a new style and click OK.
Change WordArt shape	■ Click the WordArt to select it. ■ Click the WordArt Shape button on the Objects toolbar. ■ Choose a new shape to use.
Format WordArt	■ Click the WordArt to select it. ■ Click the Text Wrapping button to wrap text in your publication around the WordArt image. ■ Click the WordArt Same Letter Heights Aa button to toggle the letter height uniformity. ■ Click the WordArt Vertical Text button to toggle vertical text. ■ Click the WordArt Alignment button, and select the new alignment setting. ■ Click the WordArt Character Spacing AV button, and choose the spacing setting.

Hands-On 3.4   Create and Format WordArt

In this exercise, you will create, move, and resize a Happy Holidays! WordArt object on page 2 of your holiday greeting card. You will also edit and change the WordArt shape.

Create WordArt

1. Click anywhere in the scratch area to make sure no objects are selected.

2. Click the Insert WordArt ![icon] button on the Objects toolbar.
   The WordArt Gallery dialog box appears.

3. Double-click the design style shown in the following figure.

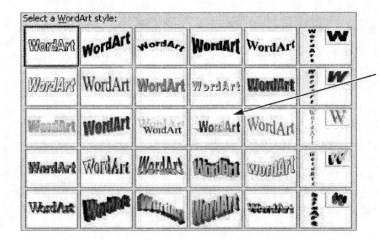

The Edit WordArt Text dialog box appears.

4. Type **Happy Holidays!**

5. Click OK.
   Your WordArt graphic appears centered across pages 2 and 3 of your greeting card.

Move and Resize WordArt

6. Follow these steps to move your WordArt graphic:

A Move your mouse pointer anywhere on the WordArt graphic so that your mouse turns into a Move pointer.

B Hold down the left mouse button and drag your WordArt so that it's roughly centered above the clip art image on page 2 of the publication.

7. Follow these steps to resize your WordArt graphic:

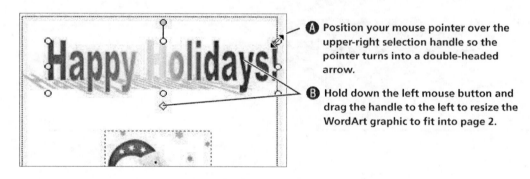

A Position your mouse pointer over the upper-right selection handle so the pointer turns into a double-headed arrow.

B Hold down the left mouse button and drag the handle to the left to resize the WordArt graphic to fit into page 2.

8. If needed, move to center the WordArt graphic over the clip art on page 2.

9. Double-click the WordArt graphic to open the Edit WordArt Text dialog box.

Edit and Format WordArt

10. Follow these steps to edit the WordArt text:

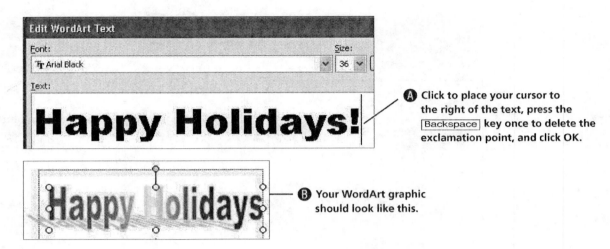

Ⓐ Click to place your cursor to the right of the text, press the `Backspace` key once to delete the exclamation point, and click OK.

Ⓑ Your WordArt graphic should look like this.

11. Follow these steps to change the WordArt shape:

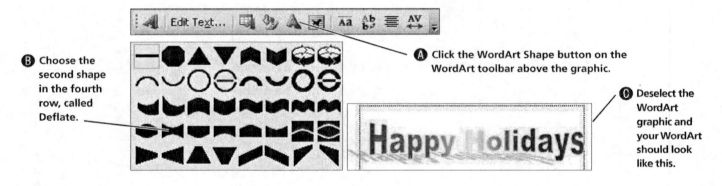

Ⓐ Click the WordArt Shape button on the WordArt toolbar above the graphic.

Ⓑ Choose the second shape in the fourth row, called Deflate.

Ⓒ Deselect the WordArt graphic and your WordArt should look like this.

Adding a BorderArt Object

Publisher has a number of special effects that can dress up a publication. In addition to standard frame borders that you learned about in Lesson 2, Creating an Invitation Using Text Boxes, you can also apply BorderArt. BorderArt is a repeated picture that serves as a border around a text box or other object. BorderArt can be overwhelming for individual text boxes, so use it sparingly.

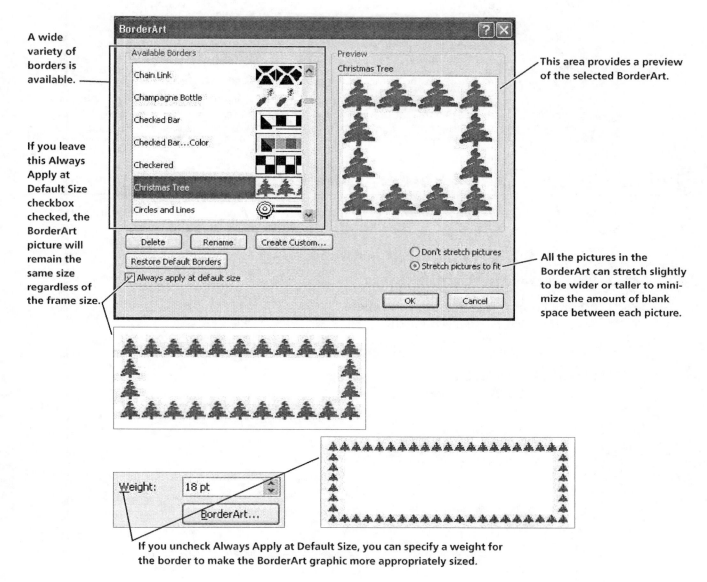

A wide variety of borders is available.

If you leave this Always Apply at Default Size checkbox checked, the BorderArt picture will remain the same size regardless of the frame size.

This area provides a preview of the selected BorderArt.

All the pictures in the BorderArt can stretch slightly to be wider or taller to minimize the amount of blank space between each picture.

If you uncheck Always Apply at Default Size, you can specify a weight for the border to make the BorderArt graphic more appropriately sized.

QUICK REFERENCE: ADDING A BORDERART BORDER

Task	Procedure
Add a BorderArt border	■ Select the text box frame so that it becomes visible.
	■ Right-click the frame border.
	■ Choose Format Text Box from the menu.
	■ Click the Colors and Lines tab in the Format Text Box dialog box.
	■ Click the BorderArt button.
	■ Click the border you want from the Available Borders list.
	■ If desired, clear the Always Apply at Default Size checkbox.
	■ Choose either Don't Stretch Pictures or Stretch Pictures to Fit.
	■ If you cleared the Always Apply at Default Size checkbox, when you click OK, the Format Text Box dialog box is visible. Enter a weight in the Weight box or use the up/down increment button ⊟ to change the weight of the border.

 Hands-On 3.5   **Add a BorderArt Object**

In this exercise, you will apply a BorderArt graphic to the text box on page 3 and change the weight of the border.

1. Click anywhere in the first text box on page 3.

2. Right-click the text box frame border.

3. Choose Format Text Box from the menu.
   The Format Text Box dialog box opens.

4. If necessary, click the Colors and Lines tab.

5. Click the BorderArt button.
   The BorderArt dialog box opens.

6. Follow these steps to choose the BorderArt graphic:

A Scroll down and click to select the Poinsettias border.

B View the preview here.

C Remove the checkmark in Always Apply at Default Size and click OK.

D In the Format Text Box dialog box, use the up/down increment buttons to choose an 8 pt weight and click OK.

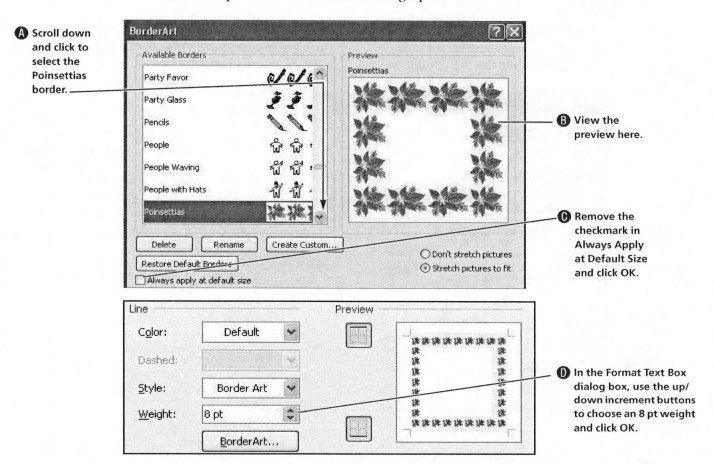

Page 3 of your greeting card should look like the following:

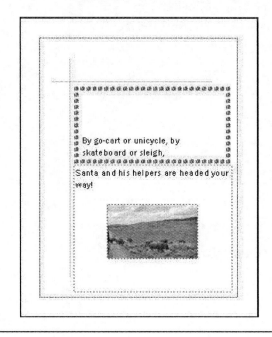

Applying a Drop Cap

You can make the first letter of a paragraph stand out with a drop cap. A drop cap is a large first letter in a paragraph. You may have seen this type of text design in books at the beginning of a chapter. Publisher can create a variety of drop cap effects.

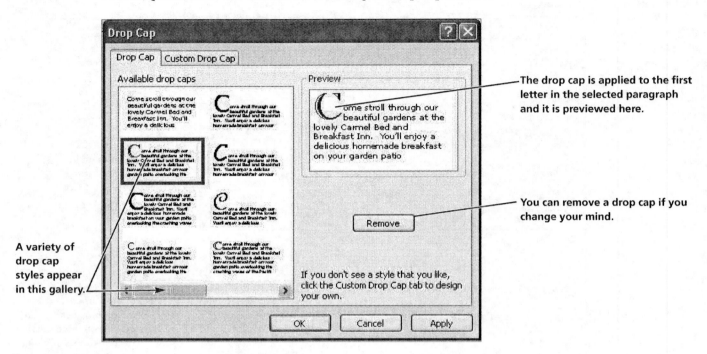

A variety of drop cap styles appear in this gallery.

The drop cap is applied to the first letter in the selected paragraph and it is previewed here.

You can remove a drop cap if you change your mind.

QUICK REFERENCE: APPLYING A DROP CAP

Task	Procedure
Apply a drop cap	■ Click in the paragraph for which you want to set a drop cap. ■ Choose Format→Drop Cap from the menu bar. ■ Choose a drop cap style.
Remove a drop cap	■ Click in the paragraph that contains the drop cap. ■ Click Format→Drop Cap from the menu bar. ■ Click the Remove button.

Hands-On 3.6　Apply a Drop Cap

In this exercise, you will apply a drop cap to the paragraph in the first text box on page 3.

1. On page 3, click in the paragraph in the first text box.

2. Click Format→Drop Cap from the menu bar.

3. If necessary, click the Drop Cap tab.

4. Choose the drop cap style shown in the following illustration and click OK.

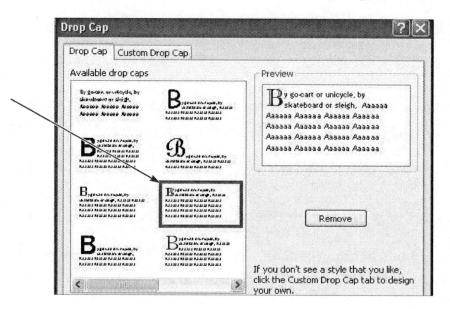

Page 3 of your greeting card should look like the following:

5. Save and close your publication.

6. Exit Publisher.

 # Concepts Review

True/False Questions

1. You can download more clip art images from Microsoft's web site.   TRUE   FALSE

2. If you resize one dimension more than another of a picture, the picture never becomes distorted.   TRUE   FALSE

3. Most of the clip art images that come with Publisher are in Windows Metafile format.   TRUE   FALSE

4. It is possible to lose image quality when you scale (resize) a clip art image in a Windows Metafile format.   TRUE   FALSE

5. Aspect ratio is the ratio of width to height.   TRUE   FALSE

6. You might be subject to legal penalties if you don't obtain permission to acquire a copyrighted picture from a web page.   TRUE   FALSE

7. Inserted pictures are embedded graphics, which means they are not stored inside the Publisher file.   TRUE   FALSE

8. BorderArt helps you format your text with arches, fancy patterns, twists, 3-D effects, and other enhancements.   TRUE   FALSE

9. WordArt formatting applies to the entire piece of WordArt.   TRUE   FALSE

10. A drop cap can be applied to the first word in a paragraph.   TRUE   FALSE

Multiple Choice Questions

1. Which of the following is not a Publisher media type?
   a. Clip Art
   b. Photographs
   c. Movies
   d. IPod

2. Which of the following is not a graphic format that Publisher accepts?
   a. TIF
   b. DOC
   c. Kodak Photo CD
   d. CorelDraw

3. Which of the following can you not do with a WordArt graphic?
   a. Resize
   b. Add a drop cap
   c. Change the shape
   d. Move

4. Which of the following is not true about BorderArt?
   a. BorderArt can be overwhelming for individual text boxes, so use it sparingly.
   b. BorderArt is a repeated picture.
   c. BorderArt can only be applied to text boxes.
   d. BorderArt is a Publisher special effect.

Skill Builders

Skill Builder 3.1   Add Clip Art and WordArt to a Valentine

It's time to create another greeting card! In this exercise, you will create a greeting card for Valentine's Day and add a clip art image.

Add Clip Art

1. Choose the Greeting Cards publication type, and then choose the Valentine's Day category at the top of the center pane.

2. Choose the Valentine's Day 9 design and click the Create button.

3. Apply the Monarch color scheme to the valentine.

4. Go to page 2 of the Valentine's card.
   Both pages 2 and 3 of the card are displayed.

5. Click the Picture Frame 🖻 button on the Objects toolbar and choose Clip Art from the menu.
   The Clip Art task pane appears.

6. Click the Results Should Be drop down arrow and check only Clip Art.

7. Type **valentine** in the Search For box and click Go.

8. Click the clip as shown in the following illustration, or if this clip art image is not available, choose another valentine-related clip.

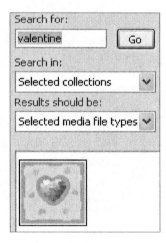

The clip art image is placed in the middle of page 2 and 3 in its own frame.

Move and Resize Clip Art

9. Position your mouse pointer over the clip art image (but not on a selection handle) so the pointer turns into a Move pointer ✥.

10. Drag the clip art image so it is approximately centered on page 2.

11. Position the mouse pointer over the upper-left corner selection handle, so the pointer turns into a double-headed arrow ↔.

12. Drag the handle down and to the right so that the clip art image is sized as shown in the following figure.

13. Position the image as shown in the previous illustration.

Add WordArt

14. Click the Insert WordArt button 🅐 on the Objects toolbar.

15. Choose the first design in the fifth row, and then click OK.

16. In the Edit WordArt Text dialog box, type **I love you!**

17. Click OK to insert the image.

18. Drag the WordArt above the clip art image, and size and position it as you see fit.

19. On page 3, leave the *Happy Valentine's Day* text box in place and delete the remaining boxes on that page.

Format Text

20. Drag the remaining text box to the middle of page 3.

21. Select the *Happy Valentine's Day* text, and change the font to Broadway, 22 pt.

22. Click the drop-down arrow on the Font Color $\boxed{\text{A}}$ · button and choose More Colors from the menu.

23. In the Colors dialog box, make sure the Standard tab is in the foreground, choose a color that blends with your valentine, and click OK.
    Feel free to experiment with a variety of colors.

24. Save $\boxed{\text{▣}}$ the file as **sb-Valentine** in your Lesson 03 folder, and then close it.

Skill Builder 3.2   Insert a Picture in a Business Card and Crop It

Your friend Marvin Washington has been in the travel business for 10 years and now he is ready to open his own boutique travel agency that specializes in Colorado's Rocky Mountains. He has asked you to help him create a business card that reflects the beauty of the area. In this exercise, you will insert a picture in a business card and crop, move, and resize it.

1. Choose Business Cards from the Publication Types list.

2. Choose the Marker design from the Newer Designs category in the center pane, and then click the Create button.

3. From the Format Publication task pane, apply the Apex color scheme.

4. Apply the Casual Comic Sans font scheme as shown in the following illustration.

5. Delete the text box in the upper-right corner of the publication as shown in the following illustration.

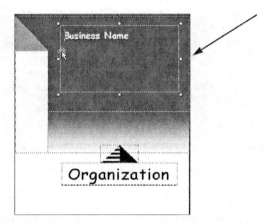

Insert a Picture

6. Click the Picture Frame button on the Objects toolbar.

7. Choose Picture from File from the menu.

8. Drag your mouse to draw a picture frame in the upper-right corner of the business card, and then release the mouse.

> **!TIP!** *Don't worry about drawing a perfect picture frame for inserting your picture. You can always move and resize the picture later.*

9. Navigate to your Lesson 03 folder and double-click to open sb-Colorado Rockies.jpg.

Crop a Picture

Next, you will crop the picture to remove the road in the lower-left corner.

10. If necessary, click the picture to select.
The Picture toolbar is displayed above the picture.

11. Click the Crop button on the Picture toolbar.

12. Position your mouse pointer over the lower-left corner cropping handle, hold down the left mouse button, and drag up and to the right until the road is cropped out.

13. Click the Crop button again to turn it off.

14. Reposition the picture to your satisfaction, and resize it as needed.

15. Replace the phone and fax area codes with **720.**

16. Delete the e-mail line and replace it with the following:
ColoradoAdventures@provider.com

17. Enter the following address in the address area and delete the extra address lines:

    1754 Mountain View
    Denver, CO

18. Position the cursor in front of the street address and tap Enter to provide some space between the e-mail address and the snail mail address.

19. Replace the text in the text box that is second from the bottom on the left side with **Marvin Washington**.

20. Replace the Your Title text with **President**.

21. Type **Colorado Adventures** in the text box below the pyramid graphic.

22. Print preview your publication, and then close the preview window.

23. Save 💾 the publication as **sb-Colorado Adventure** in your Lesson 03 folder, and then close it.

Skill Builder 3.3   Add BorderArt and a Drop Cap to a Publication

In this exercise, you will create a flyer announcing the Spring Plant Festival sponsored by the Wadsworth Senior Center. You will add BorderArt and a drop cap to your flyer.

1. Choose Flyers from the Publication Type list.

2. Scroll down to the Event category in the center pane, and double-click the Plant Sale design to open it in the text editing window.

3. Click in the Plant Sale text box at the top and type **Spring Plant Festival**.

4. Delete the two small text boxes below the top text box.

5. Select all the text in the Date text box at the bottom of the publication and type **April 13 & 14** in its place.

6. Select the 00:00 time text and type **9 to 4** in its place.

7. Delete the text box with the pyramid graphic in the bottom-right corner.

8. Select the text in the bottom text box and type **Wadsworth Senior Center** in its place.

9. Format the text with Arial 22 pt bold and center the text within the text box.

10. Follow these steps to resize and reposition the text box:

A If necessary, select the text box and position the mouse pointer on the bottom-center handle then drag up to reduce the height of the text box.

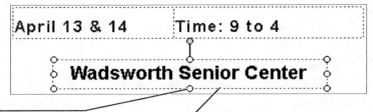

April 13 & 14 Time: 9 to 4

Wadsworth Senior Center

B Position the mouse pointer on the text box border (but not on a handle); drag down to provide some white space above the box and drag to the right to center the box below the date and time text boxes.

Add BorderArt

11. Right-click the border of the *Entice your readers* text box.

12. Choose Format→Text Box from the menu bar.

13. In the Format Text Box dialog box, make sure the Colors and Lines tab is in the foreground, and click the Border Art button.

14. Scroll down and click the Creatures...Lady Bug style border to display it in the Preview window.

15. Click OK twice to apply the BorderArt to your publication.

16. Select the text inside the Lady Bug border, and type **Get a refill for your garden while enjoying the Smith River Blue Grass Band.**

17. Tap Enter .

Insert a Drop Cap

18. Position your cursor in the text you just typed and choose Format→Drop Cap from the menu bar.

19. Choose the second drop cap style in the first column and click OK.
Hmmm, that's a bit large.

20. Click the Undo button and choose Format→Drop Cap from the menu bar again.
This time you will explore the options on the Custom Drop Cap tab.

21. Click the Custom Drop Cap tab and notice the Size of Letters option, as shown in the following illustration.

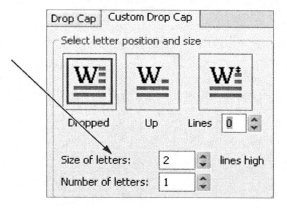

22. Use the bottom scroll arrow to specify a letter size that is two lines high, and then click OK.

23. Position the cursor on the blank line below the paragraph and type the bulleted list shown in the following illustration. Feel free to use a different bullet style if you wish.

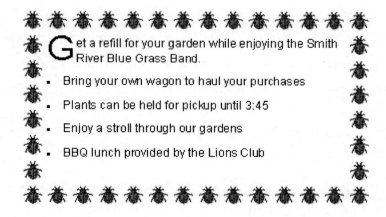

24. Save ![save icon] the publication as **sb-Plant Festival** in your Lesson 03 folder, and then close the file.

 **Assessments**

Assessment 3.1   Add Clip Art and a Picture to an Invitation

It's time for your annual BBQ by the Bay. In this exercise, you will create an invitation card to send to your friends. You will add clip art and a picture.

1. Create a BBQ 1 invitation card. You'll find it in the Theme Party category in the center pane.

2. Apply the Berry color scheme.

3. Change to the Deckle Papyrus font scheme as shown in the following illustration.

Replace the Clip Art

You've decided you would like to use a different clip art image on your invitation.

4. Delete the clip art image of the chef provided in the publication.

5. Click the Picture Frame ![icon] button on the Objects toolbar and choose Clip Art from the menu.

6. Search for a BBQ clip art image and choose one that blends well with your color scheme.

7. Size and position the image as needed.

Work with Text Boxes

8. Delete the text box below the clip art.

9. In the remaining text box, replace the sample text with `Join us for a BBQ by the Bay.`

10. Increase the font size to 22 pt.

11. Navigate to page 2 of the invitation.

12. In the top text box, type `Join us for a BBQ by the Bay.`

13. Bold the text.

14. Delete the remaining text boxes on page 2.

Insert and Format a Picture

15. Insert the picture as-San Francisco Bridge.JPG from your Lesson 03 folder.

16. Follow these guidelines to format the picture:

- Crop off approximately half of the water at the bottom of the image.
- Apply a Line/Border Style of $2^1/_4$ pts.
- Apply a line color that blends with your color scheme.

17. Resize the picture as you see fit, and then center the text box and picture on page 2.

Work with Text Boxes

18. On page 3, delete the word *Invitation* from the text box and left-align the cursor.

19. Type the following bulleted list using a bullet style of your choice.

- Sharon and Ben's
- 543 Bridgeview Drive
- September 10th, 12 noon
- RSVP 415-555-1212

20. Resize and position the text box as you desire.

21. Save 🖫 your card to the Lesson 03 folder with the name **as-BBQ**, and then close the file.

Assessment 3.2   Add BorderArt and Clip Art to a Blank Publication

You play violin in an amateur string quartet. Your group gives an annual concert as an incentive to keep practicing. In this exercise, you will create a flyer from a blank page publication. You will apply BorderArt to the page, and you will provide and format the text announcing the concert.

1. Choose an $8\frac{1}{2} \times 11$ size page from the Blank Page Sizes publication type.

2. Draw a text box the same size and shape as the blue dotted margin border on the page.

Add Border Art

3. Apply Music Notes BorderArt to the text box.

4. Apply a fill color of your choice to the text box, but be sure that it isn't so dark that the print will be difficult to read.

5. Type the following text in the text box:

   Margate String Quartet
   Tuesday, October 16 at 7:00 p.m.
   Rawlings Concert Hall
   Debussy's Quartet in G Minor
   Beethoven's Quartet in C Major

6. Center the text on the page and format the text with a font and point size of your choice.

Add Clip Art

7. Add an appropriate clip art image to your flyer, and size and position it as you see fit.

8. Save ⊞ the publication as **as-Quartet** in your Lesson 03 folder, and then close the file.

Critical Thinking

Critical Thinking 3.1　　Create an Invitation Postcard

The current President of the School Board, Heather, has just been appointed to the National School Board by the Presidential First Lady. Heather will be stepping down as the President. Jane, who will be assuming the position, decides to throw a luncheon for Heather to say congratulations and wish her the best of luck in her new job.

Jane is getting more comfortable using Publisher. She would like to create a great-looking postcard to send to the other board members inviting them to the luncheon. In this exercise, you will help Jane add a picture from the trip the School Board members took to the Grand Canyon last spring.

1. Follow these guidelines to create a postcard:

   ■ Create a postcard using the Five Blocks design in the Invitation category.

   ■ Apply the Tuscany color scheme and the Casual Comic Sans font scheme.

   ■ Add the text shown in the illustration at the end of this exercise and delete any unnecessary text boxes. Resize fonts and text boxes and reposition text boxes as necessary.

   ■ Replace the push pin graphic on the right with ct-Grand Canyon.jpg located in your Lesson 03 folder. Size and position the graphic as needed, and place a $2^1/_4$ pt border around the graphic. Apply a line color to the border that blends well with the Tuscany color scheme. Adjust the brightness and contrast of the picture to your satisfaction.

   ■ Add a school-related clip art image such as the school bus shown in the bottom-left corner of the postcard.

2. Save 💾 your postcard as **ct-Congratulations** in your Lesson 03 folder.

Critical Thinking 3.2   Create a Father's Day Card

Mike Hillicoss has always had a special relationship with his dad, Ben. They have been avid outdoorsmen since Mike was a little boy growing up in California. On one of their special hikes on a yearly trip to Montana, Mike spotted a small herd of bighorn sheep and took their picture, which his dad has never seen.

It's almost Father's Day and Mike would like to make Ben a special Father's Day card using Publisher and include a picture of the bighorn sheep, which they both enjoyed seeing on that special day in Montana a few years back. Mike is comfortable using Publisher, but he has never added pictures or clip art to his publications. In this exercise, you will help Mike add art to his Father's Day card.

1. Create a Father's Day Greeting Card that you think would look great for Mike's dad.

2. Experiment searching for and inserting a clip art image.

3. Practice creating and formatting WordArt text and placing it where you think best in your card.

4. Delete any text boxes or graphics that you don't need.

5. Insert the ct-Bighorn Sheep.jpg picture from the Lesson 03 folder and practice cropping the picture.

6. Feel free to change font and color schemes.

7. Experiment with different BorderArt graphics you think would look best on a text box of your choice in your card.

8. Save 💾 your card as **ct-Fathers Day** in your Lesson 03 folder, and then close the file.

Drawing Directions in a Flyer

In this lesson, you will expand upon the basic skills that you developed in the previous lesson. You will open a flyer and create directions using Publisher's Drawing tools. You will draw simple lines, arrows, ovals, and rectangles. You will also create more complex shapes using AutoShapes. You will see how entering text in AutoShapes is similar to entering text in text boxes. After creating these simple shapes and AutoShapes, you will format them using similar formatting features as you did with text boxes, and you will add new formats including 3-D effects and shadows. You will group, align, flip, and rotate objects as well as group and nudge them. And finally, you will insert and edit Design Gallery objects in your flyer.

LESSON OBJECTIVES

After studying this lesson, you will be able to:

- Draw lines, arrows, ovals, and rectangles
- Create AutoShapes
- Format and add 3-D effects and shadows
- Group, align, flip, and rotate objects
- Copy and nudge drawing objects
- Insert and edit a Design Gallery object

Case Study: Drawing Directions with Ease

Eleni has happily agreed to create a flyer for her friend, Ben, who just opened Ben's Fishing Haven. Ben would like Eleni to include directions to his inn as well as an interesting and catchy heading.

Eleni is feeling pretty comfortable using Publisher. She has been creating publications using clip art and pictures and is very comfortable creating text boxes and graphics. She would now like to become proficient working with drawing objects and using the AutoShape feature.

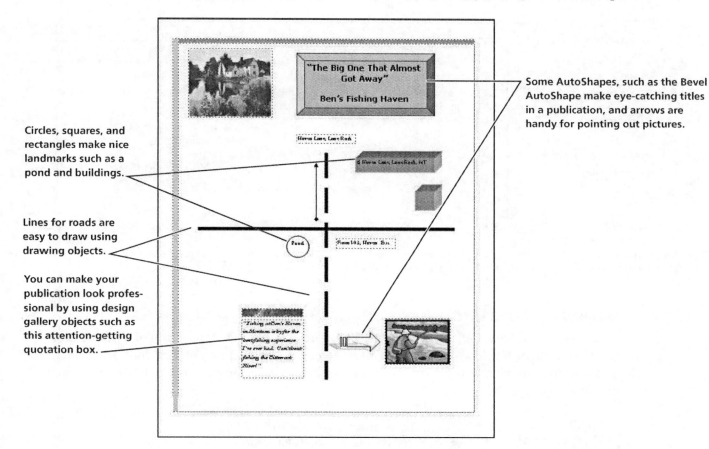

Circles, squares, and rectangles make nice landmarks such as a pond and buildings.

Lines for roads are easy to draw using drawing objects.

You can make your publication look professional by using design gallery objects such as this attention-getting quotation box.

Some AutoShapes, such as the Bevel AutoShape make eye-catching titles in a publication, and arrows are handy for pointing out pictures.

Using Drawing Objects

You are not limited to clip art, pictures, or other ready-to-use artwork in Publisher. You can draw simple lines and shapes such as ovals and rectangles using Publisher's drawing tools. These drawing tools are not sophisticated, but they can come in handy when drawing items such as directions in a publication.

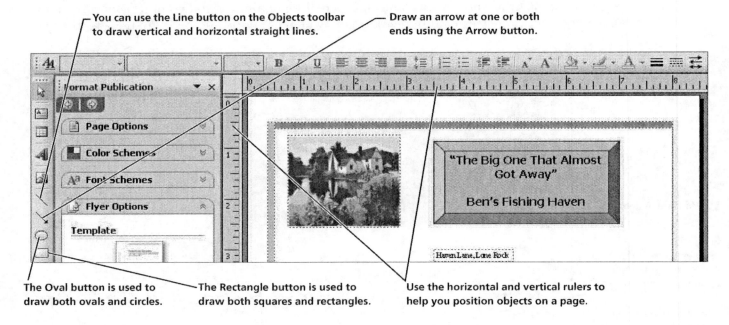

You can use the Line button on the Objects toolbar to draw vertical and horizontal straight lines.

Draw an arrow at one or both ends using the Arrow button.

The Oval button is used to draw both ovals and circles.

The Rectangle button is used to draw both squares and rectangles.

Use the horizontal and vertical rulers to help you position objects on a page.

Drawing Lines and Arrows

Lines and arrows are useful for drawing directions, separating one section of a publication from another, or for drawing arrow pointers to call attention to an object. You can draw a straight line anywhere on your publication. A straight line can be vertical, horizontal, or at any angle.

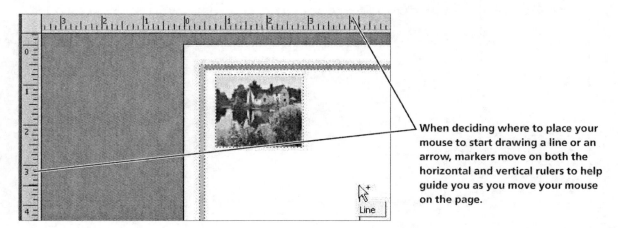

When deciding where to place your mouse to start drawing a line or an arrow, markers move on both the horizontal and vertical rulers to help guide you as you move your mouse on the page.

QR

QUICK REFERENCE: DRAWING LINES AND ARROWS

Task	Procedure
Draw lines	■ Click the Line 🖊 button on the Objects toolbar.
	■ Position the mouse pointer where you want the line to start.
	■ Hold down the left mouse button.
	■ To draw a straight vertical or horizontal line, hold down the Shift key.
	■ Drag the mouse where you want the line to end.
	■ Release the mouse button (and Shift key if necessary).
Draw arrows	■ Click the Arrow 🖊 button on the Objects toolbar.
	■ Position the mouse pointer where you want the non-arrow end of the line to start.
	■ Hold down the left mouse button.
	■ Drag the mouse where you want the tip of the arrow to be.
	■ Release the mouse button.

Drawing Ovals and Rectangles

Ovals and rectangles can be used to build simple drawings or call attention to other objects on the publication page. You can draw circles and ovals as well as squares and rectangles.

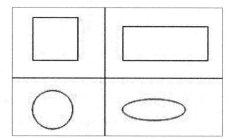

Squares, circles, rectangles, and ovals are easy to draw.

QUICK REFERENCE: DRAWING OVALS AND RECTANGLES

Task	Procedure
Draw ovals or circles	■ Click the Oval ⬭ button.
	■ Position the mouse pointer where you want the shape to start.
	■ To draw a perfect circle, hold down the Shift key.
	■ Hold down the left mouse button.
	■ Drag the mouse where you want the shape to stop.
	■ Release the mouse button (and Shift key if necessary).
Draw rectangles or squares	■ Click the Rectangle ▢ button.
	■ Position the mouse pointer where you want the shape to start.
	■ To draw a perfect square, hold down the Shift key.
	■ Hold down the left mouse button.
	■ Drag the mouse where you want the shape to stop.
	■ Release the mouse button (and Shift key if necessary).

Hands-On 4.1   Draw Lines, Arrow, Ovals and Rectangles

In this exercise, you will open a flyer and draw two lines, an arrow, an oval, a circle, a square, and a rectangle.

Draw First Line

1. Choose File→Open, navigate to the Lesson 04 folder, and open Fishing Haven.

2. Click the Line ◱ button on the Objects toolbar at the left edge of the window.

3. Position the mouse pointer ✛ so it is approximately 4¼ inches on the horizontal ruler and 3½ inches on the vertical ruler.

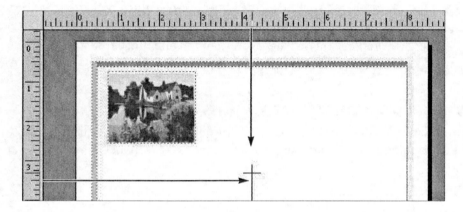

4. Hold down the left mouse button and the [Shift] key.

5. Drag the mouse pointer down to approximately 9½ inches on the vertical ruler.

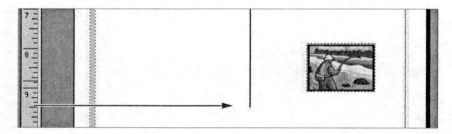

6. Release the mouse button first then release the [Shift] key.

Draw Second Line

7. Click the Line ◱ button.

8. Position the mouse pointer ✛ at approximately 1 inch on the horizontal ruler and 5½ inches on the vertical ruler.

9. Hold down the [Shift] key and the left mouse button.

10. Drag the mouse right to approximately 7½ inches on the horizontal ruler.

11. Release the mouse button first then release the [Shift] key.
    A straight horizontal line is drawn.

Draw an Arrow

12. Click the Arrow 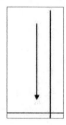 button.

13. Position the mouse pointer at approximately $3\frac{3}{4}$ inches on both the vertical and horizontal rulers.

14. Hold down the ⌗Shift⌗ key and the left mouse button, and then drag the mouse down to approximately $5\frac{1}{4}$ inches on the vertical ruler.

15. Release the mouse button first then release the ⌗Shift⌗ key.

Draw a Circle

16. Click the Oval ⬭ button.

17. Position the mouse pointer ✛ at approximately 3 inches on the horizontal ruler and $5\frac{3}{4}$ inches on the vertical ruler.

18. Hold down the ⌗Shift⌗ key and the left mouse button, and then drag the mouse down to approximately $6\frac{1}{4}$ inches on the vertical ruler and right to approximately $3\frac{3}{4}$ inches on the horizontal ruler.

19. Release the mouse button first then release the ⌗Shift⌗ key.

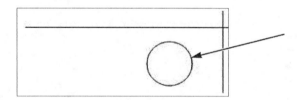

20. With the circle still selected, type the text **Pond.**

Draw an Oval

21. Click the Oval ⬭ button.

22. Position the mouse pointer ✛ approximately $5\frac{1}{2}$ inches on the horizontal ruler and 7 inches on the vertical ruler.

23. Drag the mouse down and right to approximately $6\frac{1}{2}$ inches on the horizontal ruler and $7\frac{1}{2}$ inches on the vertical ruler, and then release the mouse button.
An oval is drawn above the picture of the fisherman.

Delete the Oval

24. Click the oval to select it then tap ⎡Delete⎤.

Draw a Square

25. Click the Rectangle ⬜ button.

26. Position the mouse pointer ➕ approximately 6 inches on the horizontal ruler and $4\frac{1}{2}$ inches on the vertical ruler.

27. Hold down the ⎡Shift⎤ key and the left mouse button, and then drag the mouse down to approximately 5 inches on the vertical ruler.

28. Release the mouse button first then release the ⎡Shift⎤ key.

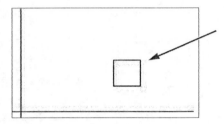

Draw a Rectangle

29. Click the Rectangle ⬜ button.

30. Position the mouse pointer ➕ at approximately 5 inches on the horizontal ruler and $3\frac{1}{2}$ inches on the vertical ruler.

31. Drag the mouse right to approximately 7 inches on the horizontal ruler down to approximately 4 inches on the vertical ruler.

32. Release the mouse button.

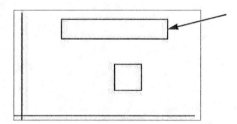

Creating AutoShapes

AutoShape graphic designs help you create more complex shapes without having to draw them with a series of lines. They include lines, connectors, basic shapes, block arrows, and stars and banners, among others. AutoShapes differ from WordArt in that they do not contain text. Some of the AutoShapes are similar to text boxes in that you can type text in the shape.

The AutoShapes button is located on the Objects toolbar.

The Basic Shapes category, for example, contains a variety of shapes to draw.

Various categories of AutoShapes are listed.

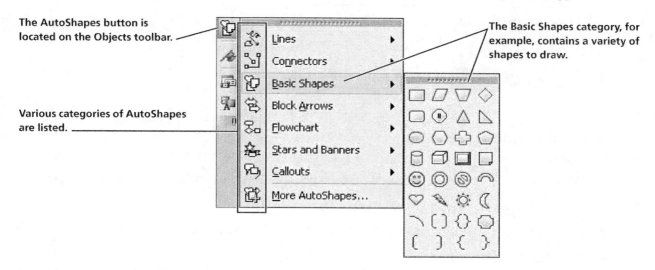

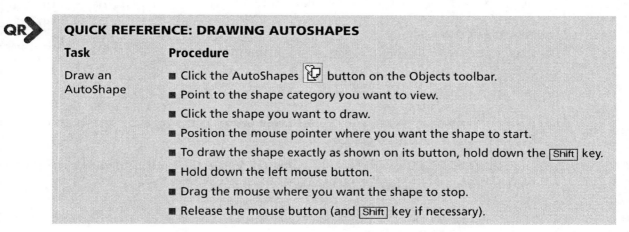

QUICK REFERENCE: DRAWING AUTOSHAPES

Task	Procedure
Draw an AutoShape	■ Click the AutoShapes button on the Objects toolbar.
	■ Point to the shape category you want to view.
	■ Click the shape you want to draw.
	■ Position the mouse pointer where you want the shape to start.
	■ To draw the shape exactly as shown on its button, hold down the Shift key.
	■ Hold down the left mouse button.
	■ Drag the mouse where you want the shape to stop.
	■ Release the mouse button (and Shift key if necessary).

 ## Hands-On 4.2   Draw AutoShapes

In this exercise, you will practice drawing three AutoShapes graphic designs, typing text in one, and then deleting another one.

Draw a Bevel Basic Shape

1. Click the AutoShapes button and point to the Basic Shapes category.

2. Choose the Bevel shape, which is in the fourth row, third shape.

3. Position the mouse pointer ┼ button approximately 3½ inches on the horizontal ruler and 1 inch on the vertical ruler.

4. Drag the mouse down to approximately $2\frac{1}{2}$ inches on the vertical ruler and right to approximately 7 inches on the horizontal ruler.

5. Release the mouse button.

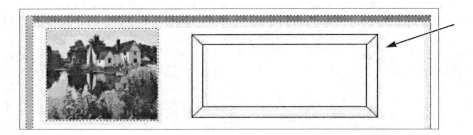

Add and Format Text

6. Type the following text:

"The Big One That Almost Got Away" Enter Enter **Ben's Fishing Haven**

7. Press Ctrl + A to select all of the text.

8. On the Formatting toolbar, select the Tahoma font and font size 16.

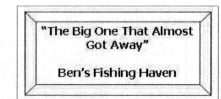

9. Click the Bold **B** button and the Center ≡ button. *Your Bevel AutoShape should look like the illustration at right.*

Draw an Arrow

10. Click the AutoShapes button and point to the Block Arrows category.

11. Click the Striped Right Arrow, which is in the fifth row, first shape.

12. Position the mouse pointer + approximately $4\frac{1}{2}$ inches on the horizontal ruler and $8\frac{1}{4}$ inches on the vertical ruler.

13. Drag the mouse to the right to approximately $5\frac{1}{2}$ inches on the horizontal ruler and down to approximately $8\frac{3}{4}$ inches on the vertical ruler.

Formatting Drawing Objects

Drawn shapes can be left with their default attributes. You can also enhance the drawn lines and shape borders by using a variety of colors and patterns. Like text boxes, it's often most effective to use the standard color scheme for the current publication. Applying 3-D and shadow effects can be dramatic on drawn shapes.

Formatting Line and Shape Borders

Just like text boxes, drawn shapes have borders. You can change a drawn shape's border color and style the same way you do text boxes (as you learned in Lesson 2, Creating an Invitation Using Text Boxes), using various tools on the Formatting toolbar.

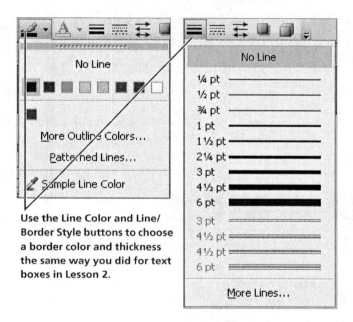

Use the Line Color and Line/Border Style buttons to choose a border color and thickness the same way you did for text boxes in Lesson 2.

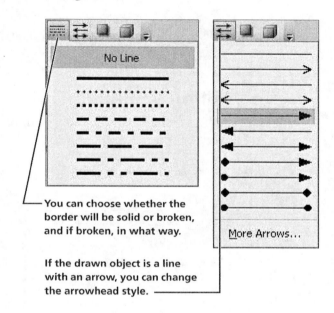

You can choose whether the border will be solid or broken, and if broken, in what way.

If the drawn object is a line with an arrow, you can change the arrowhead style.

QUICK REFERENCE: FORMATTING LINES AND BORDERS

Task	Procedure
Apply a scheme color to a line or shape border	■ Select the line or shape. ■ Click the down arrow to the right of the Line Color button on the Formatting toolbar. ■ Choose one of the scheme colors.
Change a line or shape border width	■ Select the line or shape. ■ Click the Line/Border Style button. ■ Choose one of the preset thicknesses or choose More Lines. ■ Choose a style from the Style list or type an exact thickness in the Weight box.

QUICK REFERENCE: FORMATTING LINES AND BORDERS (CONTINUED)

Task	Procedure
Apply a dash style to a line	■ Select the line. ■ Click the Dash Style ▦ button. ■ Choose a style from the list.
Add or change an arrow	■ Select a line, with or without an arrow. ■ Click the Arrow Style ⇄ button. ■ Click the arrow style you want or click More Arrows. ■ Select an arrow style (or a plain line with no arrow) from the Begin Style list. ■ Select an arrow size from the Begin Size list. ■ Select an arrow style (or a plain line with no arrow) from the End Style list. ■ Select an arrow size from the End Size list.

Filling a Shape

A drawn shape can be filled with one of the scheme colors or with any other solid color just like a text box.

Fill a shape the same way that you filled a text box in Lesson 2.

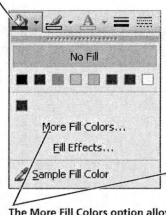

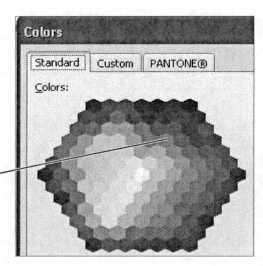

The More Fill Colors option allows you to select from many fixed colors.

QUICK REFERENCE: FILLING SHAPES

Task	Procedure
Fill a shape with a fixed color	■ Select the line or shape. ■ Click the down arrow to the right of the Fill Color ⬧ button. ■ Click More Fill Colors. ■ Choose the color you want.

Applying 3-D Effects

You can apply 3-D effects to almost any Publisher object, but they are especially effective on drawn shapes.

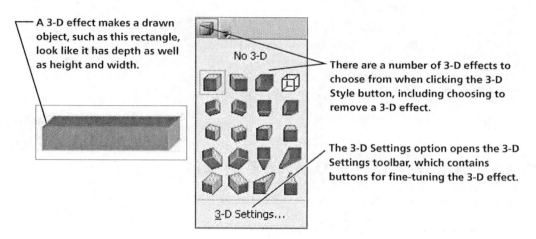

A 3-D effect makes a drawn object, such as this rectangle, look like it has depth as well as height and width.

There are a number of 3-D effects to choose from when clicking the 3-D Style button, including choosing to remove a 3-D effect.

The 3-D Settings option opens the 3-D Settings toolbar, which contains buttons for fine-tuning the 3-D effect.

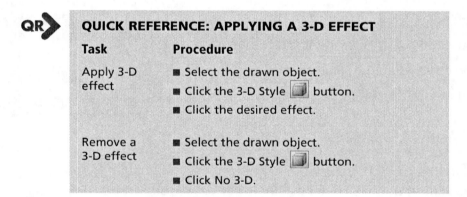

QR

QUICK REFERENCE: APPLYING A 3-D EFFECT

Task	Procedure
Apply 3-D effect	■ Select the drawn object. ■ Click the 3-D Style ▦ button. ■ Click the desired effect.
Remove a 3-D effect	■ Select the drawn object. ■ Click the 3-D Style ▦ button. ■ Click No 3-D.

Applying Shadow Effects

Shadow effects are similar to 3-D effects except a two-dimensional shadow is applied to the object instead of making a solid-looking object.

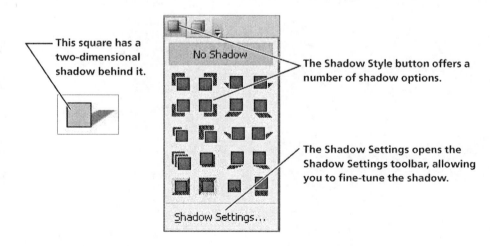

This square has a two-dimensional shadow behind it.

The Shadow Style button offers a number of shadow options.

The Shadow Settings opens the Shadow Settings toolbar, allowing you to fine-tune the shadow.

QUICK REFERENCE: APPLYING SHADOW EFFECTS

Task	Procedure
Apply a shadow	■ Select the drawn object. ■ Click the Shadow Style ⬛ button on the Formatting toolbar. ■ Choose the desired effect.
Remove a shadow	■ Select the drawn object. ■ Click the Shadow Style ⬛ button on the Formatting toolbar. ■ Choose No Shadow.

Hands-On 4.3   Format Drawn Objects

In this exercise, you will add line color and a border style.

Add Line Color and Border Style

1. Press the Ctrl key and click on both the Bevel and Arrow AutoShapes to select both, and release the Ctrl key.

2. Click the down arrow to the right of the Line Color ⬛ button.

3. Choose the seventh color in the color scheme.

4. Click the Line/Border Style ≡ button and choose the 1 pt line.

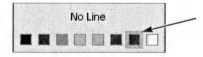

5. Click in the scratch area to deselect both the Bevel and Arrow AutoShapes.

Apply a Dash Line

6. Select the long, vertical line, click the Dash Style ⬛ button, and choose the sixth line, Long Dash.

7. Press Ctrl and click to select the long horizontal line.
Both the long vertical and horizontal lines are selected.

8. Click the Line/Border Style ☰ button and choose the 6 pt line.
The formatted vertical and horizontal lines should look the following illustration.

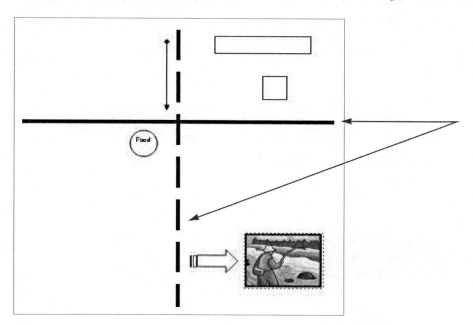

9. Click to select the short vertical arrow alongside the dashed vertical line.

10. Click the Arrow Style ⇄ button.

11. Choose the eighth arrow style, Arrow Style 8.

Apply a Fill Color

12. Click in the scratch area to deselect the arrow.

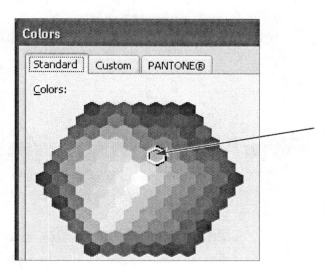

13. Press the [Ctrl] key and click to select the Bevel AutoShape, the rectangle, and the square, and then release the [Ctrl] key.

14. Click the down arrow to the right of the Fill Color button and click More Fill Colors.
Publisher displays the Colors box.

15. In the Standard tab, click to select the seven color from the left in the fifth row then click OK.

16. Click in the scratch area to deselect all the objects.

Apply a 3-D Effect

17. Press the Ctrl key and click to select the rectangle and square then release the Ctrl key.

18. Click the 3-D Style button and choose the first 3-D effect in the first line, 3-D Style 1.

19. Click in the scratch area to deselect the rectangle and square then click to select only the rectangle.

TIP! *Press F9 (zoom) to enlarge the screen to make it easier to type in text.*

20. Type the following text in the rectangle:

    6 Haven Lane, Lone Rock, MT

TIP! *Press F9 again to make the screen smaller.*

Apply a Shadow

21. Click to select the striped arrow, and then click the Shadow Style button on the Formatting toolbar.

22. Click the third shadow in the first line, Shadow Style 6.

23. Click in the scratch area to deselect the arrow.

Working with Drawing Objects

Publisher provides tools that make it easy to align and group objects. You can also rotate and flip objects as well as give them a little nudge. You can also easily copy and delete objects.

Aligning, Grouping, and Nudging Objects

You can align or distribute multiple drawn objects, clip art objects, pictures, and text boxes so that your publication looks balanced. Aligning objects helps guide the eye across the page by avoiding isolated patches of white space that might be distracting. Alignment can be left to right or from top to bottom.

You can also group images to work with them more easily. A group is a selection of multiple images that you can move or resize as one unit. When you finish working with objects as a group, you can ungroup them to work with them individually again if you wish.

An object can also be nudged to move it a precise amount in a certain direction. It's useful when you are having trouble making an object align precisely where you want it by dragging it.

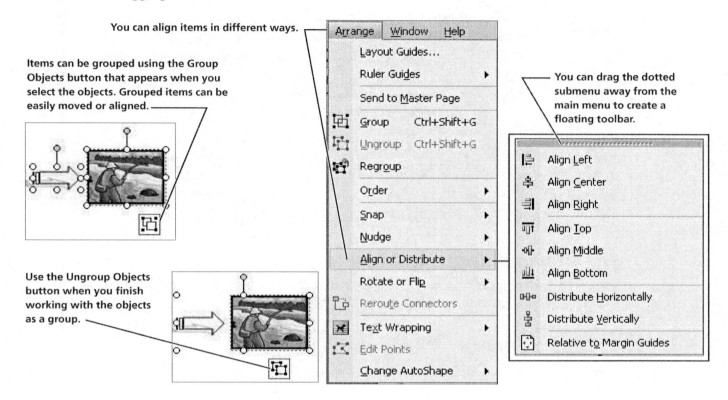

You can align items in different ways.

Items can be grouped using the Group Objects button that appears when you select the objects. Grouped items can be easily moved or aligned.

You can drag the dotted submenu away from the main menu to create a floating toolbar.

Use the Ungroup Objects button when you finish working with the objects as a group.

QR

QUICK REFERENCE: ALIGNING, GROUPING, AND NUDGING OBJECTS

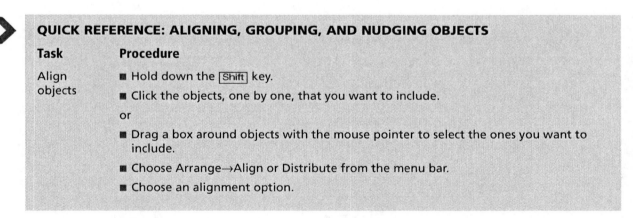

Task	Procedure
Align objects	■ Hold down the [Shift] key.
	■ Click the objects, one by one, that you want to include.
	or
	■ Drag a box around objects with the mouse pointer to select the ones you want to include.
	■ Choose Arrange→Align or Distribute from the menu bar.
	■ Choose an alignment option.

QUICK REFERENCE: ALIGNING, GROUPING, AND NUDGING OBJECTS (CONTINUED)

Task	Procedure
Group objects	■ Select the first object.
	■ Hold down the Shift key.
	■ Click the other objects, one by one, that you want to include.
	or
	■ Drag a box around objects to select the ones you want to include.
	■ Click the Group Objects 🔲 button.
Ungroup objects	■ Select the grouped object.
	■ Click the Ungroup Objects 🔲 button.
Nudge an object	■ Select the object.
	■ Press either the right or left arrow key to move the object 0.13".

Flipping and Rotating Objects

You can flip an object along its vertical or horizontal axis. You can also rotate an object to the left or right 90 degrees or Free Rotate an object by a precise amount.

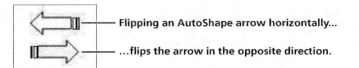

Flipping an AutoShape arrow horizontally...

...flips the arrow in the opposite direction.

QUICK REFERENCE: FLIPPING AND ROTATING OBJECTS

Task	Procedure
Flip an object	■ Select the object.
	■ Choose Arrange from the menu bar.
	■ Click Rotate or Flip.
	■ Click either Flip Horizontal or Flip Vertical.
Rotate an object	■ Select the object.
	■ Choose Arrange from the menu bar.
	■ Click Rotate or Flip.
	■ Choose either Rotate Left 90° or Rotate Right 90°.

Copying and Deleting Objects

Instead of creating a second identical object, you can quickly copy it. You can also use copied images for experimentation in manipulating their colors and cropping without changing the design of your original object. When you copy an object, the copy is held temporarily in the Windows Clipboard, a temporary storage area for copied items. Objects can also be deleted the same way as text boxes, clip art images, and pictures.

QUICK REFERENCE: COPYING AND DELETING OBJECTS

Task	Procedure
Copy an object	■ Select the object. ■ Hold down the [Ctrl] key and drag to a new location. ■ Release the mouse, and then release the [Ctrl] key.
Delete an object	■ Select the object. ■ Press the [Delete] key.

 Hands-On 4.4   **Use Drawing Objects**

In this exercise, you will align, group, nudge, flip, rotate, and copy objects.

Align Objects

1. Position your mouse pointer above the top-left corner of the rectangle and drag down and to the right to draw a dotted box around both the rectangle and square.

NOTE! *Before you start drawing, make sure that your mouse pointer is far enough above the top-left corner of the left rectangle to select both objects.*

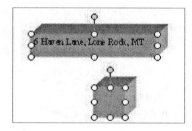

2. Choose Arrange from the menu bar, point to Align or Distribute, and choose Align Right from the submenu. *The rectangle and box are aligned to the right.*

Group Objects

3. Position your mouse pointer to the top left of the striped AutoShape arrow and to the left of the formatted vertical line. Drag down and to the right to draw a dotted box around the arrow AutoShape and the fishing picture. *Both objects are selected.*

4. Follow these steps to group the objects:

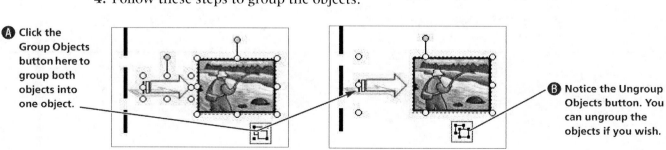

Ⓐ Click the Group Objects button here to group both objects into one object.

Ⓑ Notice the Ungroup Objects button. You can ungroup the objects if you wish.

Nudge and Ungroup Objects

5. Press the right arrow →̲ key seven times.
The group is nudged to the right.

6. Click the Ungroup Objects 🔲 button.

Flip Objects

7. Click to select the drawn arrow in the top half of the page.

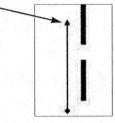

8. Click Arrange from the menu bar and choose Rotate or Flip.

9. Choose Flip Vertical from the submenu.
The arrow end is now pointing up instead of down.

Rotate Objects

10. Click to select the circle, choose Arrange from the menu bar, and choose Rotate or Flip.

11. Choose Rotate Left 90º.

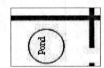

12. Choose Arrange again then choose Rotate or Flip and Rotate Right 90º.
The circle rotates back to the right 90 degrees.

Create a Text Box and Copy It

13. Click the Text Box 🔲 button.

14. Draw a box approximately $3\frac{1}{2}$ inches on the horizontal toolbar and 3 inches on the vertical toolbar to approximately 5 inches on the horizontal toolbar and $3\frac{1}{4}$ inches on the vertical toolbar.

15. Type **Haven Lane, Lone Rock** then click in the scratch area to deselect the text box.

16. Hold down the C̲t̲r̲l̲ key and place your mouse pointer on the newly drawn text box until a plus sign appears to the right of the mouse.

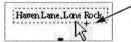

17. Drag the mouse pointer until the right side of the text box is aligned to approximately 6 inches on the horizontal ruler and the top of the text box is aligned to approximately 6 inches on the vertical ruler.

18. Release the mouse, and then release the C̲t̲r̲l̲ key.

19. Press C̲t̲r̲l̲+A̲ to select the text in the text box.

20. Type **From I-93, Haven Exit**.

21. If necessary, move the text box so it is positioned in the same location as shown in the following illustration.

Adding a Design Gallery Object

A Design Gallery is a collection of special elements that can give your publications a more professional look. The Design Gallery includes coupons, attention-getters, logos, tear-offs, boxes, quotation boxes, and much more.

Many Design Gallery categories are available.

Each category provides a variety of quotation designs you can customize and insert into your publication.

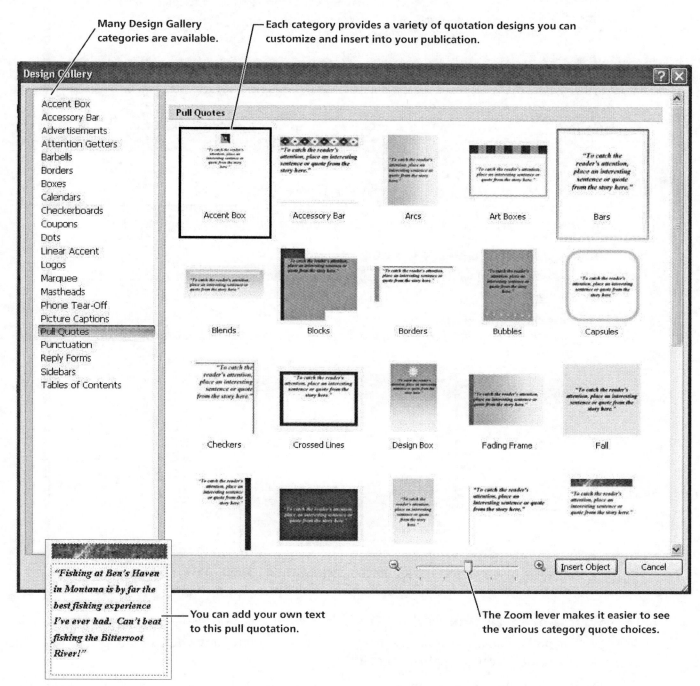

You can add your own text to this pull quotation.

The Zoom lever makes it easier to see the various category quote choices.

QUICK REFERENCE: INSERTING A DESIGN GALLERY OBJECT

Task	Procedure
Insert a Design Gallery object	■ Click the Design Gallery Object button on the Object toolbar. ■ Choose the category from which you want to select. ■ Click the object you want to insert. ■ Click the Insert Object button.
Customize a Design Gallery object (choose any of the items on the right)	■ Move or resize the object by dragging it. ■ If the drawn object has a text box, replace the text placeholder with your own text. ■ If the object has a Wizard button beneath it, click that button and use the controls in the task pane to customize the object.

 Hands-On 4.5   Add a Design Gallery Object

In this exercise, you will insert a pull quote Design Gallery object and add customized text.

Insert a Design Gallery Object

1. Click the Design Gallery Object button on the Object toolbar and choose the Pull Quotes category.

2. Click the Marble object.
   Notice that your mouse turns to a hand when placed on the Marble object and it zooms to a slightly larger size.

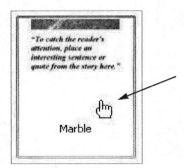

3. Click the Insert Object button in the bottom-right corner of the dialog box.
   The pull quote is placed in your publication. You will move it to the location you desire.

Customize a Design Gallery Object

4. The pull quote is a text box, so place your mouse pointer anywhere on the perimeter of the box until it turns to a Move ⊞ pointer.

5. Drag it so the top of the object is at approximately $7\frac{3}{4}$ inches on the vertical ruler and the right side of the object is approximately $3\frac{1}{2}$ inches on the horizontal ruler.

6. Select the text in the pull quote and type the following text:

"Fishing at Ben's Haven in Montana is by far the best fishing experience I've ever had. Can't beat fishing the Bitterroot River!"

7. Click in the scratch area to deselect the pull quote.

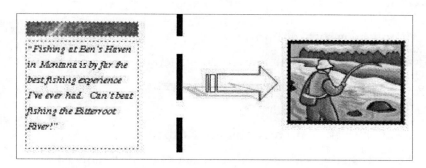

8. Choose File→Close from the menu bar and choose Yes if Publisher asks if you would like to save changes.

Publisher returns to the Getting Started with Microsoft Office Publisher 2007 window.

 # Concepts Review

True/False Questions

1. A drawn straight line can only be vertical or horizontal. **TRUE FALSE**

2. You can draw circles, ovals, squares, and rectangles in Publisher. **TRUE FALSE**

3. AutoShapes are similar to WordArt in that they can contain text. **TRUE FALSE**

4. Just like text boxes, drawn shapes have borders. **TRUE FALSE**

5. Applying 3-D and shadow effects can be dramatic on drawn shapes. **TRUE FALSE**

6. Shadow effects are similar to 3-D effects in that a three-dimensional shadow is applied behind the object instead of making a solid-looking object. **TRUE FALSE**

7. Grouping objects makes it easier to work with multiple objects as a single object. **TRUE FALSE**

8. Alignment of objects can be left to right or from top to bottom. **TRUE FALSE**

9. When you finish working with objects as a group, you don't need to ungroup them to work with them individually again. **TRUE FALSE**

10. Nudging is useful when you are having trouble making an object align precisely where you want it by dragging it into place. **TRUE FALSE**

Multiple Choice Questions

1. Which of the following is not an AutoShape?
   a. Block Arrows
   b. Stars
   c. Banners
   d. Quick Publication

2. Which of the following can you not do with objects?
   a. Align objects
   b. Rotate objects
   c. Save as clip art
   d. Group objects

3. Which of the following is not true about aligning objects?
   a. Objects can only be aligned if grouped first.
   b. Alignment can be from left to right or from top to bottom.
   c. You can align multiple drawn objects, clip art, pictures, and text boxes so that your publication looks balanced.
   d. Aligning objects helps guide the eye across the page by avoiding isolated patches of white space that might be distracting.

4. The Design Gallery does not include _____.
   a. attention-getters
   b. WordArt
   c. logos
   d. coupons

Skill Builders

Skill Builder 4.1   Draw a Dog House

Roshanda is a teenager with expensive tastes. Her mother decides that Roshanda should help out with her expenses by earning a little income. Raoshanda starts a dog-sitting business on the weekends. She wants to design a With Compliments Card that she can hand to clients when they pick up their dogs. She will note the dog's behavior in terms of what time the dog ate and how much, how long of a walk they took, and so on.

In this exercise, you will draw a dog house using the tools on the Objects toolbar and group the drawing so you can easily move it around.

Draw Rectangles

1. Choose With Compliments Cards from the Publication Type list.

2. Double-click the Linear Accent design in the center pane to open the publication in the text editing window.

3. Delete all of the text boxes on the right side of the card.

 You can draw a dotted line box around the text boxes with the mouse pointer to select all of them at once.

   Next you will draw a dog house that you will place on the card.

4. Click the Rectangle ▣ button on the Objects toolbar, and draw a rectangle on the right side of the card about 1½ inches tall and 1 inch wide.

5. Draw another rectangle inside of the existing rectangle to make a door for the dog house, as shown in the following illustration. Size and position the second rectangle as needed.

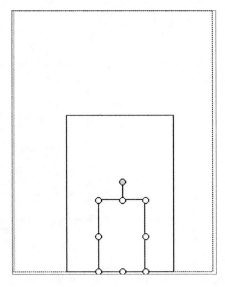

Now you are ready for the roof.

Draw a Triangle

6. Click the AutoShapes ⟨image⟩ button and slide the mouse pointer to the Basic Shapes category; in the submenu, choose the third object in the second row, the Isosceles Triangle, as shown in the following figure.

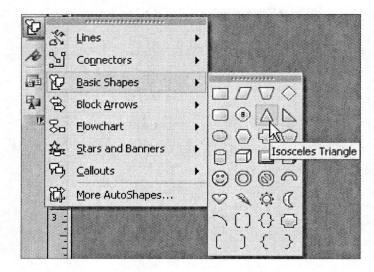

7. Drag in the card to draw the triangle and position it on top of the dog house.

8. Select all three objects.

9. Click the Group Objects button, as shown in the following illustration, so the three objects combine into one object.

10. Drag the dog house down to the bottom-right corner of the publication but within the blue dotted margins.

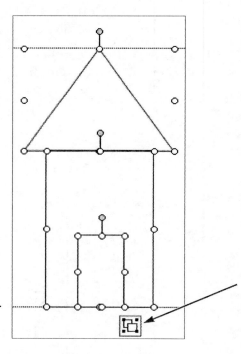

Add Clip Art

11. Locate a clip art image of a dog and position it to the left of the dog house.

12. Resize the dog and the dog house as needed.

13. Select the text in the text box below the With Compliments text box and replace it with **Roshanda's Doggie Day Care**.

14. Save ⟨image⟩ the file as **sb-Doggie Day Care** in your Lesson 04 folder, and then close the file.

Skill Builder 4.2   Draw Balloons for a Party Invitation

In this exercise, you will use a greeting card publication to personalize a birthday card for your friend Marty. You will add a bouquet of balloons to the card that you create with Publisher's drawing tools. You will add a shadow effect to the balloons, and then you will group the balloons so you can work with them as one object.

1. Choose the Greeting Cards category from the Publication Types list.

2. Click the Birthday link at the top of the center pane and double-click the Birthday 3 design.

3. Apply the Wildflower color scheme.

4. Navigate to page 2 of the publication.

5. Click the Oval button on the Objects toolbar, and draw an oval approximately 1 inch tall and $^3/_4$ inch wide, similar to the oval to the right.

6. Press and hold the Ctrl key and drag the oval to the side to make a copy of the balloon.

7. Use the same technique to make another copy.
   You should now have three balloons.

8. Move the balloons around so that they are staggered in a fashion similar to that shown in the following illustration.

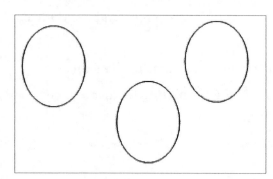

9. Click the Line 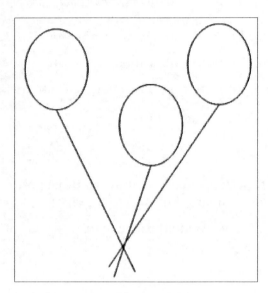 button on the Objects toolbar and draw strings similar to those shown in the following figure.

10. Click the balloon on the left to select it, click the drop-down arrow on the Fill Color button, and choose Red.

11. Use the same technique to color the center balloon blue and the right-hand balloon gold.

Add a Shadow Style

12. Press and hold the [Shift] key and click to select all three balloons.

13. Click the Shadow Style button on the formatting toolbar and choose the first style, Shadow Style 1, from the gallery.

Group the Objects

14. Select all of the lines and ovals.

!TIP! *You can draw a box around the objects with your mouse pointer to select the objects all at once.*

15. Click the Group Objects button at the bottom of the group to combine the objects into one unit.

16. Resize then position the balloons object so that it fills approximately two-thirds of the bottom of the page.

Add Word Art

17. Click the WordArt ◢ button on the Objects toolbar and select the fourth style in the third row, then click OK.

18. Type **Happy Birthday!** in the Edit WordArt Text dialog box and click OK.

19. Position the WordArt above the balloons and resize it appropriately. Remember to hold down the ⏵Shift key as you resize if you wish to maintain the aspect ratio.

20. Feel free to make any other formatting changes that you wish to the WordArt.

Work with a Text Box

21. On page 3, delete the top text box.

22. Select the text in the remaining text box and type **A bouquet of balloons for your birthday!** in its place.

23. Format the text with Broadway 18 pt and center it in the text box.

24. Save 🖫 the publication as **sb-Birthday Balloons** in your Lesson 04 folder, and then close it.

Skill Builder 4.3   Create a Gift Certificate with a 3-D Object

In this exercise, you will create a gift certificate for a 2-for-1 offer. Tony Marzetti owns the local Italian restaurant. Business has been a bit slow lately, and Tony wants to offer an incentive to attract new customers. He asks you to help him design a gift certificate. Iin this exercise, you will insert a Design Gallery Object in your certificate and apply a 3-D style, and then you will flip the object.

1. Choose Gift Certificates from the Publication Type list, and then double-click the Blends design to open it in the text editing window.

2. Apply the Tuscany color scheme and the Breve Bodoni MT font scheme.

3. Delete all of the text boxes on the right side of the certificate except the text box with the pyramid graphic.

4. Type **Tony's Trattoria** in the text box below the pyramid graphic.

5. Delete the bottom text box on the left side of the certificate.

Insert a Design Gallery Object

6. Click the Design Gallery Object  button on the Objects toolbar.

7. Choose the Attention Getters category in the left pane.

8. Choose the 2 for 1 Receding Rectangle design as shown at right then click the Insert Object button.

9. Move the object into the blank space on the right side of the certificate.

10. Resize the object to about twice its original size.

11. Position the cursor after the 1 in the text box.

12. Tap the [Spacebar] and type **Sunday Dinner**.

13. If necessary, resize the image so that all of the text is visible.

Apply a 3-D Style

14. Click the outside border of the object to select it, and click the 3-D Style ▣ button on the Formatting toolbar.

15. Choose the third style in the third row, 3-D Style 5.

Flip the Image

16. Click the outer border of the Design Gallery Object to select it.

17. Choose Arrange→Rotate or Flip from the menu bar, and then choose Flip Horizontal from the submenu.

18. Save ▣ the publication as **sb-Tony's Certificate** in your Lesson 04 folder, and then close the file.

 **Assessments**

Assessment 4.1   Create a Flyer with AutoShapes

In this exercise, you will create a flyer with AutoShapes and apply a variety of formats.

1. Create a Potluck Flyer. You'll find it in the Event category toward the bottom of the flyer gallery.

2. Delete the oven mitt picture and its background object along with the hot dog picture and its background object. Also delete the remaining two text boxes in the lower half of the flyer and any background objects behind the text boxes.

3. Replace the text Potluck with **Annual Neighborhood BBQ**.

Draw an AutoShape

4. Draw a Striped Right Arrow to the left of the top text box.

5. Edit 00/00/00 in the Date text box to **9/14/07**.

6. Delete all text in the Time text box and replace it with **4:00 pm – 11:30 pm**.

7. Delete all of the text in the Contact Person text box, and replace it with **RSVP Margarita: 555-1212**.

Format an AutoShape

8. Select the Striped Right Arrow and apply the Accent 4 fill color (fifth color in the color scheme) to the arrow.

9. Apply the 3-D Style 2 to the arrow.

Insert and Flip a Picture

10. Insert the as-Chef Marco.jpg picture from a file in the Lesson 04 folder.

11. Resize the picture to approximately 3½ inches tall and 3 inches wide and move it to the lower-left corner of your flyer.

12. Select Chef Marco and choose Arrange→Rotate or Flip from the menu bar and choose Flip Horizontal from the submenu.

Draw and Format a Callout

13. From the Callouts category in AutoShapes, draw a Cloud Callout to the right of Chef Marco.

14. Add the text **Don't miss Chef Marco's mystery dish of the summer!**

15. Change the text font to 14 pt, add Accent 4 fill color (fifth color in the color scheme), apply a Shadow Style 2, and resize the callout as appropriate.

16. Save ⊟ the file as **as-Neighborhood BBQ** in your Lesson 04 folder.
Leave the file open because you will use it in the next exercise.

Assessment 4.2   Add and Customize a Design Gallery Object

In this exercise, you insert an object from the Design Gallery and customize it to meet your needs.

1. Insert the Fading Frame design from the Sidebars category in the Design Gallery.

2. Drag the Fading Frame object above Chef Marco.

3. Click in the first line of sample text to select it and then tap Delete.

4. Click in the bulleted area to select the remaining text and type the following:

   Come with an appetite
   Bring your favorite drink
   Bring your swimsuit
   Bring your favorite dancing music—CDs

5. Resize the object if necessary.

6. Save 💾 and close the file.

 # Critical Thinking

Critical Thinking 4.1   Create a Wine Tasting Flyer

Jennica is Vice President of her local Community Dance Theatre. She has decided to get together a group of interested folks to visit a winery in the Napa Valley for lunch and wine tasting. In this exercise, you will help Jennica create a flyer for the field trip to the winery.

1. Follow these guidelines to create a flyer:

   ■ Create a Field Trip flyer. Scroll down to the Events category to locate it.

   ■ Replace Name of Field Trip with **Napa Valley Wine Tasting**.

   ■ Delete the text box with text beginning *Tell your students....*

   ■ Delete all text boxes in the bottom half of the page.

TIP! *You can draw a dotted line box around them with your mouse pointer and press the* Delete *key.*

   ■ Insert the ct-Silverado Winery.jpg picture from the Lesson 04 folder.

   ■ Resize the picture to span the width of the flyer and position it approximately in the middle of the flyer.

   ■ Draw a rectangle below your picture and type the following:
   Don't miss wine tasting and lunch at Silverado Winery
   Sunday, August 15 – 11 am until 6 pm
   We'll leave at 9 am from the Dance Theatre and return at 8 pm

   ■ Format the text with Comic Sans MS, 16 pt and bold the first two lines. If necessary, resize the rectangle to fit the text.

   ■ Apply the 3-D Style 2 to the rectangle and resize this text box so that the text fits on three lines.

   ■ Insert the ct-Silverado Winery Picnic.jpg picture from the Lesson 04 folder.

   ■ Resize and move the picture to the lower-left corner of the flyer, and add a 2¼ pt line border to the picture.

   ■ Draw a Cloud Callout AutoShape to the right of this picture that is approximately the same size as the picture.

   ■ Add the text to the callout: **Join us at the Silverado Winery for a great afternoon.**

   ■ Center the text and format it with Comic Sans MS 14 pt.

   ■ Resize and position the callout as needed.

2. Save 🖫 the file as **ct-Wine Tasting** in your Lesson 04 folder.

Critical Thinking 4.2   Draw a Bluebird with Drawing Tools

Mrs. Johnson operates the preschool in town and she just ran out of business cards. In this exercise, you will show Mrs. Johnson what a Publisher whiz you are by designing her new business cards.

1. Using the example below as a guide, create a Bluebird business card for Mrs. Johnson based on the Victorian design. Follow these guidelines to produce the card:

   - Use a color scheme that colors the design surrounding the card blue.
   - Delete unneeded text boxes.
   - Type Mrs. Johnson's contact information in a text box.
   - Use the drawing tools on the Objects toolbar to draw a bluebird. Group the objects that make up the bluebird into one unit. Add a shadow style to the bluebird. Feel free to use your imagination.

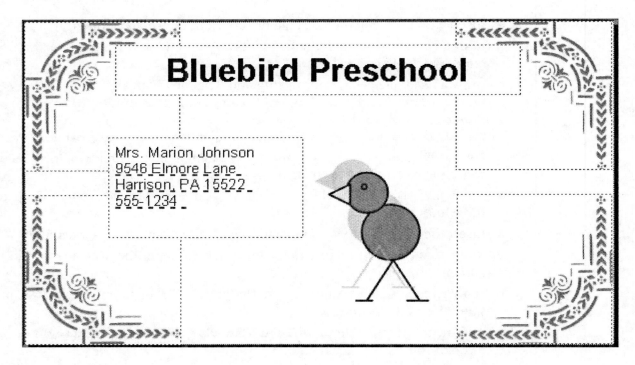

2. Save [💾] the file as **ct-Bluebird** in your Lesson 04 folder.

Creating an E-mail Letter

In this lesson, you will create an e-mail letter. You will select an e-mail letter template and edit the heading, greeting, closing, signature block, and information text boxes. You will also insert text for the body of the letter from a Word document, and then you will create e-mail hyperlinks. You will also edit a logo design. You will then preview and use the Design Checker to check for any design errors in your e-mail letter. And finally, you will prepare to send the e-mail message using Publisher.

LESSON OBJECTIVES

After studying this lesson, you will be able to:

- Select an e-mail letter template
- Edit text boxes in an e-mail letter
- Insert body text from a Word file
- Create and edit e-mail hyperlinks
- Edit a logo design
- Preview an e-mail letter
- Use the Design Checker
- Prepare to send an e-mail message

Case Study: Communicating through E-mail with Publisher

As a community member active in the Bitterroot Action Group, which is planning for controlled growth in your town, you would like to invite town residents to a special zoning meeting. The Action Group steering committee has created a listserv of e-mail addresses so they can communicate quickly with town residents. Many residents have subscribed to the committee's listserv.

Ben Hillicoss, president of the Action Group, knows of your interest in Publisher and he wants you to create an invitational e-mail letter designed to catch the recipient's eye using strong colors and fonts. Ben won't be sending the e-mail invitation for several weeks, so he would like you to create an e-mail letter and save it until he's ready to send it. He would also like you to become familiar with how to send the e-mail so you can show him how to send it when the time comes. You won't need access to the Internet or the e-mail program on your computer to create and save the e-mail letter.

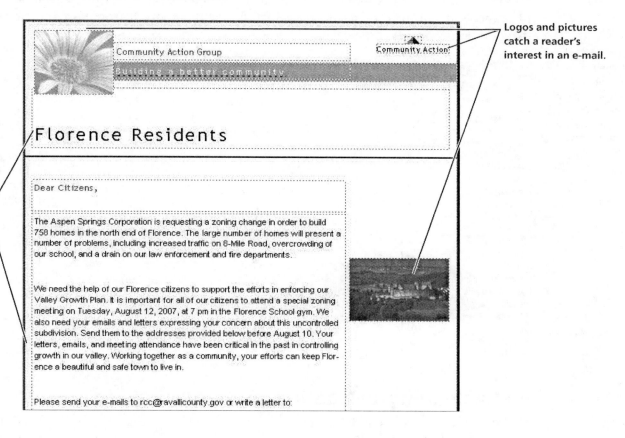

The various parts of the e-mail letter are found in text boxes that can be edited.

Logos and pictures catch a reader's interest in an e-mail.

Community Action Group

Building a better community

Community Action

Florence Residents

Dear Citizens,

The Aspen Springs Corporation is requesting a zoning change in order to build 758 homes in the north end of Florence. The large number of homes will present a number of problems, including increased traffic on 8-Mile Road, overcrowding of our school, and a drain on our law enforcement and fire departments.

We need the help of our Florence citizens to support the efforts in enforcing our Valley Growth Plan. It is important for all of our citizens to attend a special zoning meeting on Tuesday, August 12, 2007, at 7 pm in the Florence School gym. We also need your emails and letters expressing your concern about this uncontrolled subdivision. Send them to the addresses provided below before August 10. Your letters, emails, and meeting attendance have been critical in the past in controlling growth in our valley. Working together as a community, your efforts can keep Florence a beautiful and safe town to live in.

Please send your e-mails to rcc@ravallicounty.gov or write a letter to:

Using E-mail Publications

E-mail is a popular form of communication for transmitting a message to a single person or to large groups of people. You can send any Publisher publication as an attachment to an e-mail message. For quick viewing of a publication such as an announcement, letter, or card, it is best to send a single page in the body of an e-mail. When you send a single page of a publication as an e-mail message, recipients can read the message using an HTML-enabled e-mail program such as AOL, Yahoo!, or Hotmail, as well as Outlook. Recipients do not need to have Publisher installed to view the message. Also, sending a one-page publication by e-mail to a group is an efficient and inexpensive way to deliver your message. A multipage publication would need to be sent as an attachment to an e-mail.

Select an E-mail Template

Publisher provides many templates that you can use to create publications designed for e-mail. These e-mail templates are preformatted to the correct page size. The templates use place-holder text and graphics that download quickly and are suitable for the body of an e-mail message. Some of the e-mail categories include event/activity, featured product, letter, product list, newsletter, and event/speaker.

The E-mail publication type appears here. In this example, the e-mail category is Letter.

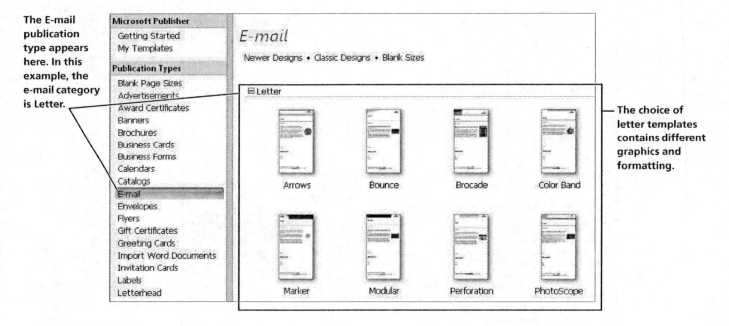

The choice of letter templates contains different graphics and formatting.

Edit a Heading, a Greeting, and a Closing

The text boxes in an e-mail letter template may include headings, a greeting, a salutation, the body of the letter, a closing, a signature block, and an informational text box at the bottom of the e-mail letter. The default text in these boxes will vary depending on the business information set (see Lesson 6, Creating Business Publications) and the template.

!NOTE! *Throughout the main part of this lesson, the following terminology will be used to describe the text boxes:*

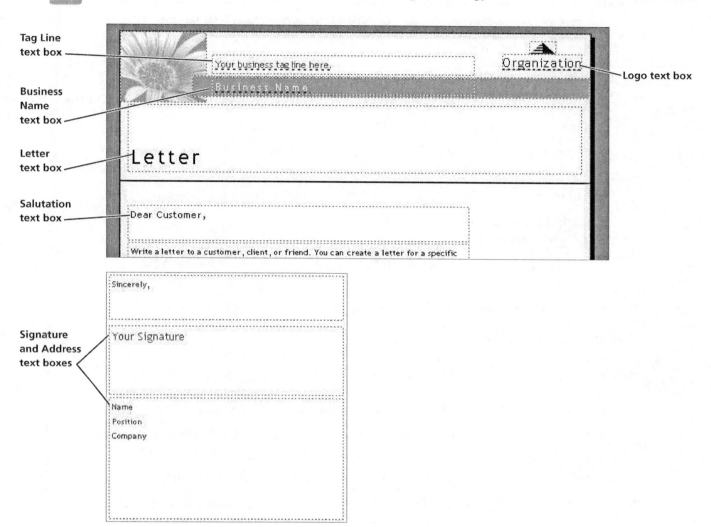

Tag Line text box — Your business tag line here.

Logo text box — Organization

Business Name text box — Business Name

Letter text box — Letter

Salutation text box — Dear Customer,

Write a letter to a customer, client, or friend. You can create a letter for a specific

Sincerely,

Signature and Address text boxes — Your Signature

Name
Position
Company

QR ▶ **QUICK REFERENCE: CREATING AND EDITING AN E-MAIL LETTER**

Task	Procedure
Create an e-mail letter	■ Click the E-mail Publication Type on the Publisher task pane.
	■ Choose a letter design.
	■ (Optional) Choose a different color scheme.
	■ (Optional) Choose a different font scheme.
Edit text in an e-mail letter	■ Edit the placeholder text with your own content.

In this exercise, you will create and edit an e-mail letter. You will add body text and informational text.

1. Start Publisher, if necessary.

Create an E-mail Letter

2. Choose E-mail from the Publication Type list in the task pane on the left side of the screen.

3. Click the Newer Designs link at the top of the center pane.

4. Scroll down to the Letter design category and choose PhotoScope.
   The PhotoScope design appears in more than one category. Be sure to choose the Letter category.

5. Choose the Color Scheme Meadow and the Font Scheme (default template font).

6. Click the Create button.
   The one-page e-mail letter is displayed.

7. If necessary, on the Standard toolbar, click the Zoom box arrow and click 100% in the zoom list.

8. If necessary, scroll to display the upper portion of the page layout.

Edit the Heading and Greeting

NOTE! *You may want to look at the illustration below step 12 to assist you in positioning the replacement text.*

9. Select the text in the Tag Line text box and replace with **Community Action Group**.

10. Select the text in the Business Name text box and type **Building a better community**.

11. Select the text in the Letter text box and type **Florence Residents**.

12. Select the text in the Salutation text box, and type the following: **Dear Citizens,**

Edit the Closing

13. Select the text in the signature text box and type **Ben Hillicoss, President**.

14. Click the text in the address text box to select it and type **Community Action Group**.

15. Press Enter and then type **51 Gunsight Lane**.

16. Press Enter and type **Florence, MT 59833**.

17. Click the Save button and save your file as **Community Action E-mail Letter** in your Lesson 05 folder.

Inserting Text from a Word File

You can insert text for the body of your e-mail letter from another program such as Word. If the text is too lengthy to fit in the text box, a message appears asking whether you want to use autoflow. Autoflow can flow text into the same text box or into a separate text box.

QR

QUICK REFERENCE: INSERTING TEXT FROM A WORD FILE

Task	Procedure
Insert text from a Word file	■ Position the insertion point in the text box where you want to import the text.
	■ Choose Insert→Text File.
	■ Navigate to the folder containing the file you want.
	■ Click the file to select it and click OK.

Hands-On 5.2　　Insert Text from a Word File

In this exercise, you will practice inserting a Word file in the body text box of your e-mail letter.

Insert Text from a Word File

1. Click the text in the body of the letter to select it.

2. Choose Insert→Text File from the menu bar.

3. Navigate to the Lesson 05 folder.

4. Click to select Zoning E-mail Letter Body Text.doc and click OK.
   A dialog box saying that Publisher is converting the file quickly flashes, and the text is placed in the text box.

> The Aspen Springs Corporation is requesting a zoning change in order to build 758 homes in the north end of Florence. The large number of homes will present a number of problems, including increased traffic on 8-Mile Road, overcrowding of our school, and a drain on our law enforcement and fire departments.
>
> We need the help of our Florence citizens to support the efforts in enforcing our Valley Growth Plan. It is important for all of our citizens to attend a special zoning meeting on Tuesday, August 12, 2007, at 7 pm in the Florence School gym. We also need your emails and letters expressing your concern about this uncontrolled subdivision. Send them to the addresses provided below before August 10. Your letters, e-mails, and meeting attendance have been critical in the past in controlling growth in our valley. Working together as a community, your efforts can keep Florence a beautiful and safe town to live in.
>
> Please send your e-mails to rcc@ravallicounty.gov or write a letter to:
>
> Ravalli County Commissioners
>
> 5 Main Street
>
> Hamilton, MT 59830

5. Save the publication and leave it open for the next exercise.

Creating and Editing Hyperlinks

E-mail letters can contain hyperlinks just as web pages do. A hyperlink is text or a graphic that you click to go to a different file, a different location in the current file, a web page, or an e-mail address. You can also edit and remove hyperlinks.

Creating a Hyperlink

Publisher makes creating hyperlinks an easy task, as shown in the following illustration. A text hyperlink can show the actual address for the link, or you can add different text.

The Insert Hyperlink button on the Standard toolbar allows you to create, edit, or remove a hyperlink.

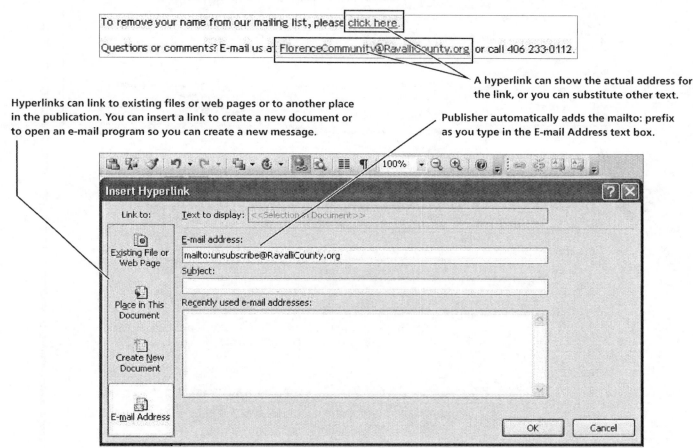

A hyperlink can show the actual address for the link, or you can substitute other text.

Hyperlinks can link to existing files or web pages or to another place in the publication. You can insert a link to create a new document or to open an e-mail program so you can create a new message.

Publisher automatically adds the mailto: prefix as you type in the E-mail Address text box.

Editing a Hyperlink

You can also edit a hyperlink, as well as remove one if you no longer need it.

You can use the Edit Hyperlink dialog box to edit an existing hyperlink.

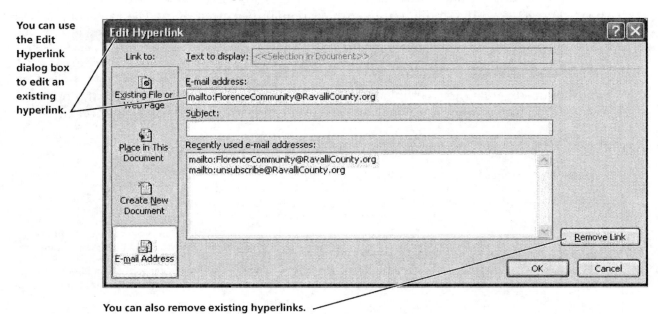

You can also remove existing hyperlinks.

QR▶

QUICK REFERENCE: CREATING AND EDITING A HYPERLINK

Task	Procedure
Create a hyperlink	■ Select the text to be underlined as the hyperlink.
	■ Click the Insert Hyperlink 🔗 button on the Standard toolbar.
	■ Click the E-mail Address box.
	■ Type the e-mail address for the hyperlink.
	■ (Optional) Click in the Subject box and type a subject, which will appear in the Subject line of the e-mail form.
Edit a hyperlink	■ Select the text that is the current hyperlink.
	■ Click the Insert Hyperlink 🔗 button on the Standard toolbar.
	■ In the Edit Hyperlink dialog box, click the E-mail Address option in the Link To bar on the left.
	■ In the E-mail Address text box, type the new text.
Remove a hyperlink	■ Select the text that is the current hyperlink.
	■ Click the Insert Hyperlink 🔗 button on the Formatting toolbar.
	■ Click E-mail Address option in the Link To bar on the left.
	■ Click the Remove Link button.

Hands-On 5.3　Create and Edit Hyperlinks

In this exercise, you will create several hyperlinks and edit one of them.

Create a Hyperlink

1. In the contact text box at the bottom of the page, click *someone@example.com* and type **FlorenceCommunity@RavalliCounty.org**.

2. Select the text *or call 555-555-5555* and type **or call 406-233-0112**.
   The new text is entered.

> To remove your name from our mailing list, please click here.
>
> Questions or comments? E-mail us at FlorenceCommunity@RavalliCounty.org or call 406 233-0112.

3. Select the *click here* text in the contact text box.

4. Click the Insert Hyperlink ▨ button on the Standard toolbar.
   The Insert Hyperlink dialog box displays.

5. Click E-mail Address in the Link To bar on the left.

6. In the E-mail Address text box, type the following e-mail address:
   unsubscribe@RavalliCounty.org
   Publisher automatically adds the mailto: prefix as you type in the E-mail Address text box.

   E-mail address:
   mailto:unsubscribe@RavalliCounty.org

7. Click OK to close the dialog box.

Create a Second Hyperlink

8. Select the text *FlorenceCommunity@RavalliCounty.org*.

9. Press ⎧Ctrl⎫+⎧C⎫ to copy the text to the Clipboard.

10. Click the Insert Hyperlink ▨ button on the Standard toolbar.
    The Insert Hyperlink dialog box displays.

11. Click E-mail Address in the Link To bar on the left.

12. Position the cursor in the E-mail Address text box.

13. Press ⎧Ctrl⎫+⎧V⎫ to paste the e-mail address in the text box.
    Publisher automatically adds the mailto: prefix as you paste in the e-mail address.

    E-mail address:
    mailto:FlorenceCommunity@RavalliCounty.org

14. Click OK to close the dialog box.

Edit a Hyperlink

15. Click to place your cursor to the right of *Community* in *FlorenceCommunity@RavalliCounty.org* and type **Action**.
The e-mail address has been edited in your e-mail letter.

16. Select the edited e-mail address and tap $\boxed{\text{Ctrl}}$+$\boxed{\text{C}}$ to copy the e-mail address to the Clipboard.

17. Click the Insert Hyperlink 🖳 button on the Standard toolbar.
The Edit Hyperlink dialog box displays.

18. Select the current e-mail address and tap $\boxed{\text{Ctrl}}$+$\boxed{\text{V}}$ to paste the edited e-mail address.
The hyperlink has been edited.

E-mail address:

mailto:FlorenceCommunityAction@RavalliCounty.org

19. Click OK to close the dialog box.

Editing the Logo

Most of the e-mail templates contain logos. A logo is a recognizable symbol that identifies a person, a business, or an organization. A logo may be composed of text, a picture, or a combination of symbols.

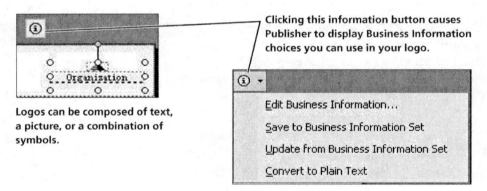

Logos can be composed of text, a picture, or a combination of symbols.

Clicking this information button causes Publisher to display Business Information choices you can use in your logo.

Edit Business Information...

Save to Business Information Set

Update from Business Information Set

Convert to Plain Text

> **!TIP!** *A Business Information Set is information about you and your business that is stored and used in various templates. Information Sets are covered in Lesson 6, Creating Business Publications.*

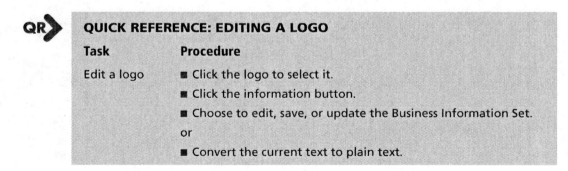

QR> **QUICK REFERENCE: EDITING A LOGO**

Task	Procedure
Edit a logo	▪ Click the logo to select it.
	▪ Click the information button.
	▪ Choose to edit, save, or update the Business Information Set.
	or
	▪ Convert the current text to plain text.

Hands-On 5.4   Edit the Logo

In this exercise, you will edit the logo in the e-mail letter.

Edit the Logo

1. Scroll to the upper-right portion of the e-mail letter.

2. Click the Logo text box to select it.
   Your logo text may not match what is shown in this lesson because the logo text may have been modified by a previous student.

3. Click the Information ⓘ button.
   The Business Information Set choices are listed.

4. Choose Convert to Plain Text. (Business Sets will be discussed in Lesson 6, Creating Business Publications.) The text is selected.

5. If necessary, press Ctrl + A to select the logo text; type **Community Action**.

Sending an E-mail Letter

An e-mail publication in Publisher is just like any other publication except for its page size and the fact that there is only one page. It is saved like any other publication in a Publisher format (.pub), and you can preview it as an e-mail before sending it. You can either attach the e-mail letter to an e-mail message or send a single-page e-mail letter in the body of an e-mail. If you *attach* the e-mail letter, your recipients must have Publisher installed on their computers in order to open it. It is safer to send the one-page e-mail letter in the body of an e-mail so all recipients can see the publication. Multipage publications must be sent as an attachment.

Listservs

E-mail letters can be sent to one or more people. Many organizations create a listserv, which is a list of interested people who use e-mail and who want to receive news and information about an organization via e-mail. A listserv e-mail is one e-mail sent to everyone on the list. Listserv e-mails should contain a link to allow recipients to remove their names from the list if they do not want to receive future e-mails.

Preview the E-mail Letter

You need to save your e-mail letter in order to preview it prior to sending.

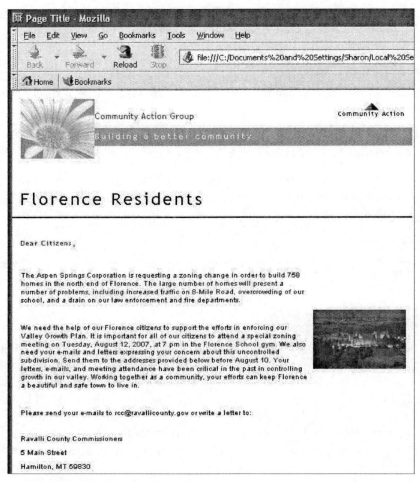

The preview displays in your browser.

Use the Design Checker

The Design Checker is very useful for identifying layout errors in a publication. It helps find and fix errors that may cause problems when the publication is printed or when it is published to the web. Depending on the nature of the problem, you can either fix it yourself or have Publisher fix it for you. The Design Checker looks for such items as spacing between sentences, disproportional pictures, objects outside the page margins, and so forth.

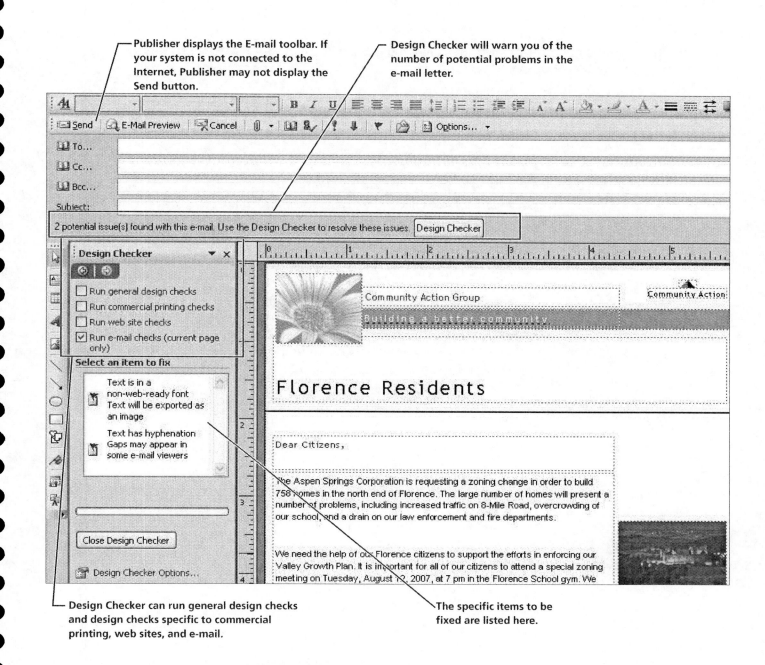

Publisher displays the E-mail toolbar. If your system is not connected to the Internet, Publisher may not display the Send button.

Design Checker will warn you of the number of potential problems in the e-mail letter.

Design Checker can run general design checks and design checks specific to commercial printing, web sites, and e-mail.

The specific items to be fixed are listed here.

Send an E-mail Letter

For purposes of this lesson, you do not have to send e-mails. You also do not have to be connected to the Internet to perform the exercise steps. It is a good idea to send the publication to yourself first to see how it will look before sending it to other recipients.

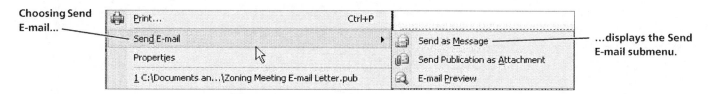

Choosing Send E-mail...

...displays the Send E-mail submenu.

QR

QUICK REFERENCE: PREVIEWING AN E-MAIL, USING THE DESIGN CHECKER, AND SENDING AN E-MAIL

Task	Procedure
Preview an e-mail publication	■ Save the publication. ■ Choose File→Send E-mail from the menu bar. ■ Choose E-mail Preview from the submenu.
Use the Design Checker	■ Click the Send as Message 🖼 button. ■ In the Design Checker task pane, select the item to be fixed. ■ Correct the error manually. or ■ Click the down arrow next to the error in the task pane. ■ Choose Fix. ■ Repeat the preceeding steps for each error. ■ Click Close Design Checker.
Send e-mail	■ If you want to send the e-mail to others, type your e-mail address in the To box. ■ Click the ✉ Send button.
Cancel e-mail	■ Click the ✖ Cancel button.

Hands-On 5.5 **Preview and Send an E-mail Letter**

In this exercise, you will save the e-mail, preview it, and use the Design Checker. You will not actually send the e-mail message.

1. Click the Save 💾 button to save your changes to the e-mail letter.

Preview the E-mail Letter

2. Choose File→Send E-mail from the menu bar.

3. Choose E-mail Preview from the submenu.
   Your browser window displays a preview of the e-mail letter.

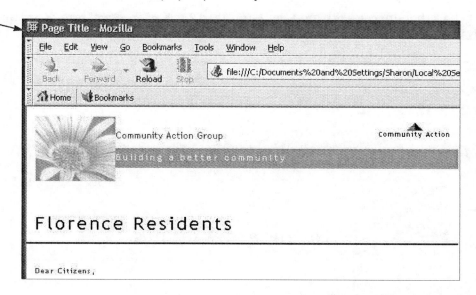

4. When finished viewing the e-mail letter, click the Close ❌ button on the browser's title bar.

Use the Design Checker

5. Click the Send as Message 🖼 button on the Standard toolbar.
   Under the Subject line is the message "3 potential issue(s) found with this e-mail. You will use the Design Checker to resolve these issues."

6. Under the Subject line, click the white Design Checker button.

7. On the Design Checker task pane, click the first item to be fixed.
   You are moved to the logo in the e-mail letter. Since this document will not be posted on a web page, you can ignore this message.

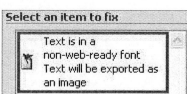

8. Click the second item to be fixed.
   You are moved to the signature in the e-mail letter. You can ignore this message.

9. Click the last item to be fixed.

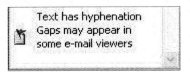

You are moved to the body text in the e-mail letter. This is fine; there is nothing to fix.

10. Click the Close Design Checker button at the bottom of the Design Checker task pane.

Send the Publication

11. Click in the Subject field and type **August 12, Aspen Springs Zoning Meeting, 7 pm.**

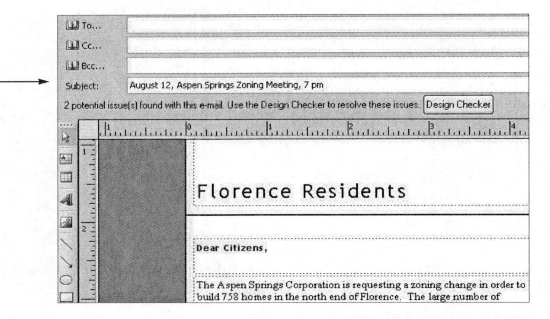

If you want to send the e-mail and your system is connected to an e-mail program, you can type your e-mail address in the To box and click the Send button.

For purposes of this exercise, you will not send the e-mail.

12. Click the Cancel button on the Standard toolbar.
The e-mail message closes and you are returned to the e-mail letter.

13. Save and close your publication, and exit Publisher.

Concepts Review

True/False Questions

1. Listserv e-mails should not contain a link to allow recipients to remove their name from the list if they do not want to receive future e-mails. **TRUE** **FALSE**

2. You can send a single page of a publication as an e-mail message and recipients can read the message using an HTML-enabled e-mail program such as AOL, Yahoo!, Hotmail, or Outlook. **TRUE** **FALSE**

3. A text hyperlink can show the actual address for the link or different text. **TRUE** **FALSE**

4. E-mail templates are preformatted to the correct page size. **TRUE** **FALSE**

5. You can edit but not remove hyperlinks. **TRUE** **FALSE**

6. A text hyperlink can show the actual address for the link, or it can show different text. **TRUE** **FALSE**

7. A logo is a recognizable symbol that identifies a person, a business, or an organization. **TRUE** **FALSE**

8. An e-mail publication in Publisher is just like any other publication except for its page size and the fact that it is only one page. **TRUE** **FALSE**

9. It is best to send a one-page e-mail letter in the body of an e-mail so all recipients can see the publication. **TRUE** **FALSE**

10. The Design Checker helps find and fix errors that may cause problems when the publication is printed or published to the web. **TRUE** **FALSE**

Multiple Choice Questions

1. Which of the following is not an e-mail publications type?
   a. Catalog
   b. Newsletter
   c. Product list
   d. Event/speaker

2. The text boxes in an e-mail letter template do not include _____.
   a. a heading
   b. a logo
   c. a signature block
   d. an information text box

3. When a hyperlink is clicked, which of the following can a viewer not do?
   a. Open a web page
   b. Open an e-mail program
   c. Open a graphic
   d. Create a new message

4. Which of the following is not part of a logo?
   a. BorderArt
   b. Text
   c. Picture
   d. Combination of symbols

Skill Builders

Skill Builder 5.1   Create an E-mail Letter

It's time to create another e-mail letter! The Contra Dancers Club is hosting a silent auction in a few weeks to raise money for this summer's Renaissance Faire. In this exercise, you will add hyperlinks to an e-mail letter and view the e-mail header form.

1. Choose E-mail from the Publication Types list on the task pane on the left side of the screen.

2. Click the Newer Designs link at the top of the center pane.

3. Scroll down to the Letter category and choose Brocade.

4. Click the Create button.

5. Apply the Sienna color scheme.

6. Apply the Dictation Lucida Sans font scheme.

7. If necessary, scroll to display the upper portion of the page layout.

Edit the Heading and Salutation

8. Follow these steps to edit the heading text boxes:

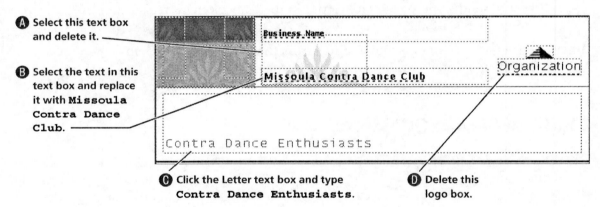

Ⓐ Select this text box and delete it.

Ⓑ Select the text in this text box and replace it with **Missoula Contra Dance Club.**

Ⓒ Click the Letter text box and type **Contra Dance Enthusiasts.**

Ⓓ Delete this logo box.

9. Click the text in the Salutation text box to select, and type the following: **Dear Contra Dancers,**

Edit the Closing

10. Click the text in the signature text box to select it and type **Jane Aldrich, President**.

11. Click the text in the text box below the signature box to select it then type the following address:

    Missoula Contra Dance Club

    24 Tie Chute Lane

    Missoula, MT 59807

Insert Text from a Word File

12. Click the text in the body of the letter to select it.

13. Choose Insert→Text File from the menu bar.

14. Navigate to the Lesson 05 folder.

15. Click to select sb-Silent Auction E-mail Letter Body Text.doc and click OK.

Create a Hyperlink

16. In the contact text box at the bottom of the page, click the text *someone@example.com* and type **jaldrich@lolowireless.net**.

17. Select the text *or call 555-555-5555* and delete it.

18. Select the text *click here* in the contact text box.

19. Click the Insert Hyperlink 🖳 button on the Standard toolbar.

20. Click E-mail Address in the Link To bar on the left.

21. In the E-mail Address text box, type **unsubscribe@contradance.net**.
    Publisher automatically adds the mailto: prefix as you type in the address.

22. Click OK to close the dialog box.

Create a Second Hyperlink

23. Select the text *jaldrich@lolowireless.net*.

24. Press ⌷Ctrl⌷+⌷C⌷ to copy the text to the Clipboard.

25. Click the Insert Hyperlink 🖳 button on the Standard toolbar.

26. Click E-mail Address in the Link To bar on the left.

27. In the E-mail Address text box, click to place your cursor.

28. Press ⌷Ctrl⌷+⌷V⌷ to paste the address.

29. Click OK to close the dialog box.

Send the Publication

30. Click the Send as Message 🖃 button on the Standard toolbar.

31. Click in the Subject field and type **Silent Auction on June 15**.
    If you want to send the e-mail and your system is connected to an e-mail program, you can type your e-mail address in the To box and click the Send button.

    For purposes of this exercise, you will not send the e-mail.

32. Click the 🖳Cancel button on the Standard toolbar.
    The e-mail message closes, and Publisher returns you to the e-mail letter.

33. Save 🖫 your publication as **sb-Silent Auction** in your Lesson 05 folder, and then close the file.

Skill Builder 5.2   Create an Event/Speaker E-mail

As a member of the Regional Speakers Association, you have been asked to prepare an e-mail announcement for next month's meeting. In this exercise, you will create an event/speaker e-mail that you will send at the beginning of next month.

1. Choose E-Mail from the Publication Types list.

2. Click the Newer Designs link at the top of the center pane.

3. Scroll to the Event/Speaker category and double-click the Color Band design to open it in the text editing window.

4. Apply the Urban color scheme and the Concourse Candara font scheme.

5. Follow these steps to begin filling in the presentation information:

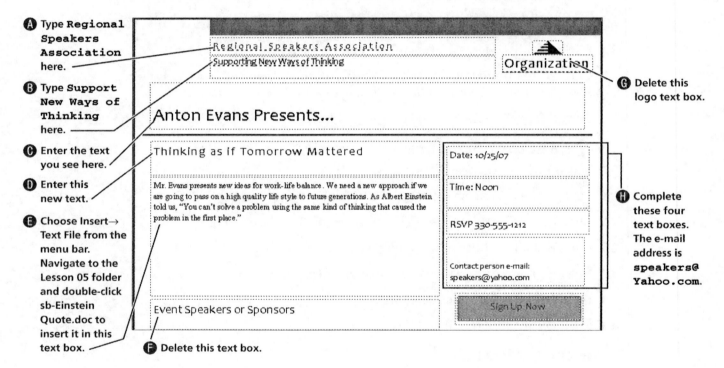

A Type **Regional Speakers Association** here.

B Type **Support New Ways of Thinking** here.

C Enter the text you see here.

D Enter this new text.

E Choose Insert→ Text File from the menu bar. Navigate to the Lesson 05 folder and double-click sb-Einstein Quote.doc to insert it in this text box.

G Delete this logo text box.

H Complete these four text boxes. The e-mail address is **speakers@ Yahoo.com**.

Regional Speakers Association
Supporting New Ways of Thinking

Organization

Anton Evans Presents...

Thinking as if Tomorrow Mattered

Mr. Evans presents new ideas for work-life balance. We need a new approach if we are going to pass on a high quality life style to future generations. As Albert Einstein told us, "You can't solve a problem using the same kind of thinking that caused the problem in the first place."

Date: 10/25/07

Time: Noon

RSVP 330-555-1212

Contact person e-mail: speakers@yahoo.com

Event Speakers or Sponsors

Sign Up Now

F Delete this text box.

6. Follow these steps to edit and rearrange the bottom section of the page as shown:

A This is a drawn line. Click it to see its handles and increase its length by resizing it.

B Type the location information on four lines.

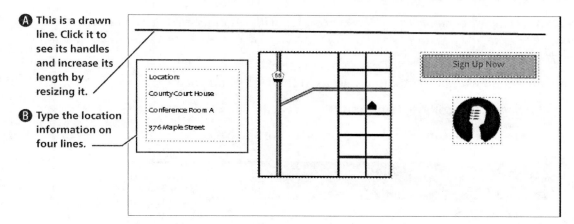

Create a Hyperlink

7. Select the text **speaker@yahoo.com** in the contact text box.

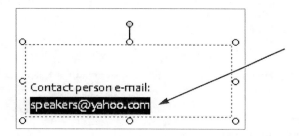

8. Press ⌨Ctrl+⌨C to copy the text.

9. Click the Insert Hyperlink 🔗 button on the Standard toolbar.

10. Click E-mail Address in the Link To bar on the left.

11. Position the cursor in the E-mail Address text box.

12. Press ⌨Ctrl+⌨V to paste the address in the text box, and then click OK.

13. Save 🖫 the e-mail as **sb-Regional Speakers** in your Lesson 05 folder, and then close the file.

Assessments

Assessment 5.1   Create a Harbor Cruise E-mail Letter

It's time to create another e-mail letter! In this exercise, you will create an e-mail letter to send to the members of the Friends of Filoli about the Harbor Cruise. You will insert a Word text file and you will create a hyperlink.

1. Create an e-mail using the Modular design in the Letter category.

2. Apply the Sagebrush color scheme and the Facet Gill Sans Mt font scheme.

3. Follow these steps to complete the upper portion of the page:

Ⓐ Select this text box and delete it.

Ⓑ Select the text in this text box and replace it with **Friends of Filoli.**

Ⓒ Click the Letter text box and type **Annual San Francisco Harbor Cruise.**

Ⓓ Click the text in this text box, and replace with **Dear Filoli Members,**

Ⓔ Type **Friends of Filoli** in the logo text box.

4. Enter **Sarah Milanos** in the signature text box.

5. In the text box below the signature text box, enter the following address:

   Friends of Filoli
   103 Sunrise Road
   Woodside, CA 94073

Insert a Text File

6. Insert the as-Cruise Text.doc file from the Lesson 05 folder in the body of the letter.

7. In the contact text box at the bottom of the page, delete the first line of text.

8. Change the sample e-mail address to **sarahmilanos@aol.net**.

9. Delete *or call 555-555-5555*.

Insert a Hyperlink

10. Copy sarahmilanos@aol.net and paste it into the E-mail Address field in the Insert Hyperlink text box.

11. Save 💾 the file as **as-San Francisco Cruise** in the Lesson 05 folder, and then close the file.

Assessment 5.2 Create a With Compliments Card

You are just getting started in an Internet sugar-free cake sales business. In this exercise, you will create a With Compliments Card to enclose with the cakes you send your customers.

1. Create a With Compliments Card using the Cascade design.

2. Apply the Casual Comic Sans font scheme.

3. Delete the cascade graphic on the left and replace it with a clip art image of a cake. Resize and position it as needed. Apply a $2^{1}/_{4}$ pt line border in the color of your choice.

4. Leave the top text box in place but delete the three text boxes below it.

5. Type **Sweet Things** in the logo text box on the right.

6. Replace the text in the top-center text box with **Sugar-Free Sweet Things** and tap ⌈Enter⌉.

7. On the second line, type **E-mail: sweetthings@sweetthings.com** and tap ⌈Enter⌉.

8. Increase the height of the text box to make room for a third line, and type the following Internet address: **www.sweetthings.com**

Insert a Hyperlink

9. Follow these guidelines to format the Internet address as a hyperlink:
   - Copy the Internet address.
   - In the Insert Hyperlink dialog box, choose Existing File of Web Page in the Link To pane on the left.
   - Paste the Internet address in the Address box at the bottom of the dialog box and click OK.

10. Save the publication as **as-Sweet Things** in the Lesson 05 folder, and then close the file.

Critical Thinking

Critical Thinking 5.1   Create a Get-Well Postcard

Your friend Jaya is in laid up with a broken leg. She's bored by the inactivity, so you decide to cheer her up. In this exercise, you will create a get-well postcard with links to several of your favorite websites. Let's hope Jaya finds them entertaining!

1. Follow these guidelines to create a get-well postcard:
   - Create a postcard using the design of your choice.
   - Apply a different color scheme and font scheme.
   - Compose a short note sympathizing with your friend's dilemma, and include links to three fun web sites.
   - Use your creativity in completing any of the other text boxes you wish.
   - Delete any unneeded text boxes, and insert a clip art picture of a girl with a broken leg. Size and position it appropriately.

2. Save ⊟ the publication as **ct-Get Well** in your Lesson 05 folder, and close the file.

Critical Thinking 5.2 Create a Family Reunion E-mail Letter

Andie Brake's family—consisting of many aunts, uncles, cousins, and grandparents—is quite large and spread out across the United States, from Maine to California. Every five years the family has a reunion in a central location in the United States so all family members can keep in touch. The family is also great about keeping in touch via e-mail. Andie is responsible for keeping the family e-mails up to date using a listserve.

Andie volunteers to coordinate the reunion next year, but she needs your help. In this exercise, you will create an e-mail letter to send out to the family about next year's family reunion.

1. Create an e-mail letter using your choice of an e-mail letter type that you think would look good for the family reunion and save it as **ct-Brake Family Reunion** in your Lesson 05 folder.

2. Experiment with adding heading information in the heading text boxes. Format the text as you wish. Delete any text boxes you do not want to use.

3. Insert the ct-Reunion Text.doc file from the Lesson 05 folder into the letter body text.

4. Add your closing information, including Andie's mailing address at **103 Mendocino Way, Redwood City, CA 94061**.

5. Edit the contact information text box with Andie's e-mail and phone number:
   andie@aol.net
   650 555-9876

6. Add a hyperlink for Andie's e-mail address.

7. Preview the e-mail letter in your web browser.

8. Check any design errors and add a subject for the e-mail letter but don't send the e-mail.

9. Save ![save icon] the letter as **ct-Brake Family Reunion,** and then close the publication.

Unit 2

Beyond the Basics

In this unit, you will work with some of Publisher's more advanced features. You will begin by creating business publications: business cards, letterhead, envelopes, and postcards. As you create a company newsletter, you will learn how to insert and delete pages, edit masthead information, import text files, add captions to graphics, and edit sidebars. You will then move on to creating mail merge documents in Publisher, which allow you to customize publications for individual customers or contacts. You will also create a catalog merge, which allows you to create publications using information other than addresses. Next you will work with Publisher tables, which are quite similar to Word tables. You will create business templates and learn how to designate them as *read-only* files, which protects them from being modified by others. Finally, in this unit you will plan, design, and create a company web site in Publisher.

Creating Business Publications

In this lesson, you will learn to use Publisher in a business environment to create business publications. You will create a Business Information Set for a company employee and then create business cards using this information. You will also create a Business Information Set for a company and create letterhead with the company information. Using the Format Painter, you will learn to quickly copy formatting in text boxes. Then you will create business envelopes, which you will find a breeze with Publisher. If you change your mind about a particular envelope design, you will see how easy it is to change to a different one. Finally, in this lesson you will create a business postcard.

LESSON OBJECTIVES

After studying this lesson, you will be able to:

- Create and edit a business set
- Create a business card
- Create business letterhead
- Use the Format Painter to copy formatting
- Create a business envelope
- Change the design template for a publication
- Create a business postcard

Case Study: Customizing Business Publications with Information Sets

Andrea recently graduated from UC-Davis. Prior to her graduation, Andrea was hired by the Dunsmuir Medical Clinic's marketing department.

The clinic's new CEO would like to change Dunsmuir's marketing look to expand the number of patients and recruit new physicians. One of Andrea's responsibilities will be to help change the clinic's marketing look. This task will include creating new business cards for the physicians and creating new letterhead, envelopes, and appointment reminder postcards. The CEO is cost-conscious and would like to keep these marketing expenses reasonable. As part of this effort, the clinic has recently purchased Publisher 2007 for Andrea to use to create these business publications.

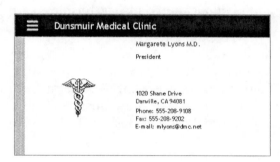

Andrea can easily create business cards and economically print them on the clinic's desktop printers.

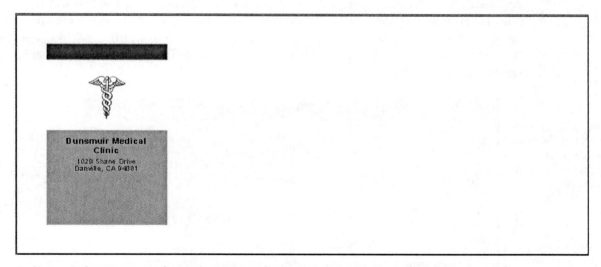

Business envelopes are one of many business publications you can create using Publisher.

Customizing Business Publications

The ability to customize business publications with unique business information expands the possibilities for using Microsoft Publisher as a complete publishing product for small- to medium-sized businesses. With the advances in desktop publishing software such as Publisher combined with the quality and convenience of desktop printers, companies have made Publisher a cost-effective choice. Companies store business information such as employee names and addresses to create and print in-house business cards, design their own letterhead and envelopes, and create mass mailings. Using these features can save companies the cost and learning time involved in other expensive programs.

About Business Information Sets

Business Information Sets are customized groups of information about an individual or an organization that can be used to quickly fill in publications, such as business cards, letterhead, and envelopes.

The Business Information Set can include an individual's name, job title, organization, address, business phone and fax numbers, e-mail address, web site, tagline, and logo. You can create as many different Business Information Sets as you want. For example, you may create one Business Information Set for the medical clinic and separate Business Information Sets for each doctor. This makes it easy to create personalized business cards, letterhead, envelopes, and appointment reminder postcards.

When you create a publication, the Business Information Set that you accessed most recently populates the new publication. Alternatively, you can choose a different information set or edit one currently being used in a publication. If you have not yet created a Business Information Set, your name and your organization name are inserted from information provided when 2007 Microsoft Office system was installed on your computer. If you no longer need a business set, you can easily delete it.

A Business Information Set can include the company and employee business information.

You can create and save as many information sets as needed.

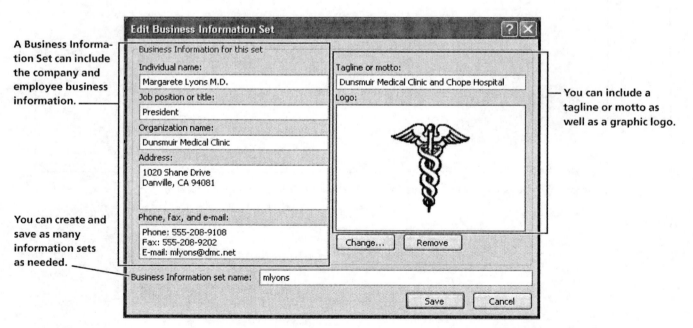

You can include a tagline or motto as well as a graphic logo.

QUICK REFERENCE: CREATING A BUSINESS INFORMATION SET

Task	Procedure
Create a Business Information Set	■ Select a publication type.
	■ Choose Create New under Business Information in the right pane.
	■ Type your business information in the Create New Business Information Set dialog box.
	■ Click the Add Logo button and choose your logo from the Insert Picture dialog box.
	■ If you want to change a logo that already appears in the dialog box, click the Change button and choose your logo from the Insert Picture dialog box.
	■ Name the Business Information Set.
Change information in a Business Information Set	■ Choose Edit→Business Information from the menu bar.
	or
	■ Click the SmartTag ⓘ button that appears when you position the mouse pointer over text or click a logo in a publication. You can then choose Edit Business Information from the SmartTag menu.
	■ Make the changes that you want and click Save.
	■ Click Update Publication to refresh the open publication.
Apply a different Business Information Set	■ Choose Edit→Business Information from the menu bar.
	■ Choose the Business Information Set that you want to apply to the open publication.
	■ Click Update Publication.
Delete a Business Information Set	■ Choose Edit→Business Information from the menu bar.
	■ Choose the Business Information Set you would like to delete.
	■ Click the Delete button.

Creating a Business Card

Companies are saving money on publishing costs by designing their own business cards. A business card is a small publication that can be printed on heavy stock paper. Business cards come in various sizes, 3.5 × 2 inches being a typical size. The card contains a name, title, business, and address information for an employee, as well as a graphic logo. Most employees also want their telephone, fax, and pager numbers on their business cards in addition to their e-mail and web site addresses. Keeping this data in a Business Information Set makes it easy to print new business cards whenever needed.

Desktop Printing of Business Cards

Printing business cards using a desktop printer instead of printing commercially gives you the flexibility to change your business cards at any time to better fit your needs. Most office supply stores carry pre-scored card sheets in a range of colors and specialty papers with preprinted designs.

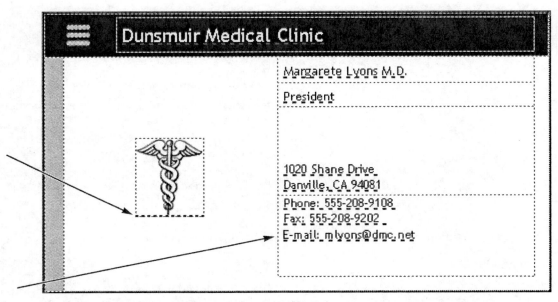

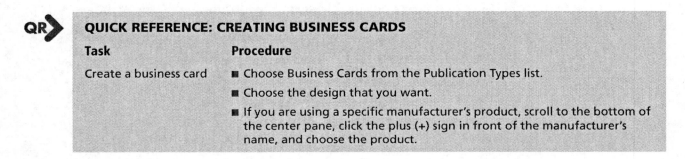

Dotted lines are text and graphic placeholders that do not appear on the printed business card.

 QR

QUICK REFERENCE: CREATING BUSINESS CARDS

Task	Procedure
Create a business card	■ Choose Business Cards from the Publication Types list.
	■ Choose the design that you want.
	■ If you are using a specific manufacturer's product, scroll to the bottom of the center pane, click the plus (+) sign in front of the manufacturer's name, and choose the product.

Hands-On 6.1 Create a Business Card and an Information Set

In this exercise, you will create a business card and Business Information Set for an employee of the clinic.

Create a Business Card

1. Start Publisher.

2. Choose the Business Cards publication type.

3. Click the Newer Designs link at the top of the center pane and click once to choose the Modular design.

4. Choose the Navy Color Scheme and the Opulent Trebuchet Font Scheme in the Customize pane at the right.

Create a Business Information Set

5. Click the Business Information drop-down box and choose Create New, as shown in the following illustration.

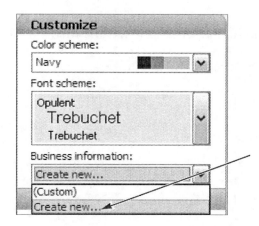

6. Type the business information as shown in the following illustration.

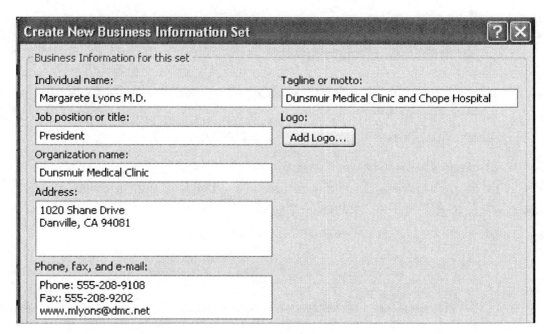

Add a Logo

7. Click the Add Logo button. (If you see a Change button instead of an Add Logo button, click the Change button.)
The Insert Picture dialog box opens.

8. Navigate to the Lesson 06 folder and double-click to insert the Medical Picture file.
The medical logo appears in the information set.

9. Press the Tab key twice to go to the Business Information Set Name field and type **mlyons,** and then click Save.

10. Click the Create button in the main Publisher window.

Change the Business Card Size

11. In the Business Card Options area of the Format Publication task pane, click the Change Page Size button at the bottom of the task pane.

12. In the Page Setup dialog box, click 3.583 x 2.165.

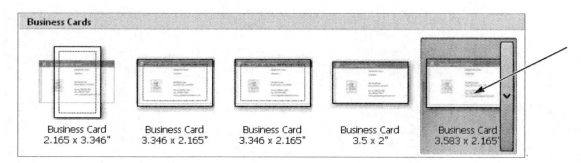

13. Click OK.

Preview the Business Card

14. Click the Print Preview 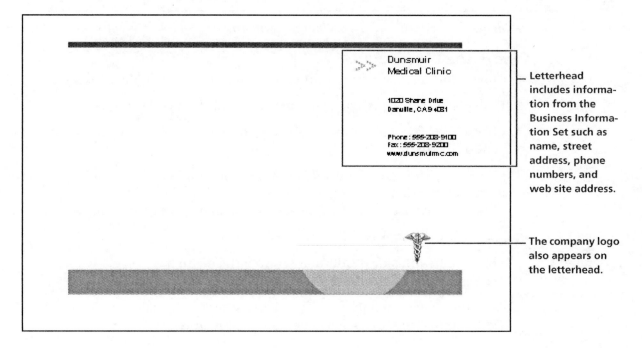 button.
    The business cards display in a printed format.

15. Close Print Preview.

16. Save the publication as **Lyons Medical Business Card** in the Lesson 06 folder.

17. Choose File→Close to close your business card and return to the main Publisher screen.

Creating a Business Letterhead

Letterhead is preprinted stationery that typically includes important facts about a company, such as address, phone, and fax. When you open a Publisher letterhead template, it includes this type of information taken from your Business Information Set. If necessary, you can change information in the current Business Information Set or create a new Business Information Set while working in a publication.

You can manipulate objects in the letterhead template, trying different colors, pictures, and other effects. Designing letterhead in-house with Publisher and then sending the file to a commercial organization for printing saves design consultation time, customization, and money.

Dunsmuir
Medical Clinic

1020 Shane Drive
Danville, CA 94531

Phone : 555-208-9100
Fax : 555-208-9200
www.dunsmuirmc.com

Letterhead includes information from the Business Information Set such as name, street address, phone numbers, and web site address.

The company logo also appears on the letterhead.

Using the Format Painter

The Format Painter is a feature that is available in other Microsoft programs, such as Word, PowerPoint, and Excel, as well as in Publisher. In Publisher, it allows you to copy formatting easily from one text box to another or to multiple text boxes. This feature can save you time creating your publications.

QUICK REFERENCE: CREATING LETTERHEAD AND USING THE FORMAT PAINTER

Task	Procedure
Create letterhead	■ Choose the Letterhead publication type from the main Publisher window.
	■ Choose a letterhead design.
	■ (Optional) Choose a different color and font scheme.
	■ (Optional) Choose a different Business Information Set in the Customize pane.
	■ Click the Create button.
Use the Format Painter to copy formatting one time	■ Select the text that is already formatted.
	■ Click the Format Painter button one time.
	■ Drag across the text to be formatted to apply the formatting.
Use the Format Painter to copy formatting more than one time	■ Select the text that is already formatted.
	■ Double-click the Format Painter button.
	■ Drag across the text to apply the formatting.
	■ Continue to apply the formatting to other text as desired.
	■ Click the Format Painter button to turn it off.

 Hands-On 6.2   Create a New Letterhead

In this exercise, you will create a new Business Information Set and new letterhead for the clinic.

Create the Letterhead

1. Choose the Letterhead publication type from the main Publisher screen.

2. Under Newer Designs, click once to choose the Arrows design.

3. Choose the Navy Color Scheme and the Basis Arial Bold Font Scheme from the Customize pane at the right.

4. Choose *mlyons* from the Business Information drop-down list if it is not already selected then click the Create button.
   The letterhead displays with the data from the information set created for Margarete Lyons.

Create a Business Information Set

5. Choose Edit→Business Information from the menu bar.
   The Business Information dialog box displays.

6. Click the New button in the upper-right corner of the dialog box.
   The Create New Business Information Set dialog box appears.

7. Follow these steps to create the information set:

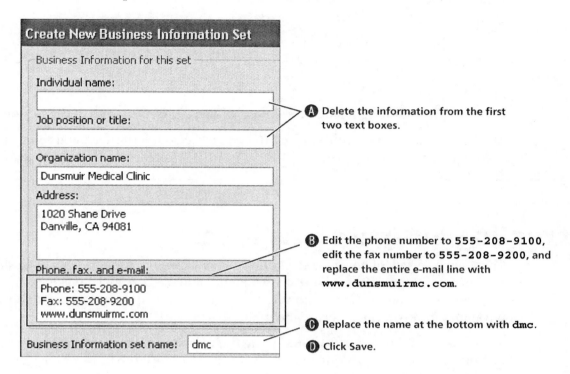

8. Click the Update Publication button at the bottom of the Business Information dialog box.

Format the Letterhead

9. Click inside the Dunsmuir Medical Clinic text box in the upper-right corner of the letterhead.

10. Press ⎡Ctrl⎤+⎡A⎤ to select the text.

11. Click the Font Size drop-down box on the Formatting toolbar and choose 12 pt.

12. Choose the third color from the Font Color drop-down box, as shown in the following illustration.

13. Select the address text in the next text box.

14. Change the Font Size to 9 pt.

Use Format Painter

15. With the text still selected, click the Format Painter 🖌 button on the Standard toolbar and position your mouse pointer inside the next text box.
The mouse pointer appears as a paintbrush icon when the Format Painter button is active.

16. Drag through all of the text in the third text box.
The formatting in this text box now matches the formatting in the second text box.

Print Preview the Letterhead

17. Resize the last text box if necessary.

18. Click the Print Preview 🔍 button.
The letterhead displays in a printed format.

19. Close Print Preview.

20. Save 💾 your letterhead as **Medical Clinic Letterhead** in the Lesson 06 folder.

21. Choose File→Close from the menu bar to close your letterhead and return to the main Publisher screen.

Creating Business Envelopes

There are a variety of envelope sizes and shapes. The most common envelope sizes are #10 business envelopes that measure 4 x 9.5 inches and #6 personal envelopes that measure 3 x 6.5 inches. You can also customize the page layout feature to instruct Publisher to print envelopes for invitations, cards, and mailers.

You can save company costs by designing the company envelope using Publisher and outsourcing only the printing of the envelopes. Most desktop printers have an envelope-feeding mechanism that works well with Publisher, so you may be able to save costs on printing, too.

Once you create an envelope design, you can always change your mind and choose a different design. Labels are often used instead of envelopes. You will use Publisher's mail merge feature in Lesson 8, Creating a Mail Merge to create labels.

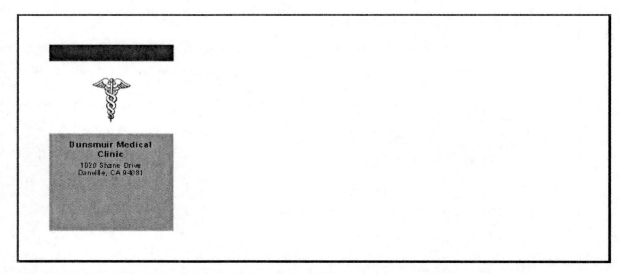

The envelope logo and address are inserted from a Business Information Set.

QR

QUICK REFERENCE: CREATING ENVELOPES

Task	Procedure
Create an envelope	■ Choose the Envelopes publication type from the main Publisher window. ■ Choose an envelope design. ■ (Optional) Choose a different color and font scheme. ■ (Optional) Choose a different Business Information Set in the Customize pane. ■ Choose the desired envelope size. ■ Click Create.
Choose a different envelope design	■ Click the Change Template button in the Format Publication Task Pane under Envelope Options. ■ Choose a different envelope design.

 Hands-On 6.3   Create a Business Envelope

In this exercise, you will create an envelope, change to a different envelope design, and format the envelope.

Create an Envelope

1. Choose the Envelopes publication type from the main Publisher screen.

2. Under Newer Designs, click once to choose the Marker design.

3. Choose the Navy Color Scheme and the Basis Arial Bold Font Scheme.

4. Click the Business Information drop-down box and choose *dmc* if it is not already selected.

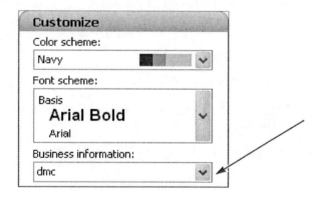

5. Under Options, click the Page Size drop-down arrow and choose #10.

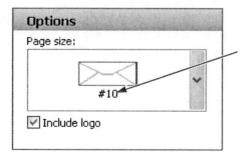

6. Click the Create button.

Change the Envelope Design

7. Click the Change Template button in the Format Publication task pane under Envelope Options.

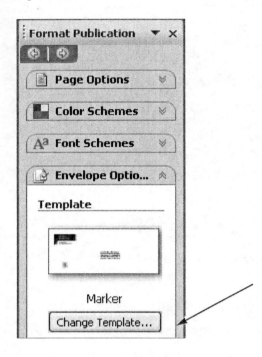

The main Publisher window appears.

8. Click the Classic Designs link at the top of the center pane, choose Bars, and click OK.

Format the Envelope

9. Select the recipient address text and press ⎡Delete⎤.

10. Click the text in the Clinic name text box and press ⎡Ctrl⎤+⎡A⎤.

11. Click the Font drop-down arrow on the Formatting toolbar, change the font size to 10 pt, and press ⎡Ctrl⎤+⎡B⎤ to bold-face the text.

12. Click the text in the return address text box and press ⎡Ctrl⎤+⎡A⎤.

13. Change the font size to 8 pt.

Print Preview the Envelope

14. Click the Print Preview 🔍 button.
The envelope displays in a printed format.

15. Click Close to exit Print Preview.

16. Click the Save 💾 button and save your envelope as **Medical Clinic Envelope** in the Lesson 06 folder.

17. Choose File→Close from the menu bar to close your envelope and return to the main Publisher screen.

Creating Business Postcards

Publisher's postcard templates help you create a variety of postcard designs, such as appointment reminders or event announcements. You can use Business Information Sets with postcards. You can print postcards on regular cardstock and cut them out by hand, or you can buy blank postcard paper and feed it into your printer as a custom paper size.

You place your message on the front and the mailing address on the back. Instead of typing an individual address on the back page, you can use Publisher's mail merge feature to print multiple addresses when you are sending out business mailings. You will learn the mail merge feature in Lesson 8, Creating a Mail Merge.

You can use business postcards as reminders or event announcements to medical patients.

Information from the business set appears in the postcard.

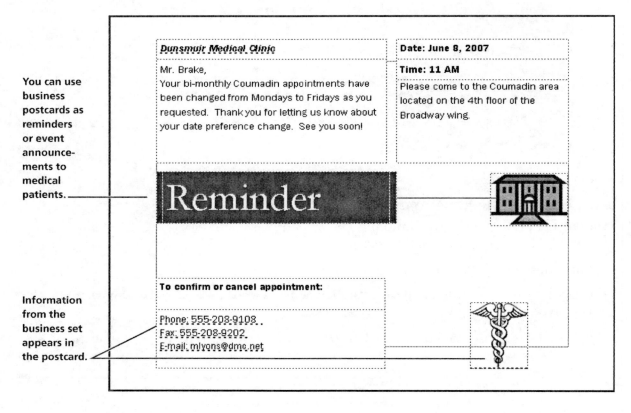

Dunsmuir Medical Clinic

Mr. Brake,
Your bi-monthly Coumadin appointments have been changed from Mondays to Fridays as you requested. Thank you for letting us know about your date preference change. See you soon!

Date: June 8, 2007

Time: 11 AM
Please come to the Coumadin area located on the 4th floor of the Broadway wing.

Reminder

To confirm or cancel appointment:

Phone: 555-208-9108
Fax: 555-208-9202
E-mail: mlyons@dmc.net

QUICK REFERENCE: CREATING POSTCARDS

Task	Procedure
Create a postcard	■ Choose the Postcards publication type from the main Publisher window.
	■ Choose a postcard design.
	■ (Optional) Choose a different color and font scheme.
	■ (Optional) Choose a different Business Information Set.
	■ Click the Create button.

Hands-On 6.4   Create a Business Postcard

In this exercise, you will create a postcard to send to a patient reminding them of a medical appointment.

Create a Postcard

1. Choose the Postcards publication type in the main Publisher window.

2. Click the Reminder link in the center pane and click once to choose the Connection design.

3. Choose the Mahogany Color Scheme and (default template fonts) Font Scheme located at the top of the Font Scheme list.

4. Choose the *mylons* Business Information Set if it is not already selected and click the Create button.

Edit the Postcard

5. Type the following text in the second text box in the upper-left corner of the postcard:

   Mr. Brake, Enter

   Your bi-monthly Coumadin appointments have been changed from Mondays to Fridays as you requested. Thank you for letting us know about your date preference change. See you soon!

6. In the upper-right corner of the postcard, change the date to **June 8, 2007** and the time to **11 AM**.

7. In the text box below the time, type the following:

   Please come to the Coumadin area located on the 4th floor of the Broadway wing.

Add an Address

8. Go to page 2 of the postcard and type the following in the recipient address box:

   Mr. Ronald Brake
   218 Crestview Drive
   Walnut Creek, CA 94881

9. Return to the first page of the postcard.

Print Preview the Postcard

10. Click the Print Preview [icon] button.
    The postcard displays in a printed format.

11. Close Print Preview.

Delete Business Information Sets

12. Choose Edit→Business Information from the menu bar.
The Business Information dialog box opens and displays mylons *as the current information set used in the postcard.*

13. Click the Delete button.

14. Choose Yes when prompted to confirm the deletion.
The mylons *Business Information Set is deleted.*

15. Check to ensure that the *dmc* Business Information Set now appears in the Business Information dialog box.

16. Click the Delete button again.

17. Choose Yes when prompted to confirm the deletion then click Close.

18. Save 🖫 your envelope as **Medical Clinic Postcard** in the Lesson 06 folder.

19. Choose File→Close from the menu bar to close your postcard and return to the main Publisher screen.

Concepts Review

True/False Questions

1. You can create a maximum of seven Business Information Sets.   **TRUE   FALSE**

2. A Business Information Set can include a graphic logo.   **TRUE   FALSE**

3. Printing business cards using a desktop printer instead of printing commercially gives you flexibility to change your business cards at any time to better fit your needs.   **TRUE   FALSE**

4. You cannot manipulate objects in the letter template.   **TRUE   FALSE**

5. The most common envelope sizes are #6 business envelopes and #10 personal envelopes.   **TRUE   FALSE**

6. If you know you will be using a specific manufacturer's business card product, you may find it listed in the design area of the main Publisher window.   **TRUE   FALSE**

7. If you want to apply formats several times in a row using the Format Painter, you must double-click the Format Painter button.   **TRUE   FALSE**

8. You can use the Format Painter to copy formatting from one text box to another text box.   **TRUE   FALSE**

9. Once you create a particular envelope design, you cannot change to a different design. You must start from the beginning if you want to use a different design.   **TRUE   FALSE**

10. You can change information in the current business set or create and delete a business set while working in a publication.   **TRUE   FALSE**

Multiple Choice Questions

1. Which of the following cannot be part of a Business Information Set?
   a. WordArt
   b. Web site address
   c. Tag line or motto
   d. Logo

2. Which of the following is not true about business cards?
   a. Business card designs come in various sizes.
   b. You cannot change the size of a business card once you select the design.
   c. You can purchase pre-scored sheets of cards in most office supply stores.
   d. You can print a business card in either portrait or landscape orientation.

3. Which of the following is not true about a Business Information Set?
   a. If no information sets have been created, your name and organization are inserted from information provided when the 2007 Microsoft Office system was installed on your computer.
   b. You can create as many different Business Information Sets as you want.
   c. An information set cannot be deleted.
   d. An information set can be used to personalize publications such as business cards, letterhead, and postcards.

4. Which of the following is true about the Format Painter?
   a. It is only used in Microsoft Publisher.
   b. It is used to copy formatting from one text box to another text box.
   c. It copies information from one Business Information Set to a different Business Information Set.
   d. It is part of the Spell Checker feature.

Skill Builders

Skill Builder 6.1 **Create a With Compliments Card Publication**

In this exercise, you will create and edit a new Business Information Set while creating a With Compliments Card publication for a law firm employee.

1. Choose the With Compliments Cards publication type from the main Publisher window.

2. Choose the Borders design.

3. Choose the Opulent Color Scheme and the (default template fonts) Font Scheme.

4. Choose Create New from the Business Information drop-down box.

5. Fill in the following information, starting with the Individual Name through the Business Information Set Name.

6. Type the tagline **Technology Mergers and Acquisitions** in the upper-right corner of the dialog box.

7. Click the Add Logo button if there currently is no logo; otherwise, click the Change button.

8. Navigate to the Lesson 06 folder and double-click the sb-Law Picture file to insert it.

9. Click the Save button to close the dialog box and save the Business Information Set.

10. Click the Create button to open the publication and insert the data from the Business Information Set in the With Compliments card, as shown in the following illustration.

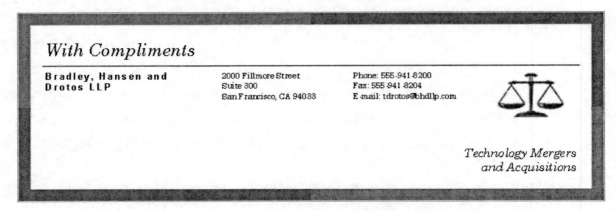

11. Save ![save icon] the publication as **sb-Law Compliment Card** in the Lesson 06 folder.

12. Choose File→Close from the menu bar to close your publication and return to the main Publisher screen.

Skill Builder 6.2   Create a Fax Cover Sheet

In this exercise, you will create a fax cover sheet for your law firm. You will use the Business Information Set you created in the last exercise.

1. Choose the Business Forms publication type from the main Publisher screen.

2. Choose the Borders design in the Fax Cover category.

3. Choose the Harbor Color Scheme and the Galley Arial Rounded Font Scheme.

4. If necessary, choose the *drotos* Business Information Set; click the Create button.

5. Click the Change Template button in the Format Publication task pane.

6. Choose a Capsules fax cover design.

7. Edit the text boxes as shown in the following illustrations. Change font size as you deem appropriate.

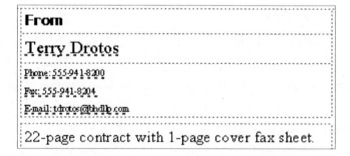

To

Sarah Jackson
Pier 45 Shipping Lines
2nd Floor
555-492-8011

Please review and fax to me by 6/28.

From

Terry Drotos

Phone: 555-941-8200
Fax: 555-941-8204
E-mail: tdrotos@bhdlb.com

22-page contract with 1-page cover fax sheet.

8. Type the following text in the message area:

Sarah,
Please review the terms of the contract and call me to schedule a conference call at your convenience.

Thanks,
Terry Drotos

9. Save 🖫 the publication as **sb-Fax Cover Sheet** in the Lesson 06 folder.

10. Choose File→Close from the menu bar to close your fax cover sheet and return to the main Publisher screen.

Skill Builder 6.3   Create a "We've Moved" Greeting Card

In this exercise, you will create a greeting card to notify clients about the law firm's move. You will also use the Information smart tag button in the publication to edit the Business Information Set.

1. Choose the Greeting Cards publication type from the main Publisher screen and click the We've Moved link at the top of the center pane.

2. Choose the We've Moved 5 design.

3. Choose the Solstice Color Scheme and choose (default font templates) from the Font Scheme menu.

4. Choose the *drotos* information set if it is not already selected; click the Create button.

5. Go to the second page of the card.

6. Hover the mouse pointer over Terry Drotos, and click the Information ⓘ button.

7. Choose Edit Business Information from the menu.
   The Business Information dialog box shows drotos *as the current information set.*

8. Click the Edit button.
   The Edit Business Information Set dialog box opens.

9. Edit the address text box to reflect the new address in the following illustration.

Address:

100 California Street
Suite 700
San Francisco, CA 94033

10. In the Phone text box, click to place your cursor at the end of the e-mail address and press ⌈Enter⌋.

11. Type the following: **www.bhdllp.com**

Phone, fax, and e-mail:

Fax: 555-941-8204
E-mail: tdrotos@bhdllp.com
www.bhdllp.com

12. Click the Save button then click the Update Publication button in the Business Information dialog box.

13. On page 2, click in the second text box, which begins with *This text can explain,* to select the text.

14. Type the following information in the text box:

    Our new offices are conveniently located in downtown San Francisco, just two blocks from BART and two blocks from the Ferry Building.

15. On page 3, click *00/00/00* in the *At new location* text box and type **8/15/2007**.

Delete the Drotos Information Set

16. On page 2, hover the mouse pointer over Terry Drotos.
    The Information button appears.

17. Click the Information ⓘ button.

18. Choose Edit Business Information from the menu.
    The drotos *set should be the default information set displayed under Select a Business Information Set.*

19. Click the Delete button. When the message appears to confirm the deletion, click Yes.

20. Close button the dialog box.
    The drotos *Business Information Set is deleted, but the* drotos *information still appears in the greeting card.*

21. Save 💾 the publication as **sb-We've Moved Greeting Card** in the Lesson 06 folder.

22. Choose File→Close from the menu bar to close your greeting card and return to the main Publisher screen.

 # Assessments

Assessment 6.1   Create an Award Certificate

In this exercise, you will create a Business Information Set for the employee of the month at Baughman Enterprises.

1. Create an Award Certificate for Employee of the Month.

2. Choose the color and font scheme of your choice.

3. Create the new business set as shown in the following illustration.

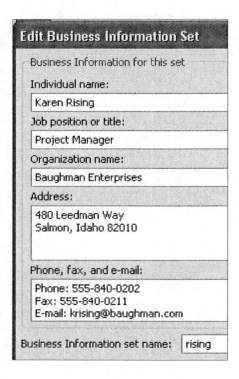

4. Click the Save button to close the dialog box.

5. Click the Create button.

6. Click in the Name of Recipient text box and type **Karen Rising**.

7. Click in the Month and Year text box and type **September 2007**.

8. Print Preview the award certificate then close the Print Preview window.

9. Save 🔲 the publication as **as-Award Certificate** in the Lesson 06 folder.

10. Close your award certificate and return to the main Publisher screen.

Assessment 6.2   Create a Luggage Tag Label

In this exercise, you will create a luggage tag label for the employee of the month because she has been awarded a trip to Hawaii!

1. Choose the Labels publication type and Luggage Tag in the Identification category of the main Publisher screen.

2. Choose whatever color and font scheme you prefer.

3. Choose the *rising Business Information Set* if it is not already selected and click the Create button.

4. Click in the phone text box and type **555-702-0305**.

5. Open the Business Information dialog box and delete the *rising* information set.

6. Save the publication as **as-Luggage Tag Label** in the Lesson 06 folder.

7. Close your luggage tag label and return to the main Publisher screen.

Critical Thinking

Critical Thinking 6.1   Create a Thank You Card for Clients

Joey's Catering Creations, a well-known catering firm located in Santa Barbara, would like you to design a thank-you card to send out to their many long-time clients to thank them for their business over the years.

1. Create a Marquee Thank You greeting card.

2. Make your own choice of color and font schemes.

3. Create the new Business Information Set shown in the following illustration. Insert the ct-Joey's Catering Picture logo from the Lesson 06 folder in the Business Information Set. Create a catchy tagline for the information set.

4. Save the invitation as **ct-Joey's Thank-You Card** in the Lesson 06 folder.

5. On page 2, delete the Thank You text box and create a Thank You using colorful WordArt.

6. On page 2, select the existing text in the text box located above the logo, and insert a Word file, ct-Joey's Catering Creations Text, located in the Lesson 06 folder.

7. Change the color scheme of the text you inserted to one that is colorful and that matches the rest of the thank-you card.

8. On page 3, delete the text in the text box.

9. Create a 3-D chocolate heart using AutoShapes to fit into this text box.

10. Look at page 4 of your thank-you card to see that the text from the information set appears there.

11. Preview your thank-you card.
   You will continue to use the joey Business Information Set in the next exercise.

Critical Thinking 6.2   Create a Calendar for Joey's Cafe

Joey's Catering Creations would like you to create a calendar for the current month. The company uses this monthly calendar to post fun items in their café about upcoming birthdays and social events.

Before You Begin: You will use the Business Information Set created in Critical Thinking 6.1.

1. Experiment with the various calendars until you find a design that best fits Joey's Catering Creations look.

2. Experiment with different color schemes and fonts until you get the look you like.

3. Joey opened a new catering location in Palo Alto. Create a new Business Information Set based on the current *joey* information set, changing the new address to **3000 El Camino Real, Palo Alto, CA 94880**. The rest of the information in this new business set is the same.

4. Experiment using either WordArt or clip art to add a colorful design to the calendar.

5. Practice choosing a different calendar template.

6. Add whatever formatting you would like to enhance the calendar.

7. Print Preview your invitation.

8. Delete the *joey* Business Information Set.

9. Save the invitation as **ct-Calendar** in the Lesson 06 folder.

10. Close your calendar and return to the main Publisher screen.

11. Exit Publisher.

Designing a Newsletter

In this lesson, you will use Publisher to create a company newsletter. You will insert new pages in the newsletter and delete pages you no longer need. You will also edit the masthead information located on the first page of the newsletter. You will find that importing text files as stories is the same as importing files in other publications and that it is easy to autoflow text files into a newsletter to accommodate larger amounts of text. You will add captions to graphics, which is just as easy as editing text in a text box. Finally, you will edit a sidebar to enhance the appeal of your newsletter.

LESSON OBJECTIVES

After studying this lesson, you will be able to:

- Create and edit a newsletter
- Insert and delete pages in a newsletter
- Edit a masthead
- Import text files as stories
- Use Autoflow with stories
- Add captions to graphics
- Edit a sidebar

Case Study: Designing a Town Newsletter

Margie Dugan is town clerk of Preston Hollow. Town Manager John Fox would like Margie to start creating a monthly newsletter to send to the citizens of Preston Hollow to keep them informed of the town's different services, community events, and meetings. John is conscious of the town's budget and realizes that creating a newsletter using Publisher would be a cost-effective way to keep citizens informed of important information about the town on an ongoing basis.

Margie is comfortable using Publisher because she has created various publications such as letters, flyers, and postcards, but she has never created a newsletter. She is anticipating that the newsletter will be easy and fun to create, given the many choices of newsletter templates that Publisher offers. She has gathered articles and pictures that she would like to include in the first newsletter. She has a layout design planned and she has decided how to print the newsletter. She is ready to begin!

Newsletters contain side-bars that add appeal, such as points of interest.

A masthead in a newsletter is similar to a masthead in a newspaper; it contains information such as the date, the volume and issue number, and the newsletter heading.

In addition to story text, newsletter articles can include graphics with captions for added visual appeal.

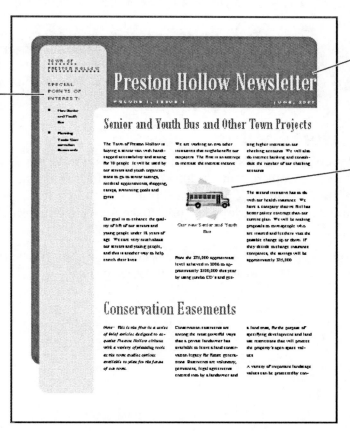

Introducing Publisher Newsletters

Newsletters provide a popular medium for companies to distribute information to their employees or clients. A newsletter is usually a multipage publication with newspaper features such as columns, a masthead, and sidebars. You can add visual appeal with pictures and graphics. You can either insert or delete pages as needed.

Newsletters have several advantages over other publications. They are easy and less costly to produce than publications such as brochures, and they are a perfect forum for delivering dated information.

Designing a Newsletter

Designing an effective newsletter involves good planning. A good newsletter should deliver a message in an attractive, clear, and effective way. You should know your audience and write to their interests, and you should clarify your purpose, such as educating your employees or clients about your organization.

You should also gather the appropriate data for your newsletter, such as articles, pictures, figures, and so on. You also need to consider how you will print the newsletter—commercially or in-house. And lastly, you need to decide the best layout for visual appeal and content delivery.

Creating a Newsletter

Publisher includes a variety of newsletter templates, each with its own design, color, font, and layout schemes. The newsletter Customize and Options pane provides choices to change colors, fonts, and Business Information Sets, as well as options to choose from one- or two-page spreads for printing. You can also choose to include space for a customer address on the back page of the newsletter.

A Publisher Newsletter template initially creates four pages of text and graphics. If appropriate for your newsletter, you can easily delete or insert extra newsletter pages.

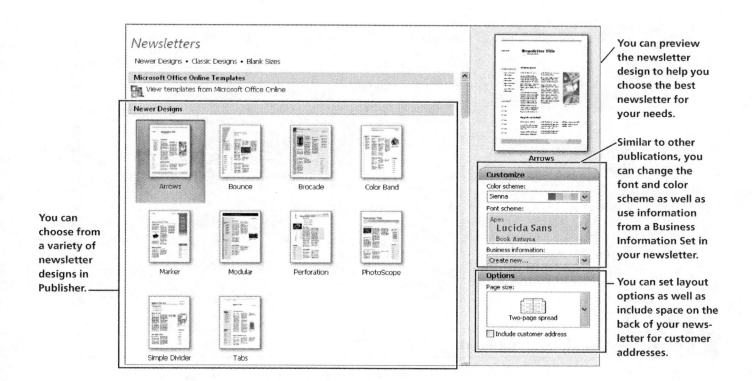

You can preview the newsletter design to help you choose the best newsletter for your needs.

Similar to other publications, you can change the font and color scheme as well as use information from a Business Information Set in your newsletter.

You can set layout options as well as include space on the back of your newsletter for customer addresses.

You can choose from a variety of newsletter designs in Publisher.

Inserting Pages in a Newsletter

When you insert pages in a newsletter, Publisher asks you to specify the type of page you want to insert, such as Story, Calendar, Response Form, Sign-up Form, and Order Form. It then sets up the new page with the appropriate elements.

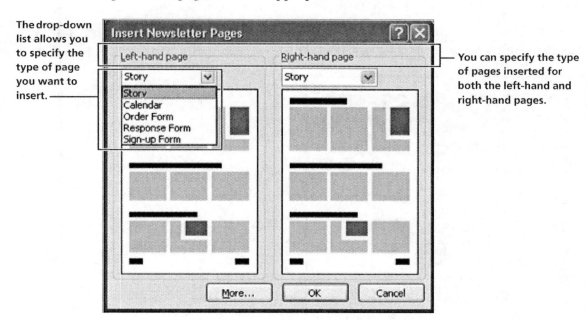

The drop-down list allows you to specify the type of page you want to insert.

You can specify the type of pages inserted for both the left-hand and right-hand pages.

QUICK REFERENCE: CREATING A NEWSLETTER AND INSERTING AND DELETING PAGES

Task	Procedure
Create a newsletter	■ Select the Newsletter publication type. ■ Select a Newsletter design. ■ Choose a Color Scheme and Font Scheme in the Customize pane. ■ Choose either a one- or two-page spread under Options. ■ Check Customer Address if you want an area on the back page for placing a customer mailing addresses.
Insert pages	■ Choose Insert→Page from the menu bar. ■ Click the Story drop-down arrow to choose what to insert in the new page on either the left-hand or right-hand page.
Delete pages	■ Choose Edit→Delete Page from the menu bar. ■ Choose Both Pages, Left Page Only, or Right Page Only from the dialog box.

 Hands-On 7.1   Create a Newsletter

In this exercise, you will create a newsletter, insert two pages, and delete four of the six pages.

Create a Newsletter

1. Choose the Newsletters publication type from the main Publisher window.

2. Click the Classic Designs link and click once to choose the Banded design.

3. Choose the Fjord Color Scheme and the Binary Verdana Font Scheme.

4. Under Options in the right-hand pane, choose Two-Page Spread; click the Create button.
   Publisher displays the first page of the newsletter.

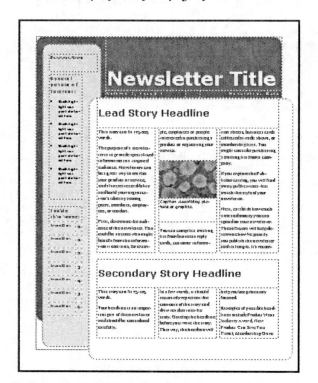

Insert Pages in a Newsletter

5. Go to page 2 in the publication.

Pages 2 and 3 appear in the workspace.

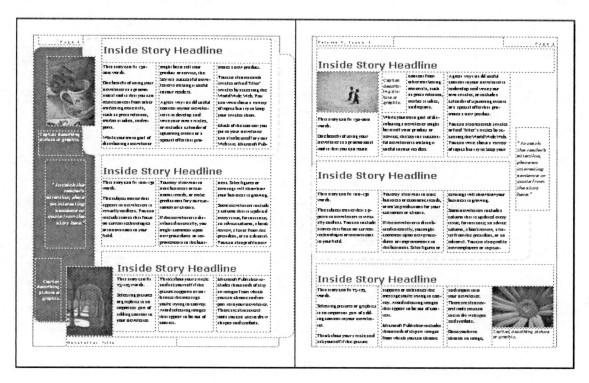

6. Choose Insert→Page from the menu bar.

The Insert Newsletter Pages dialog box displays.

7. Click the Left-Hand Page drop-down box and choose Calendar; leave the Right-Hand Page set at Story and click OK.

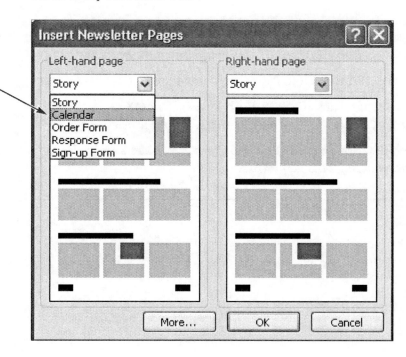

Publisher adds pages 4 and 5 to the publication. There are now six pages in the newsletter.

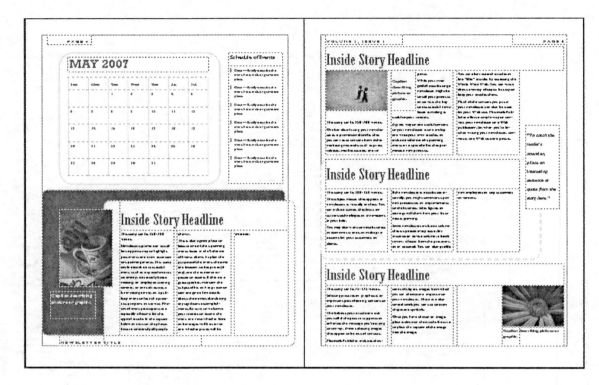

The calendar reflects the month during which you are completing this exercise.

Delete Pages in a Newsletter

8. Go to page 2 in the publication.
Pages 2 and 3 display in the workspace.

9. Choose Edit→Delete Page from the menu bar.
The Delete Page dialog box displays.

10. If not already selected, choose Both Pages; click OK.
Publisher deletes pages 2 and 3. There are now four pages in the newsletter.

11. Once again, choose Edit→Delete Page from the menu bar.

12. If not already selected, click to select Both Pages; click OK.
Publisher deletes pages 2 and 3. There are now two pages in the newsletter.

13. Save 🖫 the publication as **Preston Hollow Newsletter** in the Lesson 07 folder.
Keep your newsletter open for the next exercise.

Editing the Masthead

A masthead is a box or section printed in each newsletter issue that lists information such as the name, publisher, location, volume, and date. Most newsletters contain a masthead similar to those used in newspapers.

A Publisher masthead contains several text boxes and color-filled shapes that create an attractive, visually appealing graphic to complement the design of the newsletter. Some newsletter templates may include different shapes and text boxes in their mastheads, such as a text box that displays the organization's name. You may need to edit the masthead text boxes to convey your message.

The newsletter name automatically formats as you type it.

The newsletter volume and issue number as well as the date appear in the masthead.

QUICK REFERENCE: EDITING THE MASTHEAD

Task	Procedure
Edit the masthead	■ Click the Newsletter Title text on page 1 of the newsletter.
	■ Press the F9 key to zoom.
	■ Type the new text.
	■ Click the placeholder text in the Volume/Issue text box and type the new text.
	■ Click on the placeholder text in the Newsletter Date text box and type the date.

Hands-On 7.2   Edit the Masthead

In this exercise, you will edit the newsletter masthead. Since this is Preston Hollows' first newsletter, you will not need to edit the volume/issue.

1. Go to page 1.

2. Click on the Newsletter Title text.

3. Press the [F9] key to zoom in to view the masthead more closely.

4. Follow these instructions to edit the masthead:

A Type **Preston Hollow Newsletter.**

B Select the Newsletter Date text and type **June, 2007.**

5. Save 💾 your changes.
   Keep your newsletter open for the next exercise.

Importing Files

Importing is the term used to describe inserting text or objects from another source into a Publisher publication. In Lesson 5, Creating an E-mail Letter you imported Word text files into an e-mail newsletter. It is also common to import text and graphics from different sources into a regular newsletter. People in an organization often submit newsletter stories via e-mail in different formats, such as a Word or an Excel file.

Using Autoflow with Stories

Publisher uses the term *story* to refer to text that is contained within a single text box or a chain of linked text boxes. In a template, two or three text boxes may be linked automatically. Stories often contain graphics that can be replaced with pictures from files or clip art.

If a story is too long to fit in the linked text boxes, Publisher asks to link even more text boxes for easy reading. You then have the option of connecting to another box or continuing the story on another page. Publisher will add the *continued notices* or *jump lines* to guide readers through the story.

Senior and Youth Bus and Other Town Projects

The story headline precedes each story.

The Town of Preston Hollow is buying a senior van with handicapped accessibility and seating for 30 people. It will be used by our seniors and youth organizations to go to senior outings, medical appointments, shopping, camps, swimming pools and gyms.

Our goal is to enhance the quality of life of our seniors and young people under 18 years of age. We care very much about our seniors and young people, and this is another way to help enrich their lives.

We are working on two other initiatives that might benefit our taxpayers. The first is an attempt to increase the interest income

Our new Senior and Youth Bus

from the $75,000 approximate level achieved in 2006 to approximately $100,000 this year by using jumbo CD's and get-

ting higher interest on our checking accounts. We will also do internet banking and consolidate the number of our checking accounts.

The second initiative has to do with our health insurance. We have a company that we feel has better policy coverage than our current plan. We will be making proposals to townspeople who are insured and let them vote the possible change up or down. If they decide to change insurance companies, the savings will be approximately $35,000.

You can insert clip art or picture files with captions.

Most templates contain two or three columns for the story text.

QR ▶ **QUICK REFERENCE: IMPORTING A FILE AND EDITING A GRAPHIC CAPTION**

Task	Procedure
Import a text file	■ Position the insertion point in the text box where you want to begin the imported story. ■ Choose Insert→Text File from the menu bar. ■ Navigate to the file location. ■ Choose the file and click OK.
Edit a graphic caption	■ Click the generic caption text to select it. ■ Type the new text.

 ## Hands-On 7.3   Import Text Files

In this exercise, you will edit the Lead Story Headline text, import a text file and graphic, edit the graphic caption, and import a second story that will autoflow to a second text box.

Edit a Headline

1. On page 1, click the Lead Story Headline text to select it.

2. Type **Senior and Youth Bus and Other Town Projects**.

3. Click in the workspace area outside the newsletter to deselect the headline.

Import a Text File

4. Click the story text below the headline.

5. Choose Insert→Text File from the menu bar.

6. Navigate to the Lesson 07 folder and open the Preston Hollow Lead Story file.
A message appears explaining that Publisher is converting the file. Then the new text replaces the default text.

Senior and Youth Bus and Other Town Projects

The Town of Preston Hollow is buying a senior van with handicapped accessibility and seating for 30 people. It will be used by our seniors and youth organizations to go to senior outings, medical appointments, shopping, camps, swimming pools and gyms.

Our goal is to enhance the quality of life of our seniors and young people under 18 years of age. We care very much about our seniors and young people, and this is another way to help enrich their lives.

We are working on two other initiatives that might benefit our taxpayers. The first is an attempt to increase the interest income

Caption describing picture or graphic.

from the $75,000 approximate level achieved in 2006 to approximately $100,000 this year by using jumbo CD's and get-

ting higher interest on our checking accounts. We will also do internet banking and consolidate the number of our checking accounts.

The second initiative has to do with our health insurance. We have a company that we feel has better policy coverage than our current plan. We will be making proposals to townspeople who are insured and let them vote the possible change up or down. If they decide to change insurance companies, the savings will be approximately $35,000.

Import a Graphic

7. Right-click the flower graphic in the middle of the lead story and choose Change Picture→Clip Art from the pop-up menu.
The Clip Art task pane appears on the left side of the screen.

8. In the Clip Art task pane, type **bus** in the Search For field and click Go.
A bus clip art image appears in the task pane.

9. Click once on the image.
The bus replaces the flower graphic in the middle of the lead story.

10. Click in the scratch area outside the newsletter to deselect the graphic.

Edit the Caption

11. Click the text in the caption text box under the bus image.

12. Type **Our new Senior and Youth Bus**.

13. Center ☰ the text.
    The caption text is centered under the bus clip art.

Autoflow Text for the Second Story

14. Scroll to display the lower portion of page 1.

15. Click Secondary Story Headline to select it.

16. Type **Conservation Easements**.

17. Click the secondary story text to select it.

18. Choose Insert→Text File from the menu bar.

19. Navigate to the Lesson 07 folder and open the Preston Hollow Conservation Easements file.
    Publisher displays an autoflow warning message.

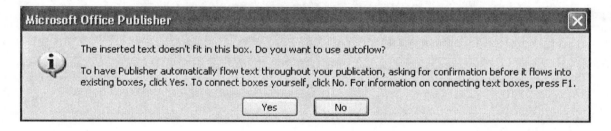

20. Click Yes.
    Publisher displays another autoflow message.

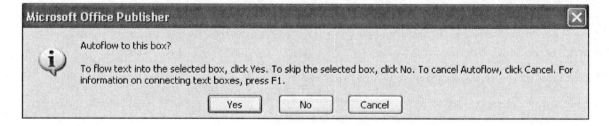

21. Again, click Yes.
    The remaining story text overflows into the back-page text box.

Edit the Second Story Caption

22. Click the text in the flower graphic caption text box.

23. Type **Leave a Conservation Legacy for Future Generations**.

24. Center ☰ the text.

25. Click the Back Page Story Headline text to select it and type the following: **Leave a Land Conservation Legacy**

Leave a Land Conservation Legacy

servation easements, such as natural areas and important habitat, water resources, scenic areas, or working lands such as farms and managed forests. Every conservation easement document is unique, tailored to the specific characteristics of each property.

Easements result in public benefit from the protections they provide to the environment, and there are financial incentives for donating an easement to a land trust. The primary incentive is state and federal income tax reductions for the value of the property rights that are given up, as determined by an independent appraisal.

Easements can also help lower or eliminate estate taxes, helping landowner's to pass land along to their heirs. There is currently no guarantee of property tax relief when donating an easement. This is decided by the local assessor.

Leave a Conservation Legacy for Future Generations

Conservation easements are enabled by state and federal law, and do not require local government approvals.

Placing a conservation easement on your land does not mean that you are automatically granting the public the right to enter onto your land. It is still your private property, and the easement does not prevent you from selling the land or passing it on to children.

The landowner is exercising their ability to put their own permanent stamp on the land. This is one of the few ways to leave something truly enduring and meaningful in this world.

26. Save 💾 your changes.
Keep your newsletter open for the next exercise.

Editing a Sidebar

A sidebar is a text element that is set off with a box or graphic and placed beside an article. It contains text that is not critical to understanding the main text but that usually adds interest or additional information. The name of a business, a table of contents, and a bulleted list of points of interest are examples of sidebar text on the first page of a newsletter. A sidebar can also contain information from a Business Information Set, such as the company name.

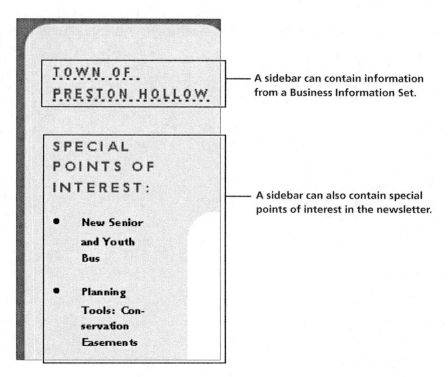

TOWN OF
PRESTON HOLLOW
— A sidebar can contain information from a Business Information Set.

SPECIAL
POINTS OF
INTEREST:

• New Senior and Youth Bus

• Planning Tools: Conservation Easements

— A sidebar can also contain special points of interest in the newsletter.

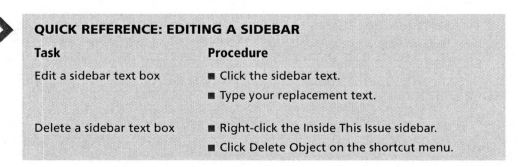

QUICK REFERENCE: EDITING A SIDEBAR

Task	Procedure
Edit a sidebar text box	■ Click the sidebar text.
	■ Type your replacement text.
Delete a sidebar text box	■ Right-click the Inside This Issue sidebar.
	■ Click Delete Object on the shortcut menu.

 **Hands-On 7.4** **Edit a Sidebar**

In this exercise, you will edit a sidebar and delete a sidebar. You will also create a Business Information Set for the newsletter.

Edit a Sidebar

1. Go to page 1 of the newsletter.

2. Scroll up to display the Special Points of Interest sidebar in the upper-left part of the page.

3. Click the text of the bulleted list.

4. Type **New Senior and Youth Bus** and press the Enter key.
   A second bullet is displayed, maintaining Publisher's same bulleted formatting.

5. Type **Planning Tools: Conservation Easements**.
   The two bullets display, as shown in the following figure.

> **SPECIAL POINTS OF INTEREST:**
>
> • **New Senior and Youth Bus**
>
> • **Planning Tools: Conservation Easements**

Delete a Sidebar

6. On page 1, scroll down to display the Inside This Issue sidebar.

7. Right-click the sidebar text.

8. Choose Delete Object from the shortcut menu.
   The Inside This Issue sidebar is deleted.

Create a Business Information Set for the Newsletter

9. On Page 1, scroll up to Business Name at the top of the sidebar.

10. Hover the mouse pointer over Business Name until the Information ⓘ button appears.

11. Click the button and choose Edit Business Information from the menu.

12. Click the New button in the dialog box to specify that you are creating a new Business Information Set.

13. Edit the generic Business Information Set as shown in the following illustration.

14. If you see an image in the Logo area of the dialog box, click the Change button; if there is no image in the Logo area, click the Add Logo button.

15. Navigate to the Lesson 07 folder and insert the Preston Hollow Town Logo file.

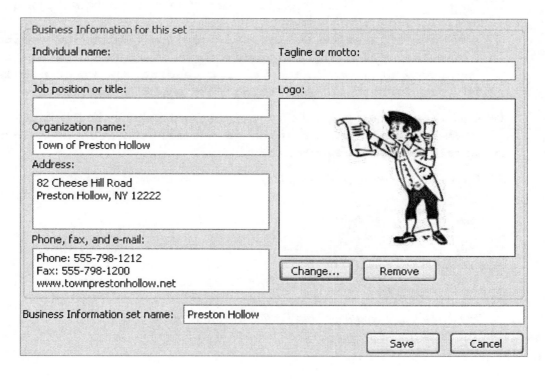

16. Click Save, and then click the Update Publication button.
Town of Preston Hollow now appears at the top of the sidebar on page 1. The information was retrieved from the Organization Name field in the Business Information Set.

17. Go to page 2 of the newsletter.
The town's information, including the logo, has also been updated in the upper-left corner of the back page of the newsletter.

**T.O.W.N. O.F.
P.R.E.S.T.O.N. H.O.L.L.O.W.**

SPECIAL
POINTS OF
INTEREST:

Town of Preston Hollow

82 Cheese Hill Road
Preston Hollow, NY 12222
Phone: 555-798-1212
Fax 555-798-1200
www.townprestonhollow.net

Complete the Back Page of the Newsletter

18. On page 2, click the first paragraph in the text box to the right of the business information to select it and type the following:
The Town of Preston Hollow services the hamlets of Preston Hollow, Rensselaerville, and Cooksburg. Town Board Meetings are every second Wednesday at 7 pm. Thank you for reading our first newsletter, and we look forward to publishing more monthly newsletters.

19. Click the paragraph below the one you just typed and type the following:
Please e-mail your articles of interest to include in our future newsletters to townpr@albany.gov.

20. Click the pull quote Design Gallery object below the two paragraphs.

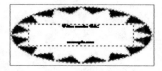

21. Tap the ⌫ Delete key.
The top of page 2 should look like the following illustration.

Town of Preston Hollow

82 Cheese Hill Road
Preston Hollow, NY 12222
Phone: 555-798-1212
Fax: 555-798-1200
www.townprestonhollow.net

The Town of Preston Hollow services the hamlets of Preston Hollow, Rensselaerville and Cooksburg. Town Board Meetings are every second Wednesday at 7 pm. Thank you for reading our first newsletter, and we look forward to publishing more monthly newsletters.

Please e-mail your articles of interest to include in our future newsletters to townpr@albany.gov.

Delete the Business Information Set

22. Hover your mouse pointer over Town of Preston Hollow.

23. When the Information ⓘ button appears, click it and choose Edit Business Information from the menu.
    Preston Hollow should appear in the Business Information dialog box.

24. Click the Delete button; click Yes when asked to delete this Business Information Set.

25. Close the dialog box.

26. Save 🖫 your changes.

27. Choose File→Close from the menu bar to close your newsletter and return to the main Publisher screen.

 # Concepts Review

True/False Questions

1. You can easily insert newsletter pages, but you cannot delete them. **TRUE FALSE**

2. A masthead is a box or section printed in each newsletter issue that lists information such as the name, publisher, location, volume, and date. **TRUE FALSE**

3. It is common in a newsletter to have linked text boxes where text flows from one text box to another. **TRUE FALSE**

4. Publisher uses the term *story* to mean text that is contained within a single text box or a chain of linked text boxes. **TRUE FALSE**

5. Graphics are often included with a story and can easily be replaced with clip art or pictures inserted from files. **TRUE FALSE**

6. A sidebar is used to add interest or additional information about a newsletter. **TRUE FALSE**

7. A sidebar can contain information from a Business Information Set. **TRUE FALSE**

8. You cannot include space for a customer address on the back page of the newsletter. **TRUE FALSE**

9. When you insert pages in a newsletter, choosing the type of page to insert from the Left-Hand Page list causes Publisher to auto-populate the same choice in the Right-Hand Page list. **TRUE FALSE**

10. A Newsletter template in Publisher initially creates three pages of text and graphics. **TRUE FALSE**

Multiple Choice Questions

1. When you insert newsletter pages, which of the following is not a type of page you can insert?
   a. Calendar
   b. Table
   c. Order Form
   d. Sign-up Form

2. Which of the following is not found in a newsletter?
   a. Sidebar
   b. Columns
   c. Masthead
   d. AutoRecover

3. Which of the following is not true about a sidebar?
   a. A sidebar is located next to an article.
   b. A sidebar contains text that is not critical to understanding the main text.
   c. A sidebar always contains a picture.
   d. A sidebar can contain a table of contents or points of interest.

4. Which is not true about a story in Publisher?
   a. A story can autoflow into different text boxes.
   b. Text boxes can be linked to stories.
   c. If a story is too long, Publisher will ask to link a story to another text box.
   d. A story is usually contained in a masthead.

Skill Builders

Skill Builder 7.1 Create a Travel Newsletter

In this exercise, you will create a newsletter for a travel agency's clients, create the travel agency's Business Information Set, and edit the masthead information.

1. Choose the Voyage Newsletter Classic Design template from the main Publisher window.

2. Choose the Lagoon Color Scheme and the Casual Comic Sans MS Font Scheme.

3. Choose Create New from the Business Information drop-down list.

Create a Business Information Set

4. Fill in the following information, starting with Organization Name through Business Information Set Name.

5. Type the tagline **On the road again**.

6. If there is an existing logo, click the Change button; otherwise, click the Add Logo button.

7. Navigate to the Lesson 07 folder and double-click to insert the sb-Travel Agency Logo file.

8. Click Save.

9. Choose Two-Page Spread under Options and click the Create button.

Edit the Default Text

10. On page 1, edit the Newsletter Title to **Voyager Newsletter**.

11. Edit the Newsletter date masthead to **September, 2007**.

12. Edit the Volume/Issue masthead to **Volume 12, Issue 14**.

13. Edit the Lead Story Headline to **California's Coastline or Bust**.

14. Edit the Secondary Story Headline to **April in Paris**.

15. Save 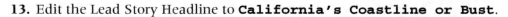 the publication as **sb-Travel Agency Newsletter** in the Lesson 07 folder. *Keep the newsletter open for the next exercise.*

Skill Builder 7.2   Edit the Sidebar

In this exercise, you will edit the sidebar on page 1.

Before You Begin: The sb-Travel Agency Newsletter file should be open from Skill Builder 7.1.

1. Click the Inside This Issue sidebar to select it.

2. Right-click and choose Delete Object from the pop-up menu.

3. Click anywhere on the perimeter of the Special Points of Interest sidebar to select it.

4. Right-click and choose Copy from the pop-up menu.

5. Move your mouse pointer to the 4-inch mark on the vertical ruler, right-click, and choose Paste from the pop-up menu.

6. Drag the new bulleted list sidebar to about midway between the Star graphic and the bottom Special Points of Interest sidebar.

Edit the Sidebar Text

7. Edit the top bulleted list sidebar as shown in the following illustration.

> **Put these on your calendar:**
>
> - Edinburgh, Scotland, September 15 to 30, 2007
>
> - Florence, Italy, May 21 to 30, 2008
>
> - Cancun, Mexico, November 25 to December 15, 2008
>
> - Kauai, Hawaii, December 20 to January 10, 2009

8. Edit the bottom Special Points of Interest sidebar as shown in the following illustration.

> **Special points of interest:**
>
> - California's Beautiful Coastline
>
> - Paris—the most romantic city in the world

9. Save 💾 your changes.
Keep your newsletter open for the next exercise.

Skill Builder 7.3   Delete Pages

In this exercise, you will delete pages, insert a Design Gallery object, and insert the travel agency's description story.

Before You Begin: *You must complete Skill Builder 7.2 before beginning this exercise. The sb-Travel Agency Newsletter file should be open on the screen.*

1. Go to page 2 of the newsletter.

2. Click Edit→Delete Page and delete both pages.

3. On the back page, click the Design Gallery object containing *We're on the Web!* Right-click and choose Delete Object.

Add a Design Gallery Object

4. Click the Design Gallery Object [icon] button on the Objects toolbar, choose Attention Getters, and double-click the Starburst object to insert it on the back page.

5. Move the Starburst object to the approximate location of the prior design object.

6. On the top of the back page, click the large text box in the right-hand column to select it.

Insert a Text File

7. Choose Insert→Text File from the menu bar.

8. Navigate to the Lesson 07 folder and double-click to insert the sb-Travel Agency Description file.

9. Save [icon] your changes.
   Keep your newsletter open for the next exercise.

Skill Builder 7.4   Import and Autoflow Text

In this exercise, you will import several text files and autoflow text. Then you will edit several captions. You will also be introduced to a new concept of editing a story directly in Microsoft Word.

Before You Begin: *You must complete Skill Builder 7.3 before beginning this exercise. The sb-Travel Agency Newsletter file should be open on the screen.*

1. Go to page 1 and click on the California Coastline or Bust story to select it.

Insert a Text File

2. Choose Insert→Text File from the menu bar.

3. Navigate to the Lesson 07 folder and double-click to insert the sb-California Coast Text file.
   Publisher converts the file and warns that the text doesn't fit in the text box.

4. Click Yes to use Autoflow.
   Publisher asks to autoflow to this box (the secondary story line).

5. Click No.
   Publisher asks again to autoflow to this box (the back page story).

6. Click Yes.

7. On the back page, edit the Back Page Story Line to **California's Beautiful Coastline**.

8. Edit the boat graphic caption by typing the following text: **Enjoy a houseboat vacation in sunny Sausalito**

9. Center ☰ your caption.

10. Go to page 1, click on the lighthouse graphic caption to select it, and type the following text: **Visit California's Coastal Lighthouses**

11. Click on the April in Paris story text to select it.

Edit a Story in Microsoft Word

12. Choose Edit→Edit Story in Microsoft Word.
    A Word document opens with the April in Paris text displayed.

13. Press Ctrl + A to select the current text and type the following text:

    I've often heard that Paris is the most beautiful and romantic city in the world, especially if you are visiting with a loved one in April. Is it Paris' long and revered history, its sidewalk cafes, the Louvre and so many other fabulous museums?

    I say it's time for you to make that decision yourself. So do join us along with a special group of "romantics" who will visit Paris next April 16 – April 30. We will be staying at the beautiful Rue St. Jean hotel in Paris across the street from the Place de la Concorde. More details in next month's newsletter.

14. In Word, click File→Close & Return to sb-Travel Agency Newsletter.
    Publisher returns you to your newsletter. The revised text appears in the April in Paris story area.

Delete a Business Information Set

15. Choose Edit→Business Information from the menu bar.
    The Travel Agency set should be the default information set displayed under Select a Business Information Set.

16. Click Delete; click Yes when asked to delete this Business Information Set.

17. Click the Close button to close the dialog box.

18. Save 💾 your changes.

19. Choose File→Close from the menu bar to close your travel agency newsletter and return to the main Publisher screen.

Assessments

Assessment 7.1   Create an Employee Holiday Newsletter

In this exercise, you will create a company employee holiday newsletter.

1. Create a Fading Frame Classic Design newsletter using a two-page spread.

2. Choose a color scheme and a font scheme that fits a holiday theme.

3. Save your newsletter as **as-Holiday Newsletter** in the Lesson 07 folder.

4. Go to page 2 and delete pages 2 and 3.

Edit a Design Gallery Object

5. On page 2, click on the Design Gallery object text to select it and type the following:
   www.goldengateferrytransit.net

6. Enlarge the Visit Us At text box and reduce the font size as needed.

7. On page 2 in the upper-right corner, delete any text boxes.

8. Create a WordArt object of your choice that says **Happy Holidays** in the upper-right portion of page 2.

Create a Business Information Set

9. Create a new Business Information Set with the following information:

10. Delete the tagline, and if there is a logo, remove it.

11. Save and Update the Publication.
    Keep your newsletter open for the next exercise.

Assessment 7.2   Add Captions, Text, and Masthead

In this exercise, you will continue creating the company employee holiday newsletter by adding captions, sidebars, and a masthead.

Before You Begin: *You must complete Assessment 7.1 before beginning this exercise. The as-Holiday Newsletter file should be open on the screen.*

1. On page 2, add the following text as a caption for the ice skating graphic:
   Join us for ice skating at Embarcadero Center on Saturday, December 23, from 4 - 6 pm

2. Center the text.

3. Go to page 1 and add the following text as a caption for the snowman:
   Thank you for all that you do for our company throughout the year

4. Center the text.

5. Edit the masthead to **Seasons Greetings, Volume 12, Issue 12, December 2007**.

6. Delete both the Special Points of Interest and Inside This Issue sidebars on the right side of the newsletter.

Add an AutoShape

7. Draw a Stars and Banners Horizontal Scroll AutoShape approximately 2 inches long and wide enough to fit centered in the sidebar area of the newsletter.

8. Type the following text in the AutoShape:
   As our thanks to you, please enjoy 4 tickets to the Phantom of the Opera playing in San Francisco in January, 2008

9. Center and bold the text and change the font size to 12 pt. If necessary, resize the AutoShape so that all the text is showing.
   Save your publication and keep your newsletter open for the next exercise.

Assessment 7.3   Insert Text

In this exercise, you will continue creating the company employee holiday newsletter by adding text and AutoShapes.

Before You Begin: *You must complete Assessment 7.2 before beginning this exercise. The as-Holiday Newsletter file should be open on the screen.*

1. On page 1, edit the Lead Story Headline to say **Thank You to Our Outstanding Employees**.

2. Replace the associated lead story text by inserting the file, Employee Holiday Newsletter Text, and autoflow the text into the Back Story Headline of page 2.

3. Edit the Back Page Story Headline to read **Our Outstanding Employees**.

4. On page 1, delete the Second Story Headline text box and the three text boxes below.

5. Draw a Heart AutoShape to replace the Second Story Headline and the three text boxes.

6. Type the following text in the heart:
   Thank You to All Our Valued Golden Gate Ferry Transit Employees

7. Center the text and change the font to 12 pt. Resize the heart if necessary so that the text fits and no words are hyphenated.

8. Apply a 3-D Style 1 effect to the heart. If needed, move the heart so that it is centered underneath the lead story.

9. Open the Business Publication dialog box and delete the *Golden Gate Ferry* Business Information Set. Do not update the publication.

10. Save and close your company holiday newsletter and return to the main Publisher screen.

Critical Thinking

Critical Thinking 7.1   Create North Beach Espresso Newsletter

North Beach Espresso is an up-and-coming chain of espresso shops featuring delicious Italian baked goods with recipes originating from northern Italy. The restaurant manager would like to send a newsletter to the café's clients. In this exercise you will create a client newsletter for North Beach Espresso clientele.

1. Open ct-North Beach Espresso Newsletter from the Lesson 07 folder.

2. Choose a font and color scheme that you feel complement the newsletter.

3. Delete pages 2 and 3.

4. On page 1, delete the Inside This Issue and Special Points of Interest sidebars and insert a WordArt or AutoShape that complements the newsletter.

5. Edit the lead story, How North Beach Espresso Started, in Word and add a paragraph of text inviting the public to enjoy a free espresso with the purchase of an Italian baked good during the months of February and March.

6. When you are finished typing the text, return to your newsletter.

7. On page 2, add a design gallery object you like that offers a 2-for-1 promotion.

8. Close your newsletter and save your changes.

Critical Thinking 7.2   Create a Sample Newsletter

The Human Resources department of your advertising firm, Firenze and Associates, would like you to create a two-page bimonthly newsletter for clients and potential clients, but they would like to see a design sample first. The firm represents local retail stores such as bookstores and restaurants. In this exercise, you will create the newsletter samples.

1. Experiment with the various newsletter design templates until you find one that best fits the look of an advertising firm.

2. Experiment with different color schemes and fonts until you get the look you like.

3. Create a new Business Information Set based on the following information:

    Firenze and Associates
    3004 El Camino Real, Palo Alto, CA 94880
    Phone: 555-730-1122
    Fax: 555-730-1124
    www.firenzeassociates.net

4. Create a tagline that best suits your advertising firm.

5. Save your newsletter as **ct-Firenze Newsletter** in the Lesson 07 folder.

6. Delete pages 2 and 3.

7. Add a calendar page.

8. Practice adding appropriate WordArt or Design Gallery objects on either page 1 or 2 that would add visual appeal to the newsletter.

9. Edit the masthead information.

10. Add a logo to the Business Information Set from the ct-Advertising Classifieds Image file in the Lesson 07 folder.

11. Add a sample lead story headline for a restaurant your firm represents—**Flaherty's Fish Market Restaurant**.

12. On the back page, draft a short paragraph about your advertising firm next to the business information. There are suggestions as to what to include in the text box in the upper-right side on the back page. Add whatever formatting you think will make it look visually appealing.

13. Delete the Business Information Set.

14. Save and close your newsletter and return to the main Publisher screen.

15. Exit Publisher.

LESSON 8

Creating a Mail Merge

In this lesson, you will learn how to use Publisher to create individual postcards to customers using Publisher's mail merge feature. You will find that creating a list of customer addresses (known as a data source) is easy in Publisher. You can also keep your customer addresses stored in other data source files such as Excel or an Outlook Contact List and use these to create individual postcards to customers. You will learn how to add merge codes, which are placeholders that allow you to add each individual customer address during the mail merge process, in your postcard. You will then learn how easy it is to merge both the postcard and addresses to create an individual postcard for each customer. In addition to creating an individual publication for each customer, you will create mailing labels for each customer. You will also create a catalog merge, which allows you to create publications using information other than addresses, such as product information.

LESSON OBJECTIVES
After studying this lesson, you will be able to:
- Create a Publisher address data source
- Insert merge codes into publication
- Create a mail merge using a Publisher data source
- Generate mailing labels
- Create a catalog merge
- Create a mail merge using an Excel data source

Case Study: Creating a Postcard Mail Merge

Larisa Benovich is owner of Larisa's Designs, a very successful and well-known interior design store. Larisa's Designs has been in business for the last 15 years, and Larisa would like to send a thank-you postcard to her loyal customers. She asks you to create an individual postcard for each of her customers using Publisher's mail merge feature.

You are comfortable using Publisher because you have created various publications such as letters, flyers, and company newsletters, but you have never used the mail merge feature. You are anticipating that the mail merge should be easy to use. Larisa has used it at home, and she tells you that you will have no trouble using it to create customer postcards.

The postcard will contain the same message for each customer.

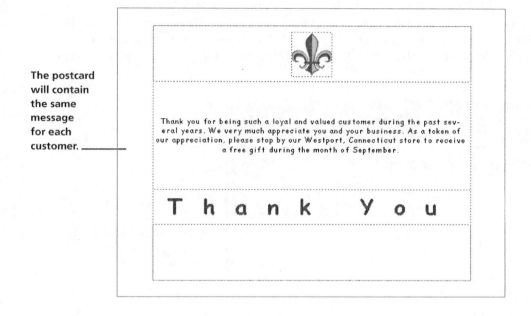

This information is taken from the Business Information Set.

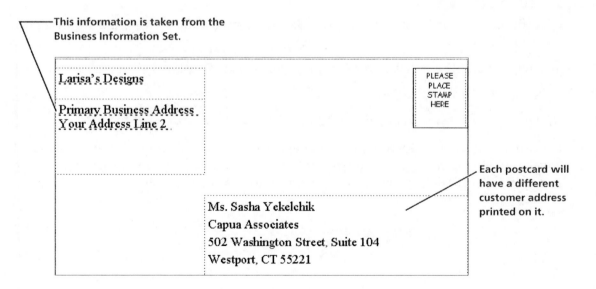

Each postcard will have a different customer address printed on it.

Introducing Mail Merge

If you create publications to send to your customers, most likely you will need to mail them. You can use Publisher to print customer mailing addresses directly on each copy of individual publications such as postcards, gift certificates, invoices, and newsletters. You can also create and print mailing labels to attach to your publications.

Mail Merge Defined

Merging is the process of combining the contents of a data source with a main publication. The main publication contains the constant or unchanging text, punctuation, spacing, and graphics. The data source contains the variable or changing information in each publication, such as address information. A mail merge combines the records from a database (usually names and addresses) with a publication template, such as a postcard, to produce individual versions of the publication. Publisher's Mail and Catalog Merge feature performs the mail merge.

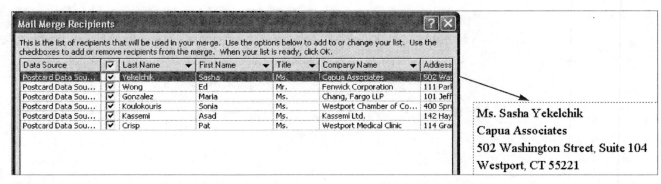

The Mail Merge Recipients data source provides the information that appears in the address text box.

Data Sources

In addition to the publication, every merge must have a data source. Publisher supports three types of data sources:

1. An external file created in another program such as Word, Excel, or Access

2. A contact list from Outlook

3. An address list you create in Publisher

Publisher's address list feature offers an easy way to create a database of names and addresses without having to rely on an external program. You cannot use a Publisher address list for a catalog merge; catalog merges must use external data sources only.

Merge Types

Publisher allows you to perform two types of merges:

- **Mail Merge**—A mail merge is used for publications where you will have one record for each copy of the publication. For example, a mail merge is used to address labels, postcards, newsletters, and similar mailings where each publication is addressed to a different person.

- **Catalog Merge**—A catalog merge is used where multiple records will appear within a single publication. For example, a catalog merge is used for price lists, product inventories, and reports that list the items in a database without placing each one on its own page.

Conducting the Merge

Following are the steps involved in creating and merging a data source with a publication.

1. **Open the publication and the recipient list document**—The recipient list can be created as part of the mail merge or selected from an existing list.

2. **Insert merge codes**—This tells Publisher where to place the unique information, such as names and addresses.

3. **Perform the merge**—Publisher merges the address list with the publication based on the inserted merge codes.

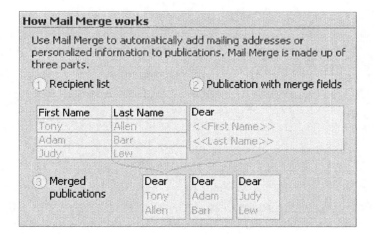

 Hands-On 8.1   Create a Postcard

In this exercise, you will create a postcard and an address list, which is referred to as the data source.

Create a Postcard

1. If necessary, start Publisher.

2. Choose the Postcards publication type.

3. Click the Thank You link and click once to choose the Symmetry design.

4. Choose a Tidepool Color Scheme and the Casual Comic Sans MS Font Scheme.

5. Under Options, choose Address Only from the Side 2 Information list if not already selected and click Create.
   Publisher displays the first page of the postcard.

Edit the Postcard

6. Click on the text in the text box above Thank You to select it.

7. Type the following:

Thank you for being such a loyal and valued customer during the past several years. We very much appreciate you and your business. As a token of our appreciation, please stop by our Westport, Connecticut store to receive a free gift during the month of September.

8. Click the Organization logo to select it and press ⌈Delete⌉.
Your postcard should look like the following illustration.

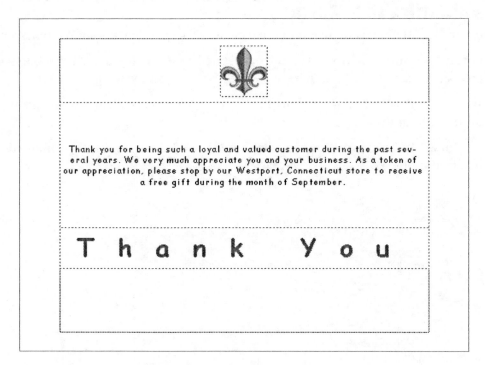

9. Click the page 2 Navigation icon to go to page 2.
The back page of the postcard contains placeholders for Larisa's Designs return address and customer address.

10. Edit the return address with **Larisa's Designs** as the Business name and the following address:

104 East End Street
Westport, CT 55221

11. Save 🖫 the publication as **Postcard Mail Merge** in the Lesson 08 folder.

Creating a Publisher Address List

Publisher's data sources are called Publisher address lists. Each customer is an entry in Publisher's address list. An entry is all of the information about one person or business, which is similar to a *record* in other database applications.

In the following table, an entry is equivalent to a row of information. Entries are broken down into pieces of information called *fields*. As you can see in the following table, fields in a typical Publisher address list include Title, First Name, Last Name, Company, Address Line 1, Address Line 2, City, State, and Zip Code.

Entries are broken down into pieces of information called fields such as Title, First Name, and Last Name.

Table 8-1 Customer Address List

Title	First Name	Last Name	Company	Address Line 1	Address Line 2	City	State	Zip Code
Ms.	Sasha	Yekelchik	Capua Associates	502 Washington Street	Suite 204	Westport	CT	55221
Mr.	Ed	Wong	Fenwick Corporation	111 Park Boulevard		Westport	CT	55221
Ms.	Maria	Gonzalez	Chang, Fargo LLP	101 Jefferson Avenue	Suite 100	Westchester	NY	55440
Ms.	Sonia	Koulokouris	Westport Chamber of Commerce	400 Spruce Street		Westport	CT	55221
Mr.	Asad	Kassemi	Kassemi Ltd.	142 Hayward Drive	Suite M	Westport	CT	55221
Ms.	Pat	Crisp	Westport Medical Clinic	114 Grant Avenue	2nd Floor	Westchester	NY	55442

Each piece of customer address data is located in the intersection of a row and a column.

QUICK REFERENCE: CREATING A MAIL MERGE AND CREATING AND EDITING AN ADDRESS LIST

Task	Procedure
Create an Address List in Publisher and merge it with a publication	■ Create or open a publication. ■ Choose Tools→Mailings and Catalogs→Mail Merge from the menu bar. ■ Choose the Type New List option in the Mail Merge task pane. ■ Type the name and address information in the new Address List dialog box, using the ⎡Tab⎤ key to move from field to field. Click the New Entry button to display the next new row. ■ Save the address list. ■ Close the Mail Merge recipient dialog box. ■ Delete the generic text in the name and address text box. ■ Drag a name and address merge code into the address text box or click a merge code once to insert it. ■ Click the Next button in the Mail Merge task pane to preview the recipients. ■ Click the Next: Create Merged Publications link. ■ Click the Merge to a New Publication Link.
Edit an address list in Publisher	■ Open a publication. ■ Choose Tools→Mailings and Catalogs→Edit Address List from the menu bar. ■ Open the address file. ■ To find an entry, click the Find button and use the dialog box that appears to find a data record. ■ To add a new address, click the New Entry button and enter a new name and address. ■ To delete an entry, click to select it and click the Delete Entry button. ■ Click OK when you are finished editing the entries.

Hands-On 8.2   Create the Address List

In this exercise, you will enter and edit customer address information.

Create a Publisher Address List

1. Choose Tools→Mailings and Catalogs→Create Address List from the menu bar.
   The New Address List dialog box appears. The cursor is positioned in the line for the first contact.

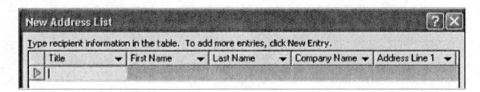

2. Type the following customer name and address in the appropriate fields, using the `Tab` key to move to subsequent fields:

   Ms. in the Title field
   Sasha in the First Name field
   Yekelchik
   Capua Associates
   502 Washington Street
   Suite 104
   Westport
   CT
   55221

3. Click the New Entry button.
   The first customer address is completed. The cursor is now positioned to begin typing the second customer address.

4. Continue to type in the remaining customer addresses as shown in the following table.

TIP! *Remember to press the* `Tab` *key to go to the next field. If a field should remain blank, press the* `Tab` *key to skip to the next field. When finished with an address, click the New Entry button to go to a new line.*

Mr. Ed Wong Fenwick Corporation 111 Park Boulevard Westport, CT 55221	Ms. Maria Gonzalez Chang, Fargo LLP 101 Jefferson Avenue Suite 100 Westchester, NY 55440
Ms. Sonia Koulokouris Westport Chamber of Commerce 400 Spruce Street Westport, CT 55221	Mr. Asad Kassemi Kassemi Ltd. 142 Hayward Drive Suite M Westport, CT 55221
Ms. Pat Crisp Westport Medical Clinic 114 Grant Avenue 2nd Floor Westchester, NY 55442	

5. When finished, click OK.
   The Save Address List dialog box opens.

6. Navigate to the Lesson 08 folder and save the file there as **Postcard Data Source**.
   Publisher saves the address list as a file that you can open and edit in the future.

Inserting Merge Codes in a Publication

A publication, such as a postcard (main publication), that will be merged with customer addresses (data source) must contain merge codes. A merge code is a placeholder in the publication that shows Publisher where to insert the address from the data source. You can format, copy, move, or delete a merge code just as you would regular text. You need to add the appropriate punctuation and spacing around merge codes.

Managing Field Codes

After the merge codes are added to the postcard, you can preview the customer addresses to make sure they are correct prior to performing the mail merge. You can also edit these addresses prior to performing the merge between the postcard and the list of customer addresses.

The Mail Merge task pane provides features where you can customize merge codes, and you can individually exclude recipients, if desired, as you preview the addresses prior to the merge.

 TIP! *If you intend to use the address list again, you may prefer to edit the list directly as described in the Creating a Mail Merge and Creating and Editing an Address List Quick Reference table on page 227.*

Publisher walks you through adding merge codes to the postcard.

These merge codes are available to insert into the publication.

You can prevent a record from merging by clicking the Exclude This Recipient button.

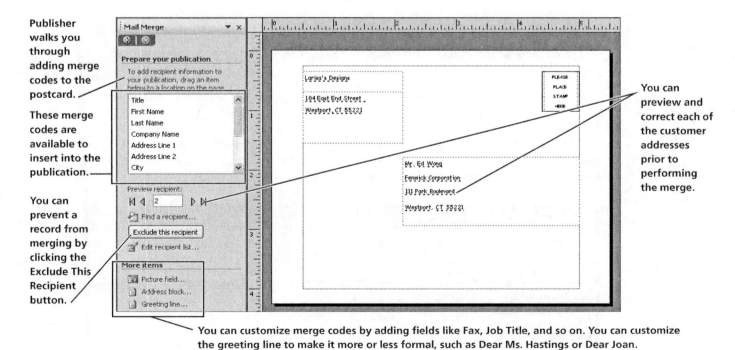

You can preview and correct each of the customer addresses prior to performing the merge.

You can customize merge codes by adding fields like Fax, Job Title, and so on. You can customize the greeting line to make it more or less formal, such as Dear Ms. Hastings or Dear Joan.

In this exercise, you will open the Publisher address list (data source) and insert merge codes in the postcard (main publication).

Open the Publisher Address List

1. Choose Tools→Mailings and Catalogs→Mail Merge from the menu bar.
   The Mail Merge task pane appears on the left side of your screen.

2. Choose Use an Existing List, if necessary, as shown in the following illustration.

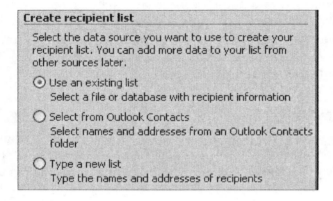

3. Click Next: Create or Connect to a Recipient List as shown in the following illustration.

Step 1 of 3

→ Next: Create or connect to a recipient list

⊚ Help with Mail Merge

The Select Data Source dialog box appears. Notice that My Data Sources is the default Look In folder.

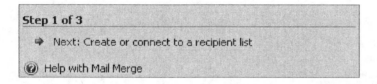

4. Navigate to the Lesson 08 folder.

5. Double-click to open the Postcard Data Source file.
   The Mail Merge Recipients dialog box displays, listing the customer names and addresses that you will merge with the postcard. At this point you have the option to add, edit, or remove recipients from the merge. Here you will include all of the names and addresses.

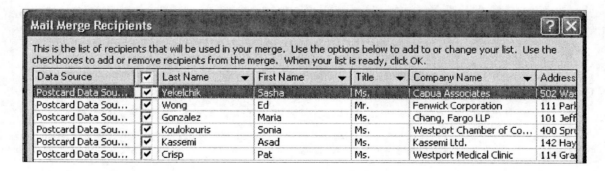

6. Click OK.

The Mail Merge task pane appears with instructions for adding the recipient information under Prepare Your Publication.

Insert Merge Codes in the Postcard

7. Go to page 2.

8. Click the text in the postcard address text box to select it and press `Delete`.

9. Follow these steps to insert the address merge codes:

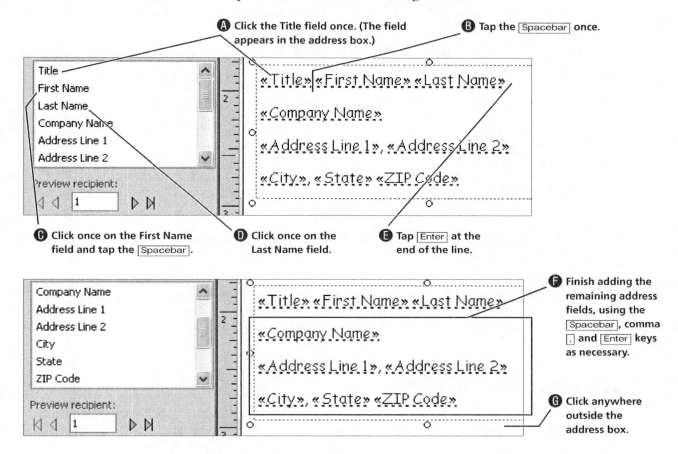

Ⓐ Click the Title field once. (The field appears in the address box.)

Ⓑ Tap the `Spacebar` once.

Ⓒ Click once on the First Name field and tap the `Spacebar`.

Ⓓ Click once on the Last Name field.

Ⓔ Tap `Enter` at the end of the line.

Ⓕ Finish adding the remaining address fields, using the `Spacebar`, comma `,` and `Enter` keys as necessary.

Ⓖ Click anywhere outside the address box.

The first customer address previews in the postcard.

Preview and Edit Addresses

10. Click twice on the Next button, as shown in the following illustration.

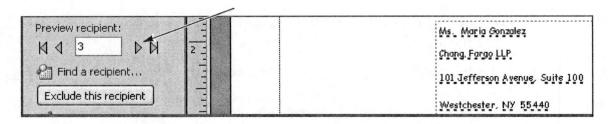

Publishers displays a preview of the third customer address.

11. Continue to click Next until you arrive at the sixth address, Ms. Pat Crisp.

12. Click the Exclude This Recipient button, as shown in the following illustration.

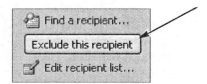

A postcard will not be created for Pat Crisp when the merge is performed, but this customer address is still included in the data source to be used in future publications.

13. Save 💾 your changes.

Now that the address fields are in place, you are ready to perform the final phase of the merge.

Performing the Merge

By default, Publisher uses a font that can be scanned at the post office; however, you can change the font if you wish. Once you have inserted the merge codes and previewed the names and addresses, it is time to merge the publication with the data source. When the merge is complete, you can decide whether or not to save the merged file as described below.

Working with Address Field Fonts

You can format the fonts for merge codes, and that will affect the way they print after merging. The preset font for merge codes is OCR (optical character recognition) A Extended. This means that the post office can scan the address easily with electronic equipment, thereby speeding up the mailing process.

Saving a Merged File

Publisher allows you to save the newly created publication when you perform a merge. However, it is not necessary to save a merged file because it is easy to merge a publication and address list again if you need to print at a later time and because you can include updates to the address list. If you are planning to print the same customer labels on a regular basis, it would save time if you save a mailing label merge file so you can print these same labels when needed without having to perform the merge each time.

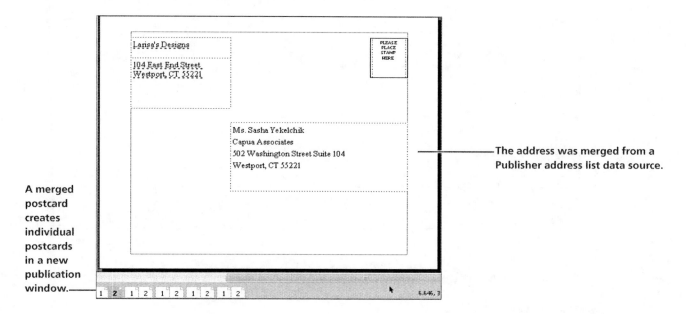

The address was merged from a Publisher address list data source.

A merged postcard creates individual postcards in a new publication window.

Hands-On 8.4   Merge the Postcard with Addresses

In this exercise, you will merge the postcard with the customer addresses.

Merge the Postcard and Addresses

1. Click Next: Create Merged Publications, as shown to the right.
   Options for creating the merged publication appear in the Mail Merge task pane. You could print this directly, save it as a new publication, or add it to an existing publication.

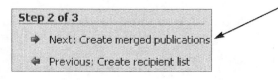

2. Click the Merge to a New Publication link.
   Publisher may display a prompt if a font is not available on your computer or is not part of your publication.

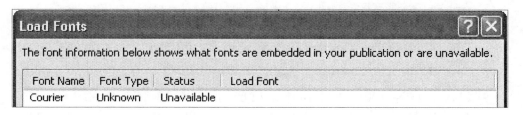

3. Click OK if a Load Fonts prompt appears.

A new publication consisting of all five postcards is created. Any of the individual postcards can be edited.

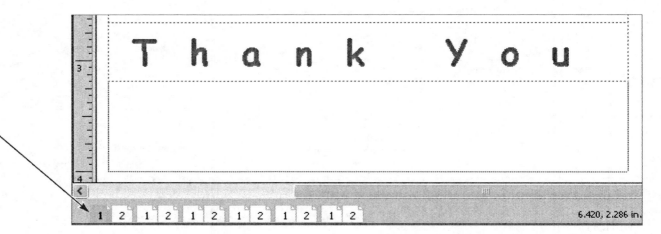

Publisher is now displaying the front of postcard #1.

Edit a Merged Postcard

You can still make revisions to a merged publication. In this case, only a single postcard needs revision.

4. Display page 1 of the fifth postcard.

5. In the text box above Thank You, select the text *the month of September* and type **August and September**.

6. Click in the scratch area to deselect this text box.

Save the Merged Postcards for Later Use

7. Click the Save This Publication link, as shown in the following illustration.

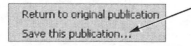

Publisher displays the normal Save As dialog box as it would for any other publication.

8. Save the file as **Postcard Mail Merge Final** in the Lesson 08 folder.

9. Choose File→Close from the menu bar. Choose Yes if prompted to save any changes.
   The Postcard Mail Merge publication appears again. It was in the background when you merged to a new publication.

10. Choose File→Close from the menu bar. Choose Yes if prompted to save any changes.

Opening a Publication with a Data Source

If you conduct a mail merge with a publication, its data source remains associated with the publication. When you open the publication, you have the choice of opening it with or without its original data source. In the latter instance, you might choose to open the publication without its original data source and re-merge it with a different data source.

If you choose to open the publication with the data source, you only need to open the Mail Merge task pane and follow the steps to perform the merge. If you do not choose to use the data source, when you open the publication, you can select a different existing data source or you can choose to type a new list.

 Hands-On 8.5   Open the Postcard

In this exercise, you will open your merged postcard and observe the dialog box that gives you the choice of using the associated data source or not using it.

1. Choose File→Open from the menu bar, navigate to the Lesson 08 folder, and open Postcard Mail Merge.
   Publisher's dialog box informs you that you can open and insert the customer addresses into the postcard from the file where the customer addresses are stored or open the postcard without inserting customer addresses.

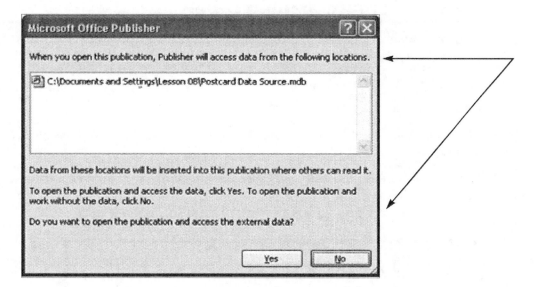

2. Click No.
   You can now create a new data source or use a different existing data source.

3. Choose File→Close from the menu bar to close your postcard and return to the main Publisher screen.

Creating Mailing Labels

Publisher's Mail Merge feature provides the option to create mailing labels so you can have matching labels for your merged publications. You can use the very same data source that you used for your publication.

QUICK REFERENCE: CREATING MAILING LABELS	
Task	**Procedure**
Create mailing labels using an existing data source	■ Choose the Labels publication type.
	■ Choose the desired label design.
	■ Choose Tools→Mailings and Catalogs→Mail Merge from the menu bar.
	■ Choose Use an Existing List.
	■ Click the Next: Create or Connect to a Recipient List link.
	■ Choose the data source from the Select Data Source dialog box.
	■ Delete the default text from the mailing label address text box.
	■ Insert the merge codes in the address box.
	■ Click the Next: Create Merged Publications link.
	■ Save the publication if you want to generate the same list of labels again.

Hands-On 8.6   Create Mailing Labels

In this exercise, you will create mail merge labels using the same customer addresses so that you will have them ready for a future mailing.

Create a Mailing Label

1. Choose the Labels publication type.

2. Click the Mailing Address link and click once to choose the Ambassador (Avery 5160) design.

3. If necessary, choose the Tidepool Color Scheme and the Casual Comic Sans MS Font Scheme; click Create.
   The mailing address label appears as shown in the following illustration.

> Type address here or use Mail
> Merge (under Tools) to
> automatically address this
> publication to multiple
> recipients.

4. Click the Lion graphic to the left of the address text and press ⌐Delete⌐.

5. Choose Tools→Mailings and Catalogs→Mail Merge from the menu bar.

6. On the Mail Merge task pane under Create Recipient List, if necessary, click to choose Use an Existing List.

7. At the bottom of the task pane, click Next: Create or Connect to a Recipient List.
   The Select Data Source dialog box displays.

8. Navigate to the Lesson 08 folder and double-click to open Postcard Data Source.

9. Click OK to close the Mail Merge Recipients dialog box.
   You are returned to the mailing label.

Insert Merge Codes in the Mailing Label

10. Click the text in the mailing label address text box to select it and press [Delete].

11. Follow these steps to insert the address merge codes:

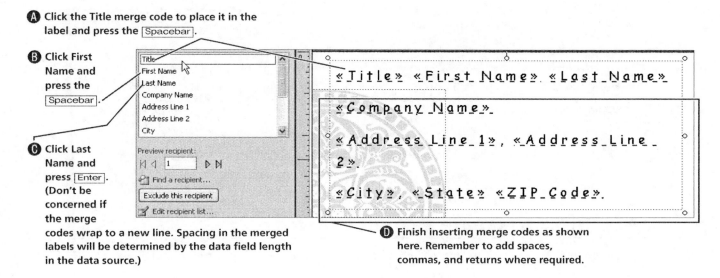

Ⓐ Click the Title merge code to place it in the label and press the [Spacebar].

Ⓑ Click First Name and press the [Spacebar].

Ⓒ Click Last Name and press [Enter]. (Don't be concerned if the merge codes wrap to a new line. Spacing in the merged labels will be determined by the data field length in the data source.)

Ⓓ Finish inserting merge codes as shown here. Remember to add spaces, commas, and returns where required.

Merge the Mailing Label and Addresses

12. Click Next: Create Merged Publications at the bottom of the task pane.

13. Click the Merge to a New Publication link.
    A new publication consisting of all six mailing labels is created. Any of the individual mailing labels can be edited.

Save the Merged Mailing Labels for Later Use

14. Click the Save This Publication link on the task pane.

15. Navigate to the Lesson 08 folder, type **Mailing List Merge Final** in the File Name box, and click Save.

16. Choose File→Close from the menu bar to close Mailing List Merge Final.
    You are returned to the Mailing Label.

17. Choose File→Save As from the menu bar. Navigate to the Lesson 08 folder and save the file as **Mail List Merge**.

18. Close the Mail List Merge publication.

Performing a Catalog Merge

You can use a catalog merge for different purposes. As the name implies, you can use it to produce a catalog type of publication, such as a parts catalog or a product list.

A catalog merge is also useful for creating a name and address list of recipients that you use in a mail merge. For example, if you performed a mail merge for 100 recipients, you may not want to waste the paper necessary to keep a file copy of each letter. Instead you could print one copy of the letter and attach the list of recipients to it.

QUICK REFERENCE: CREATING A CATALOG MERGE

Task	Procedure
Create a catalog merge using an existing data source	■ Choose the publication you want for the merge.
	■ Choose Tools→Mailings and Catalogs→Catalog Merge from the menu bar.
	■ Click the Next: Create or Connect to a Product List link.
	■ Open the data source and click OK.
	■ Insert the merge codes into the Catalog Merge Area.
	■ Position and resize the text box that Publisher inserts in the Catalog Merge Area as needed.
	■ Resize the Catalog Merge Area as desired to control the spacing of the items in the list.
	■ Click the Next: Create Merged Publications link.
	■ Click the Merge to a New Publication link.

 ## Hands-On 8.7   Create a Catalog Merge

In this exercise, you will create a recipient list for your postcard mailing using a catalog merge.

1. Choose the Blank Page Sizes publication type.

2. Double-click Letter (Portrait) 8.5 x 11".

3. Choose Tools→Mailings and Catalogs→Catalog Merge from the menu bar.
   The Catalog Merge task pane opens and the Catalog Merge Area is inserted in the publication.

4. Click the Next: Create or Connect to a Product List link at the bottom of the task pane.

5. Open the Postcard Data Source file from the Lesson 08 folder.

6. Click OK in the Catalog Merge Product List dialog box to close it.

7. Click the Title merge code in the task pane to insert it in the Catalog Merge Area.
   The merge code appears in its own text box.

8. Position the Title text box in the upper-left corner of the Catalog Merge Area.

9. Widen the text box until it takes up approximately half the width of the Catalog Merge Area, as shown in the following illustration.

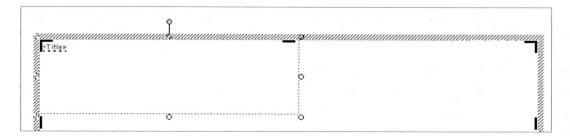

10. Tap the [Spacebar] and insert the First Name merge code.

11. Continue adding merge codes as shown in the following illustration, remembering to include the necessary spacing and punctuation.

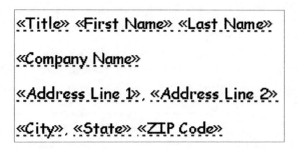

12. Resize the Catalog Merge Area by dragging its bottom handle up to the bottom of the text box, as shown in the following illustration.

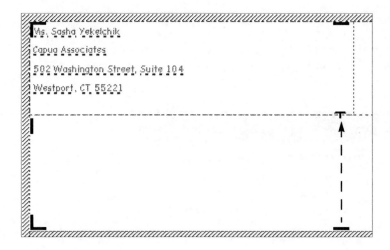

This determines the spacing between records. If you left the Catalog Merge Area at its original size there would be a large gap between addresses. The resizing coincidentally provides a preview of the list of recipients.

13. Click the Next: Create Merged Publications link at the bottom of the task pane.

14. Click the Merge to a New Publication link.

15. Save 🖫 the file as **Postcard Mailing List** in the Lesson 08 folder.

16. Print the publication then close it.

17. Close the original publication without saving it.

Merging a Publication with an Excel File

In addition to creating merge lists within Publisher, you can attach an Excel data file to a publication. This is particularly convenient if the Excel file already exists—it won't be necessary to retype the list in Publisher.

This topic provides a brief introduction to Excel data sources, but a complete discussion is beyond the scope of this course.

Following is an example of an Excel file that can be used as a data source in a Publisher mail merge. The merge code names that you see during the merge process are taken from the column headings: Title, First Name, Last Name, and so forth.

	A	B	C	D	E	F	G	H
1	Title	First Name	Last Name	Company	Address	City	State	Zip
2	Ms.	Ilsa	Morales	Canal Dredging, Inc.	768 Harbor Drive	San Rafael	CA	94947
3	Mr.	Arlo	Washington	Top Sails, Ltd.	90 Bayside Street	Sausalito	CA	98760
4	Mr.	Alan	Murphy	Margate Sailmakers	687 C Street	San Rafael	CA	94947
5	Ms.	Minako	Morioka	Ship Welding, Inc.	789 Warren Street	Oakland	CA	98764
6	Ms.	Galit	Baum	West Coast Sailing Academy	128 Mariner Way	Sausalito	CA	98760
7								

When you connect to the data source during the merge process, the Select Table dialog box appears, allowing you to specify the page of the Excel workbook that contains the list you want to use.

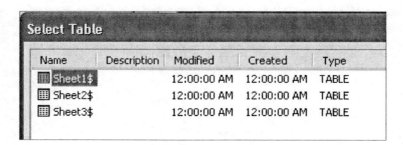

Conventions for Creating Excel Lists

When creating a name and address data source in Excel, there are some conventions that are important to consider.

- The data source is made up of adjacent columns and rows. You cannot have blank rows and columns within the list.

- Columns such as a Name column are more flexible when separated into multiple columns such as Title, First Name, and Last Name. You cannot merge part of a column. If you want to use the data source in a letter publication, for example, this technique provides the flexibility to say Dear Ms. Morales rather than Dear Ms. Ilsa Morales. The former is considered more appropriate.

 Hands-On 8.8   Merge a Publication with an Excel File

In this exercise, you will merge a postcard publication with an existing Excel data file.

1. Open Angel Island Yacht Sales from your Lesson 08 folder.

2. Go to page 2 of the postcard.

3. Choose Tools→Mailings and Catalogs→Mail Merge from the menu bar.

4. Make sure Use an Existing List is chosen in the Mail Merge task pane.

5. Click the Next: Create or Connect to a Recipient List link at the bottom of the task pane.

6. Open Boat Sales Mailing List from your Lesson 08 folder.
   The Select Table dialog box opens.

7. Click OK to accept Sheet1 of the Excel file as your data source.

8. Click OK to close the Mail Merge Recipients dialog box.

9. Go to page 2, click in the address text box in the publication, and tap $\boxed{\text{Delete}}$.

10. Click the Title merge code in the task pane to insert it in the address text box.

11. Insert the remaining merge codes as shown in the following illustration. Remember to add the appropriate spacing and punctuation.

12. Click the Next: Create Merged Publications link at the bottom of the task pane.

13. Click the Merge to a New Publication link.
    Publisher merges the five names and addresses from the Excel file into the publication.

14. Save the file as **Angel Island Yacht Sales Final** in the Lesson 08 folder.

15. Close the file.

16. Close the original publication, Angel Island Yacht Sales, without saving it.

Concepts Review

True/False Questions

1. You can create and print mailing labels using Publisher's Mail Merge feature.   TRUE   FALSE

2. You can use a Publisher address list for a catalog merge.   TRUE   FALSE

3. Catalog merges can be used for price lists, product inventories, and reports.   TRUE   FALSE

4. The Exclude This Recipient feature allows you to exclude names and addresses prior to the merge without deleting them from the data source.   TRUE   FALSE

5. You can preview customer addresses after merge codes have been added to the publication.   TRUE   FALSE

6. Merge codes do not need to be spaced and punctuated.   TRUE   FALSE

7. You can edit addresses in a data source prior to performing a merge.   TRUE   FALSE

8. A mail merge is used for publications where you will have one record for each copy of the publication.   TRUE   FALSE

9. The preset font for merge codes is OCR (optical character recognition), which allows the address to be scanned at the post office.   TRUE   FALSE

10. You can print a merged publication without saving it.   TRUE   FALSE

Multiple Choice Questions

1. Which of the following external files is not usable as a data source?
   a. Access
   b. Excel
   c. Outlook address book
   d. PowerPoint

2. Which of the following is not true about a mail merge?
   a. Merging combines the data source contents with a main publication.
   b. The main publication contains the variable or changing information like addresses.
   c. A main publication could be a postcard, a form letter, or a newsletter.
   d. Publisher's Mail and Catalog Merge feature performs the mail merge.

3. Which of the following is not true about a Publisher address list?
   a. Publisher's data sources are called publisher address lists.
   b. Each customer is an entry in Publisher's address list.
   c. An entry is equivalent to a row of information.
   d. Entries are broken down into pieces of information called tables.

4. Which is not true about merge codes?
   a. You cannot format, copy, move or delete a merge code as you would regular text.
   b. Merge codes need to be spaced and punctuated.
   c. A merge code is a placeholder text in the publication that shows Publisher where to insert the address from the data source.
   d. A publication that will be merged with a data source must contain merge codes.

Skill Builders

Skill Builder 8.1   Create an Award Certificate Mail Merge

In this exercise, you will create award certificates for your employees.

1. From the main Publisher screen, choose the Appreciation 5 Award Certificate.

2. Choose the Sunset Color Scheme and the Galley Arial Rounded Font Scheme.

3. Click the Create button.

Create Names to Insert in the Certificates

4. Choose Tools→Mailings and Catalogs→Mail Merge from the menu bar.
   The Mail Merge task pane displays to guide you through the merge. In this exercise, you will create a new recipient list rather than using an existing list.

5. Choose the Type a New List option, then click Next: Create or Connect to a Recipient List at the bottom of the task pane.
   The New Address List dialog box opens. It displays a standard list of fields for an address list. Now you will rename one of the standard fields to store data specific to your certificates.

6. Click the Customize Columns button in the lower-left corner of the New Address dialog box.
   The Customize Address List dialog box opens and Title is selected.

7. Click the Rename button.
   The Rename Field dialog box opens.

8. Type **Contribution** as the new name and click OK.

9. Click OK again to return to the New Address List dialog box.

10. Follow these steps to widen the Contribution column and add the data:

Ⓐ Place your mouse on the dividing line between Contribution and First Name until your mouse turns to a two-headed arrow and drag so the column is about twice the width of the First Name column.

Ⓑ Type **Sales-woman of the Year** in the contribution box, press Tab and type **Keisha**, press Tab and type **Banks**.

Ⓒ Click the New Entry button.

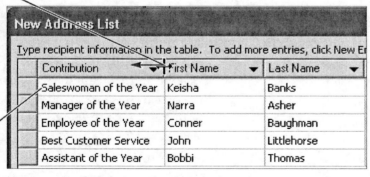

Ⓓ Type the remaining records as shown in the illustration, using the Tab key and New Entry button as needed.

Save the Data Source

11. Click OK.

12. In the Save Address List dialog box, navigate to the Lesson 08 folder.

13. Save your data source as **sb-Award Certificate Data Source**.

14. Save  the Award Certificate as **sb-Award Certificate Mail Merge** in the Lesson 08 folder.

    Keep the award certificate open if you are going on directly to the next exercise.

Skill Builder 8.2   Insert Merge Codes and Merge

In this exercise, you will insert merge codes, merge the award certificate with the people's names and contributions, and print the certificates.

Before You Begin: You must complete Skill Builder 8.1 before beginning this exercise. The sb-Award Certificate Mail Merge publication should be open in Publisher.

1. In the lower-right corner of the award certificate, select the word *Signature* in each signature text box and delete it.

2. To the right of the signature text boxes, select the word *Date* in each date text box and delete it.

Insert Merge Codes in the Award Certificate

3. Click the *Name of Recipient* text and delete it.

4. Follow these steps to add the merge codes:

Ⓐ Place the First Name field in the text box, then tap the Spacebar.

This certificate is awarded to

«First Name» «Last Name»

Ⓑ Place the Last Name field to the right of the space following First Name.

«Contribution»

Ⓒ Place the Contribution field in the text box above the first signature line.

Preview the Names

5. Click the Next button under Preview Recipient until you have viewed all the names and contributions.

Merge and Print the Award Certificates

6. Click Next: Create Merged Publications at the bottom of the task pane.

7. Click Print Preview in the task pane.

8. Click the Page Up button to view all five certificates.

9. Close ☒ the Print Preview.

10. Click Print in the task pane to display the Print dialog box.

11. Follow these steps to print a test page:

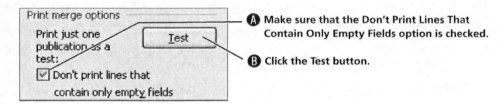

Publisher prints one test certificate for you to review. Assuming all looks good, you could go ahead and run a full print job. In this case, you will cancel out of the dialog box.

12. Click the Cancel button to close the dialog box and save any changes.

13. Choose File→Close from the menu bar. Choose Yes if you are asked to save any changes.

Skill Builder 8.3   Create a Catalog

In this exercise, you will create a floral catalog using the catalog merge feature that accesses product information in an Excel file data source.

1. Open the sb-Catalog Mail Merge from the Lesson 08 folder.

Edit the Catalog

2. Use the task pane on the left side of the screen to apply the Lilac color scheme.

3. Use the task pane to apply the Aspect Verdana font scheme.

4. On page 1, change the Catalog Title to **Hardesty's Flowers**.

5. On page 1, change the Catalog Subtitle to **Luxury Floral Gifts**.

6. On page 1, replace all of the text in the Date text box to **Mother's Day 2008**.

7. Add the Dot Attention Getter from the Design Gallery and place it in the lower-left corner of page 1.

8. Apply an Accent 1 fill color to the Attention Getter.

9. Edit the Attention Getter to read **100% Satisfaction Guaranteed**.

10. If necessary, move the Attention Getter to the approximate location shown in the following illustration.

Open Catalog Merge

11. Go to page 2.

12. Choose Tools→Mailings and Catalogs→Catalog Merge from the menu bar.
    Two new pages are added after page 1. Notice that the Catalog Merge Layout toolbar opens near the Catalog Merge Area. You will not use the toolbar in this example; you can just ignore it.

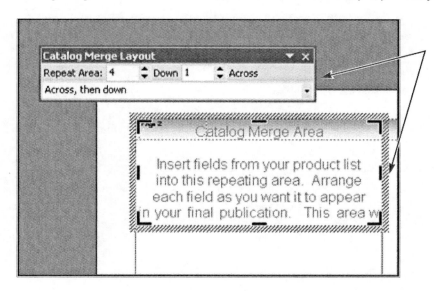

13. If necessary, choose the Use an Existing List option in the task pane.

14. Click Next: Create or Connect to a Product List at the bottom of the task pane.
The Select Data Source dialog box displays, where you can choose a data source file. For this exercise, you will use an Excel spreadsheet.

Open Catalog Merge Data Source

15. Navigate to the Lesson 08 folder and double-click to insert sb-Catalog Mail Merge Data Source.
The Select Table dialog box appears. Notice the Mothers Day table that is currently selected.

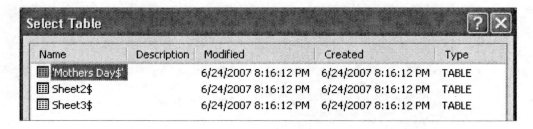

16. Click OK.
The Catalog Merge Product List window displays a preview of the data.

17. Click OK.

18. Save your changes.
Keep your catalog open if you will go directly to the next exercise.

Skill Builder 8.4 Perform a Catalog Merge

In this exercise, you will insert merge codes for products and then perform the catalog merge.

Before You Begin: *You must complete Skill Builder 8.3 before beginning this exercise. The sb-Catalog Mail Merge publication should be open in Publisher.*

1. Follow these steps to insert the merge codes:

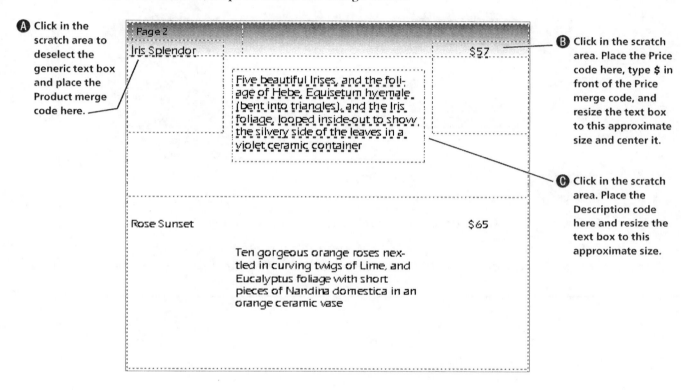

A Click in the scratch area to deselect the generic text box and place the Product merge code here.

B Click in the scratch area. Place the Price code here, type $ in front of the Price merge code, and resize the text box to this approximate size and center it.

C Click in the scratch area. Place the Description code here and resize the text box to this approximate size.

2. Go to page 3.

3. Open the sb-Flowers for Catalog Mail Merge in the Lesson 08 folder.

4. Select, copy, and paste the flower graphics onto page 3 of the catalog. If necessary, move the image to center it on the page.

   The flower graphics should line up across from the product descriptions on page 2.

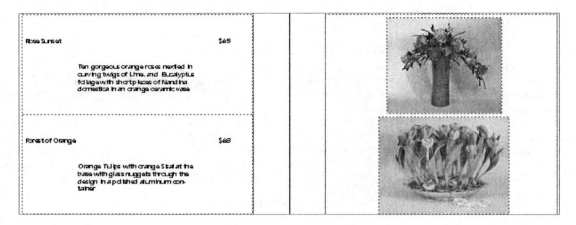

5. Save 💾 your changes.

6. Choose File→Close from the menu bar to close your catalog.

7. Close sb-Flowers for Catalog Mail Merge and return to the main Publisher screen.

   Publisher returns to the Getting Started with Microsoft Office Publisher 2007 window.

 # Assessments

Assessment 8.1   Create a University Form Letter

In this exercise, you will open a form letter for a university, add your own personal information in the data source, and insert merge codes.

1. Open as-University Form Letter from the Lesson 08 folder.

2. Open the Mail Merge task pane.

3. Open as-University Form Letter Data Source from the Lesson 08 folder.

4. Add your address information in the data source.

Insert Merge Codes

5. In the address text box, insert the merge codes as shown in the following illustration.

«Title» «First Name» «Last Name»
«Address Line 1»
«Address Line 2»
«City», «State» «ZIP Code»
«Country or Region»

6. Replace the greeting line text with **Dear** and the First Name merge code.

7. Preview the addresses and make any necessary changes to the placement of the merge codes. Notice that the Italy address has an extra line with a comma. You will correct this after you perform the mail merge.

Edit an Address

8. On the Mail Merge task pane, click Edit Recipient List.
   Although you won't use phone numbers in these letters, you would like to include home phone numbers to use at a future time.

9. Click on the Data Source name and click edit. Add the following phone numbers to the data source:

   Fayeh Hassan: 555-221-1133
   Francesca Porto: 011-39-347-245-6670
   Liam O'Conner: 555-770-1100
   Your home phone

10. Save your changes.
    Keep your letter open for the next exercise.

Assessment 8.2   Merge and Print the Form Letter

In this exercise, you will merge, edit, and print one letter. You will also print a list of addresses to give to student housing.

Before You Begin: You must complete Assessment 8.1 before beginning this exercise. The as-University Form Letter publication should be open in Publisher.

1. On the Mail Merge task pane, click Next: Create Merged Publications.

2. On the Mail Merge task pane, click Merge to a New Publication.
   Notice that you haven't entered the date on the letter yet.

Return to the University Letter and Add a Date

3. On the Mail Merge task pane, click Return to Original Publication.

4. Select the text in the date text box, click Insert→Date and Time, and replace this text with the highlighted date format found in the following illustration.

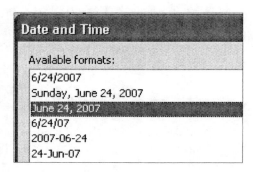

5. On the Mail Merge task pane, click Merge to a New Publication.

Edit a Merged Letter

6. Go to Francesca Porto's letter.

7. Delete the address line containing the comma above Italy. Your address should now look like the address as seen in the following illustration.

8. Print preview the four letters.

9. Print only your letter.

10. Close and don't save the merged letters.

Print a Recipient List

11. Go to the original University form letter.

12. Click Print Recipient List in the task pane.

13. Click to place a check in the columns under Select Columns as shown in the following illustration.

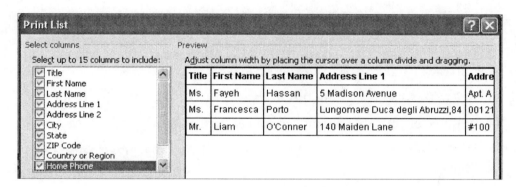

14. Click the Print button in the Print List dialog box.

15. Close and save your university form letter.

Assessment 8.3   Create CD/DVD Labels

In this exercise, you will create CD and DVD Labels for your home movie collection.

1. Create CD/DVD Booklet labels.

2. Apply the Glacier Color Scheme and the Virtual Trebuchet MS Font Scheme.

3. Save the file as **as-CD_DVD Labels Mail Merge** in the Lesson 08 folder.

Create Your Own Business Information Set

4. Create a Business Information Set for yourself using your home information. Be sure to include your name, address information, and phone number(s).
Your information will be included on the label so that if the CD or DVD gets lost or is borrowed, it can be returned to you.

5. Delete the logo picture graphic box below your address information.

Add WordArt and a Picture

6. Delete the text box that starts with *This inside panel....*

7. Create a WordArt image of your choice using the word **Movies** and center it in place of the text box that you deleted in step 5.

8. Replace the picture of the man playing a violin under CD Title with as-Movies Picture in your Lesson 08 folder.

9. If necessary, resize and center the picture under CD Title.

Create Your List of Movies

10. Open the Mail Merge task pane.

11. Create a new recipient list.

12. Use the Customize Columns in the New Address List dialog box to add two new columns: **DVD Name** and **Movie Stars**.

13. Delete the rest of the columns in the Customize Address List dialog box.

14. Add five of your favorite movies and at least one movie star in each movie.

15. Save your movie list data source as **as-DVD Movies Data Source** in the Lesson 08 folder.

Insert Merge Codes

16. Delete the text CD Title text on the right side of the label.

17. Place the DVD Name merge code in the CD Title text box.

18. Delete the text Performer's Name on the right side of the label.

19. Insert Movie Stars in the Performer's Name text box.

Merge Your DVD Labels

20. Delete your Business Information Set.

21. Save and close your CD/DVD labels and return to the main Publisher screen.

Critical Thinking

Critical Thinking 8.1   Create a Menu

Richard Ho, owner of Café Changs, has asked you to prepare a menu for this week's entrées. Richard keeps a list of his entrées in Excel. In this exercise, you will create this week's menu using the entrée items in this Excel list and Publisher's Catalog Merge feature.

1. Create the Gingham Wine/Dessert menu.

2. Choose a font and color scheme that you feel complement the menu.

3. On page 1 replace Wine List with **Chef Chang's Daily Specials**.

4. Practice adding whatever formatting you like to this text box.

5. On page 1 replace the graphic with any clip art that you think would look good on your menu.

6. On page 1 delete any other graphics or text boxes you would like.

7. Save the menu as **ct-Menu Catalog Merge** in the Lesson 08 folder.

8. Use the following guidelines to perform the merge:
   - Go to page 2.
   - Be sure to choose the correct merge type.
   - In the Catalog Merge Layout box above the publication, change the Repeat Area from 4 to **5**.
   - Merge data from the ct-Menu Excel Data Source file.
   - If additional pages are created in the merge, delete them.
   - Make sure that the menu contains all the items in the data source.
   - Prices should be clearly marked with dollar signs.
   - The menu should not contain any empty pages.

9. Print the menu.

10. (Optional) Compare your menu design and layout with that of another student who's performed this exercise. Consider the following questions together:
    - Does one menu design stand out?
    - What difference do font choices make?
    - What other layout decisions made a menu more or less effective?

Critical Thinking 8.2   Create a Friends' Addresses List

You have just graduated from the university and landed your ideal job as a CPA with a Chicago accounting firm. You would like to keep track of your university friends by creating an address list that you use on an ongoing basis to create mailing labels as well as create updates on how you are doing. You decide to let your friends know about your new job in Chicago and your new address.

1. Experiment with the various publications until you choose a simple one that you think would look best to notify your friends of your recent move and new job.

2. Experiment with different color schemes and fonts until you get the look you like.

3. Create a new Business Information Set for yourself.

4. Save your publication as **ct-Friends Mail Merge** in the Lesson 08 folder.

5. Add whatever text you would like to your publication letting your friends know about your new job and new home.

6. Practice drawing a simple map to your new home.

7. Experiment with the different clip art and add one that you think would look best.

8. Create a list of your friend's addresses (at least three addresses) and save the address data source as **ct-Friends Mail Merge Data Source** in the Lesson 08 folder.

9. Practice inserting merge codes for your friends' addresses as well as any other field codes you think appropriate.

10. Merge your publication with your friends' addresses and experiment with either printing or merging to a new publication.

11. If you decide to merge to a new publication, close that publication without saving the changes.

12. Close your publication and save the changes.

13. Create mailing labels for your friends using ct-Friends Mail Merge Data Source.mdb and experiment with choosing one of the Avery mailing labels.

14. Save the mailing labels as **ct-Friends Mailing Labels** in the Lesson 08 folder.

15. Insert the merge codes and perform the merge.

16. Save your new mailing labels as **ct-Friends Mailing Labels Merge** in the Lesson 08 folder.

17. Close your new mailing labels.

18. Delete your Business Information Set.

19. Close your mailing label publication and Save the changes.

20. Exit Publisher.

Creating Tables and Business Forms

In this lesson, you will learn to use Publisher to create and format tables. If you currently work with Word tables, you will see a great deal of similarity to creating and formatting Publisher tables. You will also learn to create calendars, which are essentially tables with a special purpose. You will also see that Publisher business forms, such as expense reports, contain tables, which makes it easy to work with these forms. In order to protect your business form template so that changes cannot be made to it by users, you will learn to make a business form *read-only*. And lastly, you will learn to add tabs to business form text boxes to make it easier to align data.

LESSON OBJECTIVES

After studying this lesson, you will be able to:

- Create a table
- Format a table
- Create a calendar
- Create an expense report business form
- Make a business form read-only
- Add tabs to business forms

Case Study: Creating a Table, a Calendar, and Business Forms

Sandy Baughman is the district manager of the Park Service at Glacier National Park. She is in charge of park employees, services, marketing, and public relations.

Sandy would like you to use Publisher to create a nice-looking flyer that lists Glacier Park's various entrance fees. She would also like you to create a monthly calendar of park events. These flyers will be distributed to hotels and restaurants for use by tourists. And finally, she would like you to create an employee expense report for park employees to use.

In addition, you have a friend who works for a newspaper in North Carolina, and you promised to create a fax cover sheet for her.

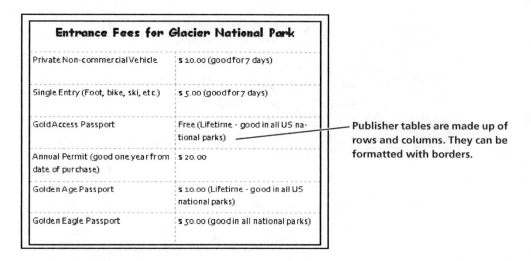

Publisher tables are made up of rows and columns. They can be formatted with borders.

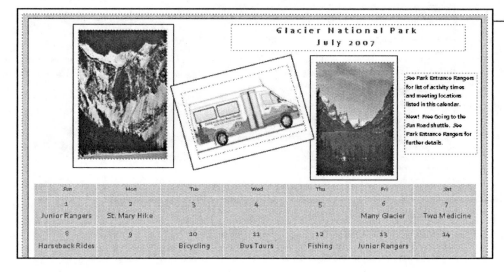

Tables are found in calendars as well as in most business forms.

Creating Tables

A table is a collection of rows and columns designed to help organize information. Publisher tables are very similar to Word tables. They are useful if you need to align lists of numbers and text. For example, you can use tables to align data in invoices, price lists, expense reports, schedules, résumés, and so on.

The intersection of a row and column is called a *cell*. Cells contain your data and text. You can also insert pictures in cells.

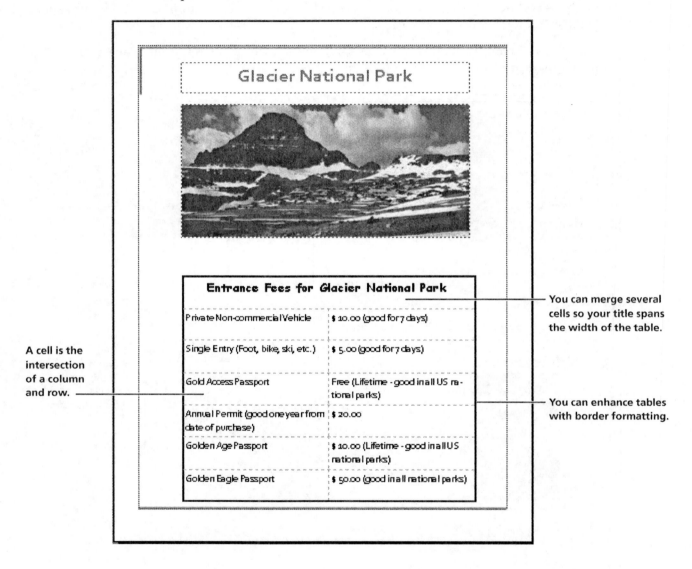

A cell is the intersection of a column and row.

You can merge several cells so your title spans the width of the table.

You can enhance tables with border formatting.

QUICK REFERENCE: CREATING A TABLE AND SELECTING CELLS

Task	Procedure
Create a table	■ Click the Insert Table 🔳 button on the Objects toolbar. ■ Drag the mouse pointer to draw a box on the publication where you want the table to appear. ■ Enter the Number of Rows. ■ Enter the Number of Columns. ■ Select a format from the Table Format list.
Type in a table and move the cursor	■ Click to position the cursor in the cell in which you want to type. ■ Type your text. ■ Move to another cell using any of the following techniques: ◆ Press `Tab` to move to the next cell. ◆ Press `Shift`+`Tab` to move to the previous cell. ◆ Press an arrow key to move one cell in the direction of the arrow.
Select cells	■ Position the mouse pointer at left edge of a cell so that the pointer becomes a black arrow pointing up and to the right. ■ Click the mouse button.
Select a range of cells	■ Drag the mouse pointer across the cells. ■ Click to select the cell that will become the upper-left corner of the range. Hold down the `Shift` key and click the cell that will become the bottom-right corner of the range.
Select a row	■ Position mouse pointer at left edge of a row so that the pointer becomes a black arrow pointing to the right. ■ Click to select the row.
Select a column	■ Position the mouse pointer at the top edge of a column so that the pointer becomes a black arrow pointing down. ■ Click to select the column.
Select the entire table	■ Position cursor inside a cell in the table. ■ Press `Ctrl`+`A` to select the current cell. ■ Press `Ctrl`+`A` again to select the entire table.

Formatting Tables

Formatting a table gives it a professional look. Effects, such as fill color, draw the reader's attention to a particular area of the table that you want to emphasize. With Publisher tables, you can easily rearrange columns and rows, and you can change column widths and row heights. You can also add and delete columns and rows. Merging cells is useful when you want text to span the width of several columns. Adding borders to a table is similar to adding a border to a text box.

Some of the tools that you have worked with in formatting text boxes are also used to format tables.

- The Line/Border Style ☰ button applies borders to table cells.
- The Line Color 🖌 ▾ button changes border color.

QUICK REFERENCE: FORMATTING A TABLE

Task	Procedure
Insert a row or multiple rows	■ Select a row. ■ To insert multiple rows, select multiple rows. ■ Choose Table→Insert→Rows Above (or Rows Below) from the menu bar.
Insert a column or multiple columns	■ Select the column adjacent to the point where the new column should appear. ■ To insert multiple columns, select multiple columns. ■ Choose Table→Insert→Columns to the Left (or Columns to the Right) from the menu bar.
Delete a row	■ Select the row(s) to delete or click anywhere in a row. ■ Choose Table→Delete→Rows from the menu bar.
Delete a column	■ Select the column(s) to delete or click anywhere within a column. ■ Choose Table→Delete→Columns from the menu bar.
Change cell height or width	■ Position the mouse pointer between two rows or columns so that the pointer becomes a double-headed arrow. ■ Drag the row or column to a new height or width. ■ You can also double-click a divider between two rows or columns to AutoFit to the contents.
Turn off automatic hyphenation	■ Position the cursor within the table. ■ Choose Tools→Language→Hyphenation from the menu bar. ■ Deselect Automatically Hyphenate This Story.
Merge cells	■ Select the cells to merge. ■ Choose Table→Merge Cells from the menu bar.
Split a cell	■ Select the cell. ■ Choose Table→Split Cells from the menu bar.

In this exercise, you will create a table in a flyer that lists activities offered in Glacier National Park. You will add a border, insert a row, and merge cells. Lastly, you will turn off automatic hyphenation.

Create a Flyer

1. Choose the Quick Publications publication type.

2. Click the Classic Designs link and click once to choose the Edge design.

3. Choose the Meadow Color Scheme and the Module Corbel Font Scheme, and click Create.

4. Save the flyer as **Glacier Park Table** in your Lesson 09 folder.

Insert Picture and Text

5. Delete all text boxes and the picture.

6. Follow these steps to complete the top portion of the flyer:

Ⓐ Draw a text box similar to the one shown here and type **Glacier National Park**. Format the text as 28 pt bold, centered. Change the font color to Accent 2.

Ⓑ Draw a picture frame to insert a picture from a file. Make it approximately this size and location. Open the Glacier Park file from the Lesson 09 folder. Resize and position the picture as necessary.

Create a Table

7. Click the Insert Table ▦ button on the Objects toolbar.

8. Draw a box starting from approximately 1 inch on the horizontal toolbar and 6 inches on the vertical toolbar to 7½ inches on the horizontal toolbar and 10 inches on the vertical toolbar.

9. Type **6** in the Number of Rows field and press the ⌗Tab⌗ key.
   The number of rows is now six and the number of columns is selected.

10. Type **2** in the Number of Columns field and click OK.

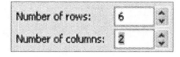

Your table appears as in the following illustration.

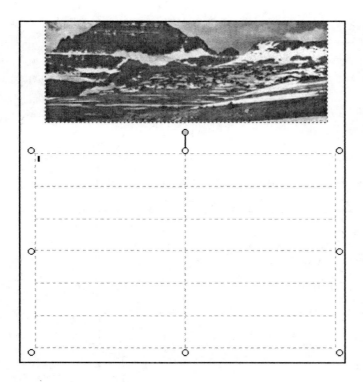

Type in a Table

11. Click the top-left cell.

The cursor appears in the cell.

12. Type **Private Non-commercial Vehicle**, press the [Tab] key, and type **$ 10.00 (good for 7 days)**.

13. Press the [Tab] key.

14. Zoom the screen if necessary, and continue typing in the table as shown in the following table.

Private Non-commercial Vehicle	$ 10.00 (good for 7 days)
Single Entry (Foot, bike, ski, etc.)	$ 5.00 (good for 7 days)
Gold Access Passport	Free (Lifetime - good in all US national parks)
Annual Permit (good one year from date of purchase)	$ 20.00
Golden Age Passport	$ 10.00 (Lifetime - good in all US national parks)
Golden Eagle Passport	$ 50.00 (good in all national parks)

Format a Table

15. Click anywhere inside a table cell and press ⏎ Ctrl + A twice.
This selects the entire table.

16. Change the font size to 14 pt.

17. Click the outside border of the table to select it.

18. Click the Line/Border Style ☰ button and choose 2¼ pt.

19. Click the Line Color ✎ ▾ button and choose the Hyperlink (Dark Blue) color.

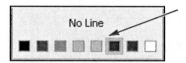

Insert a Row

20. Position the mouse pointer at the left edge of the first row so that the mouse pointer becomes a black arrow. (You may need to zoom out.)

21. Click the mouse button.
The first row of the table is selected.

22. Choose Table→Insert→Rows Above from the menu bar.
A new row appears, and the new row is selected.

Merge Cells

23. Choose Table→Merge Cells from the menu bar.
The cells in the first row merge into one cell.

24. Type **Entrance Fees for Glacier National Park** in the merged cell.

25. Press ⏎ Ctrl + A to select the cell in which you typed your text.

26. Change the font to Comic Sans MS 18 pt bold.

27. Center ☰ the text.

28. Change the font color to Hyperlink (Dark Blue).
Your table should look like the following illustration.

Entrance Fees for Glacier National Park	
Private Non-commercial Vehicle	$ 10.00 (good for 7 days)
Single Entry (Foot, bike, ski, etc.)	$ 5.00 (good for 7 days)
Gold Access Passport	Free (Lifetime - good in all US national parks)
Annual Permit (good one year from date of purchase)	$ 20.00
Golden Age Passport	$ 10.00 (Lifetime - good in all US national parks)
Golden Eagle Passport	$ 50.00 (good in all national parks)

Turn off Automatic Hyphenation

29. Click anywhere in the table.

30. Choose Tools→Language→Hyphenation from the menu bar.

31. Deselect Automatically Hyphenate This Story and click OK.
Hyphens disappear from any cells containing hyphenated words.

32. Close your flyer and save your changes.

Working with a Calendar Table

A calendar is a specialized table that can be used for various reasons, such as creating a company calendar of special events or a personal calendar containing family pictures. As with any table, you can insert rows and columns, merge cells, and change row height and column width. You can also format calendar cells with color and borders.

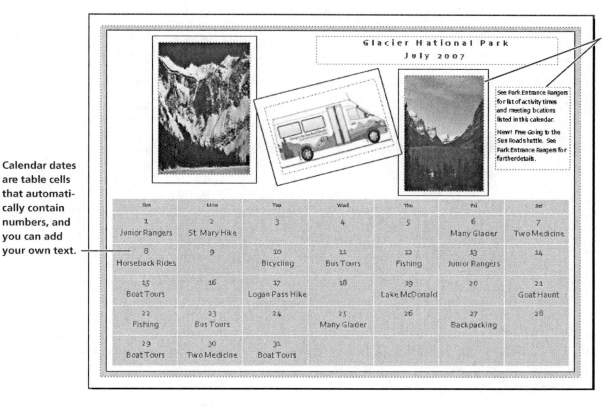

Calendar dates are table cells that automatically contain numbers, and you can add your own text.

You can add pictures and text boxes to a calendar to make it more interesting.

Hands-On 9.2   Create a Calendar

In this exercise, you will create a calendar for Glacier Park's activities. You will add pictures and a text box, and then you will edit the calendar to add your own text.

Create a Calendar

1. Choose the Calendars publication type.

2. Click once to choose the Travel design in the Full Page category.

3. Customize the calendar using the Trout Color Scheme and the Module Corbel Font Scheme.

4. Choose One Month per Page under Options and click Create.

5. Save your calendar as **Glacier Park Activities Calendar** in the Lesson 09 folder.

Add Pictures

6. Delete the picture of the flowers in the left-hand frame but leave the frame.
You'll use the current picture frames in order to maintain the original arrangement of the pictures.

7. Click the Picture Frame button, choose Picture from File, and draw a box to approximately fill the frame. Open the Avalanche Lake file from the Lesson 09 folder and resize the picture to fit the frame.

8. Delete the middle picture and insert the Shuttle picture file in its place. Click and turn the green circle to rotate the picture and then resize it to fit the picture frame.

9. Continue with the last picture, using the Wild Goose Island picture file.

Add a Text Box

10. Follow these steps to add a text box to the right of the pictures you just added:

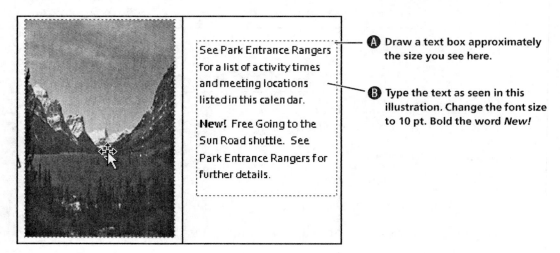

Ⓐ Draw a text box approximately the size you see here.

Ⓑ Type the text as seen in this illustration. Change the font size to 10 pt. Bold the word *New!*

Edit the Calendar

11. In the date text box above the pictures, place your cursor to the left of the current month, type **Glacier National Park**, and press Enter.

12. Select all the text in the date text box and change the font to 14 pt bold.
    Your title displays the current month and year.

```
Glacier National Park
     July 2007
```

13. Click to the right of the number 1 in the first date cell and press Enter. Type **Junior Rangers** and press Tab to go to the second date cell.

14. Click to the right of the number 2.

15. Continue typing in the remaining cells as you see in the following table. Remember to press Tab to move to the next field and mouse-click to the right of the calendar number.

1 Junior Rangers	2 St. Mary Hike	3	4	5	6 Many Glacier	7 Two Medicine
8 Horseback Rides	9	10 Bicycling	11 Bus Tours	12 Fishing	13 Junior Rangers	14
15 Boat Tours	16	17 Logan Pass Hike	18	19 Lake McDonald	20	21 Goat Haunt
22 Fishing	23 Bus Tours	24	25 Many Glacier	26	27 Backpacking	28
29 Boat Tours	30 Two Medicine	31 Boat Tours				

16. Preview your calendar and close Print Preview.

17. Close and save your changes.

Using Business Forms

Publisher offers a variety of forms for general business use. These include invoices, customer statements, fax cover sheets, purchase orders, expenses reports, employee time cards, and inventory lists. Other types of business publications are specific to certain industries. For example, a travel company may use a reservation form while a university might need a student registration form.

A customer statement is a form sent to customers at regular intervals that may include invoice numbers, charges, and payments. An expense report is a means of itemizing an employee's business expenses for reimbursement. A purchase order is a formal request to buy a product from a vendor and to bill a business account. An invoice is an itemized list of goods or services stating quantities, fees, prices, and other charges with a request for payment. Businesses use time cards to keep track of the exact time employees begin and complete their workdays. And finally, an inventory list usually includes quantities, serial numbers, descriptions, and values.

Creating an Expense Report

Expense Report templates are one of a variety of business form templates that you can use for your business. Most expense reports have several elements in common. They display information about the business such as its name, location, and contact information. This information is most often taken from the Business Information Set.

When you create a business form such as an expense report, you create a master form that employees will make copies of. It is a good idea to protect the expense report so employees don't mistakenly make changes to it. You can do this by making the publication *read-only,* which forces users to save it with a different filename. Thus, your original file remains unchanged.

The company name is inserted from the Business Information Set.

Employees enter information into text boxes and tables.

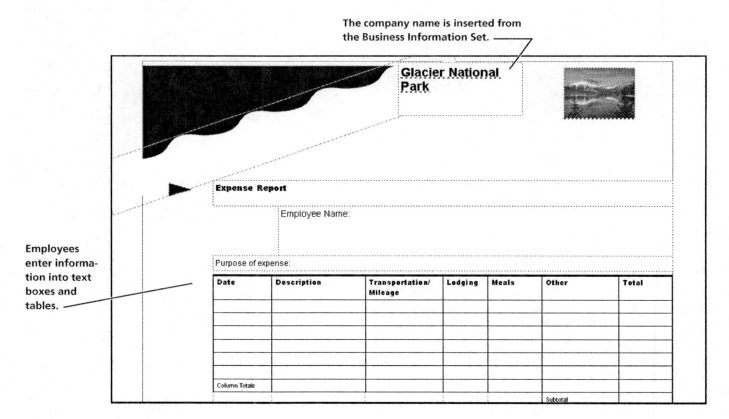

Glacier National Park

Expense Report

Employee Name:

Purpose of expense:

Date	Description	Transportation/ Mileage	Lodging	Meals	Other	Total
Column Totals						

Subtotal

QUICK REFERENCE: USING AN EXPENSE REPORT

Task	Procedure
Create an expense report from a template	■ Choose the Business Forms publication type. ■ Choose a design. ■ Edit the business form as necessary.
Make the publication read-only	■ Right-click the file in Windows Explorer or the Open Publication dialog box. ■ Click Properties on the shortcut menu. ■ Check the Read-Only checkbox.

 Hands-On 9.3 **Create an Expense Report from a Template**

In this exercise, you will create an expense report that will be used by all park employees. You will make it read-only. You will also create a copy of the expense report.

Create an Expense Report

1. Choose the Business Forms publication type.

2. Click the Expense Report link at the top of the screen and click once to choose the Waves design.

3. Choose the Wildflower Color Scheme and the Basis Arial Bold Font Scheme.

4. Create a Business Information Set for your department that includes the information in the following illustration. Insert the Lake McDonald file in the Lesson 09 folder as the logo.

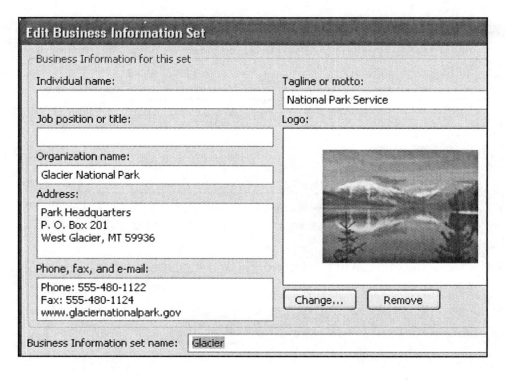

5. If necessary, check the Include Logo checkbox under Options; click Create.

6. Click the text in the Employee text box below the Expense Report text box to select all the text then type **Employee Name:** and press the ⌨Spacebar two times.

```
Expense Report

              Employee Name:
```

7. Save your expense report as **Employee Expense Report** in the Lesson 09 folder.

Make the Expense Report Read-Only

8. Choose File→Open from the menu bar and navigate to the Lesson 09 folder.

9. Right-click the Employee Expense Report file and choose Properties from the menu.
   The Employee Expense Report Properties dialog box displays.

10. Check the Read-Only checkbox and click OK.
    The Open Publication dialog box is still displayed.

Create Your Own Copy of the Expense Report

11. Open Employee Expense Report from your Lesson 09 folder.
    The read-only version of the publication appears in the Publisher window. Notice the title bar indicates that the Employee Expense Report is read-only.

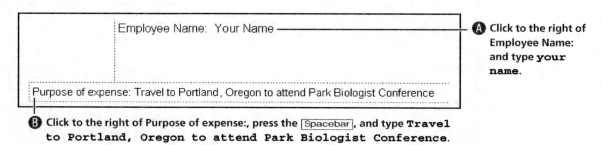

12. Save your expense report as **Personal Expense Report** in the Lesson 09 folder.
    Now you are working with a copy of the read-only publication; the copy is editable.

13. Follow these steps to fill in the expense report:

```
Employee Name:  Your Name ──────────────────────     Ⓐ Click to the right of
                                                         Employee Name:
                                                         and type your
                                                         name.

Purpose of expense: Travel to Portland, Oregon to attend Park Biologist Conference
```

Ⓑ Click to the right of Purpose of expense:, press the ⌨Spacebar, and type **Travel to Portland, Oregon to attend Park Biologist Conference.**

14. Click in the first cell of the second row and fill out the expense report using the following information.

Date	Description	Transportation/ Mileage	Lodging	Meals	Other	Travel
8/1-6/07	Biologist Conference	$352.00	$552.00	$210.00	$52.00	$1,166.00

15. Click the text box cell at the bottom of the table and to the right of Total Due and type **$1,166.00**.

Do not delete the Business Information Set for Glacier Park yet. You will use it later in a Skill Builder exercise later in this lesson.

16. Save your changes and close your expense report.

Working with Tabs

It is important to make business forms as user-friendly as possible so people can easily enter data in the correct places. You can use tabs in a text box to help correctly position the cursor inside the text box.

Working with tabs in Publisher is similar to working with tabs in Word. A tab stop is a horizontal location on the page as noted by a tab marker on the Publisher ruler. Tab stops ensure that the data entered in the text box is properly aligned.

As in Word, there is a default tab grid in Publisher with tabs set every one-half inch. Default tabs do not display marks on the ruler to indicate their location. Tabs that you set manually do have tab symbols on the ruler.

Special Characters Button

Turning on the Special Characters ¶ button makes special non-printing characters visible, helping you locate tab characters, end-of-frame marks, and paragraph marks. This feature is very helpful when creating tables and editing documents.

Understanding Tab Alignment

Publisher allows you to set tabs using four different alignment options: Left, Right, Center, and Decimal. You can choose the type of alignment in the Tabs dialog box.

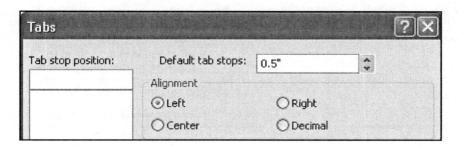

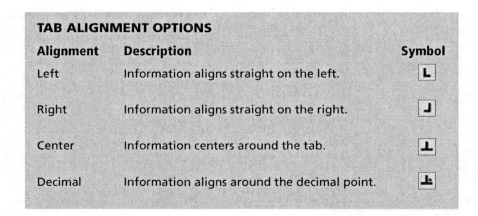

TAB ALIGNMENT OPTIONS

Alignment	Description	Symbol
Left	Information aligns straight on the left.	L
Right	Information aligns straight on the right.	⌐
Center	Information centers around the tab.	⊥
Decimal	Information aligns around the decimal point.	⊥.

A left tab appears at 1" on the ruler.

The arrow indicates that the Tab key was pressed. The cursor stops at the tab stop marker displayed on the ruler.

Paragraph marks appear in the text box; in this example, each line is a paragraph.

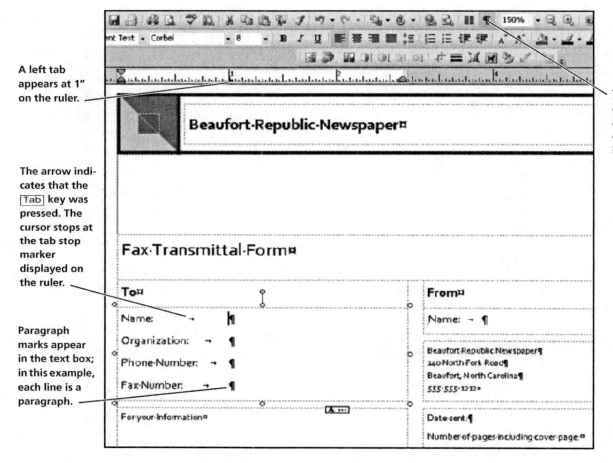

The Special Characters button is active and special characters appear in the publication.

QUICK REFERENCE: INSERTING, MOVING, AND DELETING TAB STOPS IN TEXT BOXES

Task	Procedure
Insert a tab stop from the menu bar	■ Place the cursor in the text box. ■ Choose Format→Tabs from the menu bar. ■ Type the Tab Stop Position. ■ Choose the Alignment and click Set.
Insert a tab stop using the mouse	■ Place the cursor in the text box. ■ Place tip of mouse pointer on the ruler and click to insert a tab.
Move a tab stop	■ Place the cursor in the text box. ■ Place tip of mouse pointer on the tab stop on the ruler and drag the tab stop to the right or left on the ruler.
Delete a tab stop	■ Place the cursor in the text box. ■ Drag the tab stop off the ruler then release the mouse button.

Hands-On 9.4   Insert Tabs in a Publication

In this exercise, you will open a fax cover sheet and add tabs in text boxes.

Insert a Tab in a Text Box

1. Open the Tabs file from the Lesson 09 folder.

2. Click the drop-down arrow on the Zoom button on the Standard toolbar.

3. Choose 150% from the menu.

4. Press ⎡Ctrl⎤+⎡F1⎤ to turn off the Format Publication task pane.
   It can be helpful to close the task pane when you zoom your publication to a larger size.

5. Click the Special Characters ¶ button on the Standard toolbar.
   The nonprinting characters appear.

6. Place your cursor to the right of the colon following *Name:* below the To text box.

7. Choose Format→Tabs from the menu bar.

8. Follow these steps to add a left tab stop:

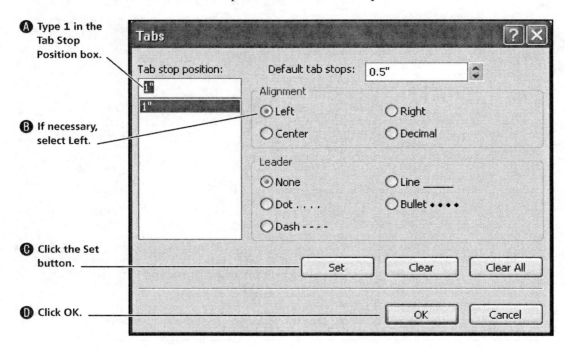

A Type **1** in the Tab Stop Position box.

B If necessary, select Left.

C Click the Set button.

D Click OK.

A left tab stop marker appears on the ruler.

9. With your cursor to the right of the colon, press the [Tab] key. *The cursor aligns at the 1" mark.*

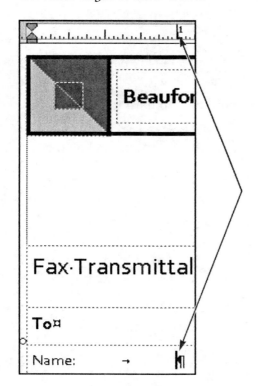

10. Follow these steps to finish typing in this text box:

A Press Enter to go to the next paragraph, type **Organiza-tion:**, press Tab, and press Enter.

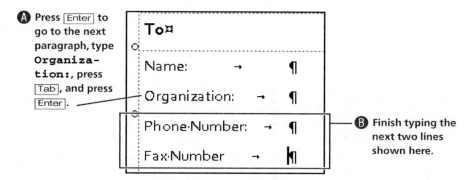

B Finish typing the next two lines shown here.

Insert a Second Tab

11. In the Name text box below the From text box, place your cursor to the right of the colon following Name and press the Tab key.
    Since you did not specify a tab stop in this text box as you did in the previous text box, Publisher moves to the next default tab stop at the half-inch mark. This default tab stop does not display a tab stop marker on the ruler.

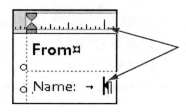

12. Click to the right of the tab symbol following To Name and type **Suzanne Frost**.

13. Click to the right of the tab symbol following From Name and type **John Walker**.

14. Click the Special Characters ¶ button on the Standard toolbar.
    The nonprinting characters no longer appear.

15. Close and save your changes.

Concepts Review

True/False Questions

1. When you create a business form such as an expense report, you create a master form that employees will make copies of. TRUE FALSE

2. A table is a collection of rows and columns designed to help organize information. TRUE FALSE

3. You can change the height of a row in a table. TRUE FALSE

4. Merging cells is useful when creating a title for your table. TRUE FALSE

5. Calendar cells, unlike table cells, cannot be formatted with text color and borders. TRUE FALSE

6. You can protect a business form template by making it read-only. TRUE FALSE

7. You use the Special Characters button to insert symbols, such as a copyright symbol, in a publication. TRUE FALSE

8. Publisher's default tabs are set at every inch. TRUE FALSE

9. The intersection of a column and row in a table is called a cell. TRUE FALSE

10. Once a tab is set on the ruler, you position the cursor at a tab stop by tapping the Spacebar . TRUE FALSE

Multiple Choice Questions

1. Which of the following is not a Publisher business form?

   a. Expense report

   b. Fax cover sheet

   c. Purchase order

   d. Labels

2. Which of the following is not true about tables?

   a. You can add a border.

   b. You can change a column width.

   c. You cannot insert pictures.

   d. You can format cells.

3. Which of the following is not true about an expense report?

   a. It is a good idea to protect the expense report template so users don't mistakenly make changes to the template.

   b. Information about a business such as a name and address is usually not taken from the Business Information Set.

   c. In an expense report, information about incurred expenses, the employee signature, and the date are usually contained in table formats.

   d. Once the employee is finished filling out the expense report, they will save their changes as a copy of the expense report template.

4. Which of the following is not true about tabs?

   a. Triangles and rectangles on the ruler are called tab stops.

   b. Tab stops ensure that the data entered in a text box will be properly aligned.

   c. A tab stop is a horizontal location on the page as noted by a tab marker on the Publisher ruler.

   d. Once the tab is set, you position the cursor at a tab stop by pressing the Tab key.

Skill Builders

Skill Builder 9.1   Create a Photo Album Calendar

In this exercise, you will create your own personal photo album calendar for the last six months of the year. You will add your own photos and events to the calendar.

Create a Photo Album Calendar

1. Choose the Full Page Photo Album in the Calendar publication-type category from the main Publisher screen.

2. Apply the Wildflower Color Scheme and the Casual Comic Sans MS Font Scheme.

3. Under Options, choose Landscape and the One Month per Page Timeframe if it is not already chosen.

4. Click the Set Calendar Dates button.

5. Choose July, 2008 as the Start Date.

6. Choose December, 2008 as the End Date and click OK.

7. Click the Create button.

Add Photos

8. Delete the photo on the July calendar.

9. Click the Picture Frame ▨ button and choose Picture from File from the menu.

10. Draw a frame that approximately fills the area of the deleted picture.

11. Insert the July file from your Lesson 09 folder.

12. Resize and move the picture as needed.

13. Go to the August page, delete the current picture, and add the August file from the Lesson 09 folder.

14. Resize and move the picture to fit in the frame.

15. Continue replacing the pictures for September through December, resizing and moving the pictures as you deem appropriate.

Add Calendar Events

16. Zoom the calendar to 100 percent.

17. Go to the July calendar and position the cursor to the right of the number 12.

18. Change the font size to **6** pt, press Enter, and type **Family BBQ**.

19. Go to the August calendar and position the cursor to the right of the number 23.

Resize a Calendar Cell

20. Change the font size to 6 pt, press [Enter], and type **Fishing Trip**.
If you cannot see Fishing Trip after you have typed it, you will need to resize the calendar cell for August 23.

21. If necessary, place your mouse on the white cell border under the number 23 until your mouse turns to a double-headed arrow; drag down until you see Fishing Trip.

22. Go to the September page; click to place your cursor to the right of the number 19 and press [Enter].

23. Change the font size to 5 pt and type **Family Reunion**.

24. Go to the October page; click to place your cursor to the right of the number 26 and press [Enter].

25. Change the font size to 6 pt and type **Balloon Trip**.

26. Go to the November page; click to place your cursor in the empty text box above November 2, change the font size to 5 pt, and type **Trip to Scotland**.

27. Go to the December page; click to place your cursor to the right of the number 25 and press [Enter].

28. Change the font size to 6 pt and type **Family Xmas**.

29. Save the publication as **sb-Photo Album Calendar** in the Lesson 09 folder.

30. Close your calendar.

Skill Builder 9.2   Create a Time Card

In this exercise, you will create and edit an employee time card to be used by all the Glacier Park employees. You will create and edit a table, and you will make the time card read-only.

Before You Begin: *You will use the Glacier Business Information Set created for the expense report in Hands-On 9.3 on page 271.*

Create a Time Card

1. Choose the Quadrant Time Billing Business Form.

2. Choose Waterfall Color Scheme and the Office Classic 2 Arial Font Scheme.

3. If necessary, choose the Glacier Business Information Set.

4. Under Options, choose to include the logo, and click Create.

5. Save your time card as **sb-Employee Time Card** in the Lesson 09 folder.

Edit a Text Box

6. Select the Time Billing text at the top of the time card and type **Employee Time Card**.

7. Select the text again and bold it.

Edit a Row Heading

8. Follow these steps to edit the column headings in the table:

A Select the text in the first cell and replace it with **Date**.

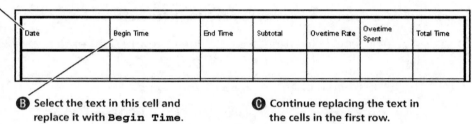

Date	Begin Time	End Time	Subtotal	Overtime Rate	Overtime Spent	Total Time

B Select the text in this cell and replace it with **Begin Time**.

C Continue replacing the text in the cells in the first row.

Delete a Column

9. Place your cursor in the Overtime Rate cell.

10. Choose Table→Delete→Columns from the menu bar.
The Overtime Rate column is deleted.

Resize a Column Width

11. Place your mouse pointer on the dividing line between Begin Time and End Time until your mouse turns into a double-headed arrow, and then drag to the left to narrow the column.

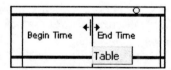

Move the Table

12. Place your cursor anywhere in the table and press Ctrl + A twice to select the table.

13. Place your mouse on the perimeter of the table so your mouse pointer changes to a move pointer, and then drag the table to the right until the right edge of the table is at approximately $7\frac{1}{2}$ inches on the horizontal ruler.

Resize Text Boxes

14. In the lower-left corner of the time card, select both text boxes containing the park's address and phone numbers and group them.

15. Widen the text boxes so that they look like the following illustration.

```
Park Headquarters
P. O. Box 201
West Glacier, MT 59936
Phone: 555-480-1122
Fax 555-480-1124
www.glaciernationalpark.gov
```

16. In the lower-left corner of the time card, center the park logo picture above the address.

17. Save your changes.

Make the Time Card Read-Only

18. Choose File→Open from the menu bar and navigate to the Lesson 09 folder.

19. Right-click the sb-Employee Time Card file and choose Properties from the menu.
The sb-Employee Time Card Properties dialog box displays.

20. Check the Read-Only checkbox and click OK.

21. Open the sb-Employee Time Card file again and notice that it is read-only.

22. Delete the Glacier Park Business Information Set.

23. Close the time card template.

Skill Builder 9.3   Create a Sign

In this exercise, you will create a sign announcing the Gourmet Chocolate Shop's business hours. You will edit the hours in an existing table, and you will create a new table.

1. Choose the Business Hours sign.

2. Choose the Urban Color Scheme and the Galley Arial Rounded Font Scheme, and click Create.

3. Save your sign as **sb-Gourmet Chocolate Shop Sign** in the Lesson 09 folder.

Edit the Sign

4. Follow these steps to complete the upper portion of the sign:

Ⓐ Select the text in this text box and replace it with **Gourmet Chocolate Shop Business Hours.**

Gourmet Chocolate Shop Business Hours

Monday	8:30	to	5:30
Tuesday	8:30	to	6:00
Wednesday	9:00	to	5:30
Thursday	8:30	to	5:30
Friday	8:30	to	6:00
Saturday	8:00	to	6:00

Ⓑ Select the time text in this cell and replace it with **8:30.**

Ⓒ Select the time text in this cell and replace it with **5:30.**

Ⓓ Continue to replace the time in the cells through Saturday.

Ⓔ Click to place your cursor in the Sunday cell and choose Table→Delete→Rows.

Place additional information here,

Create a New Table

5. Delete the text box at the bottom of the sign.

6. Click the Insert Table ⊞ button on the Objects toolbar.

7. Draw a box to fill most of the space below the table.

8. Indicate **2** as the number of rows and **2** as the number of columns then click OK. *Your new table should look similar to the following illustration.*

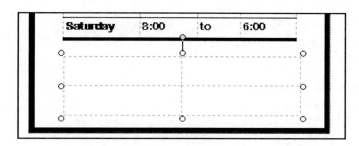

Add Text and Pictures in the Table

9. Follow these steps to add text and pictures in the table:

Ⓐ Type the text shown in these two text boxes. Change the font to Tahoma 12 pt bold, centered.

Let us Tempt you with our large selection of Delicious Chocolate Truffles

One of our best sellers is our rich dark chocolate cupcakes topped with an espresso chocolate icing

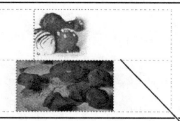

Ⓑ Add the sb-Chocolate Truffles image in the top row and the sb-Chocolate Cupcakes image in the bottom row. The picture files are in the Lesson 09 folder. Resize the pictures to fit from top to bottom in their cells.

10. Click the Print Preview 🄰 button to preview the sign then close Print Preview.

11. Save your changes and close your sign.

 **Assessments**

Assessment 9.1 Create a Fundraiser Invitation Card

In this exercise, you will create a fundraiser invitation card.

1. Create a Mobile Fundraiser Invitation Card.

2. Choose a Color Scheme and a Font Scheme.

3. Create a Business Information Set that includes the information in the following illustration. Insert the as-Park file from the Lesson 09 folder as the logo.

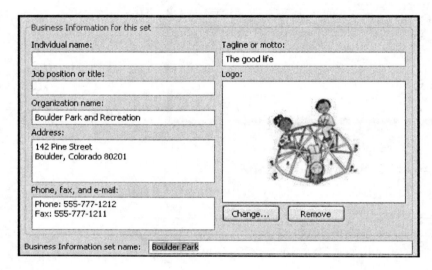

4. Save your newsletter as **as-Boulder Park Invitation** in the Lesson 09 folder.

5. Go to page 2 and edit the text boxes to look like the following illustration.

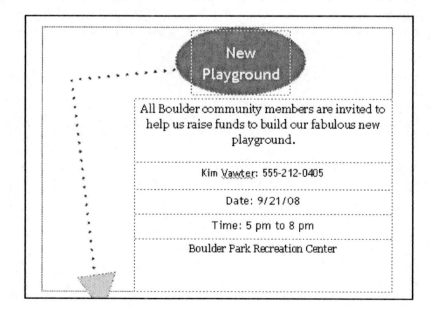

6. Go to page 3, select the text box containing *And have a good time!* and delete it. *This also deletes the border around the text box.*

7. Draw a five-row, two-column table to fit within the margins.

8. Follow these steps to complete table:

Ⓐ Merge the cells in the first row and type **Silent Auction Prizes**. Change the font to Comic Sans MS 12 pt bold. Center the text and change the font color to Hyperlink Blue.

Ⓑ Type the rest of the table as shown, centering the text within the cells.

Ⓒ Apply a BorderArt design of your choice.

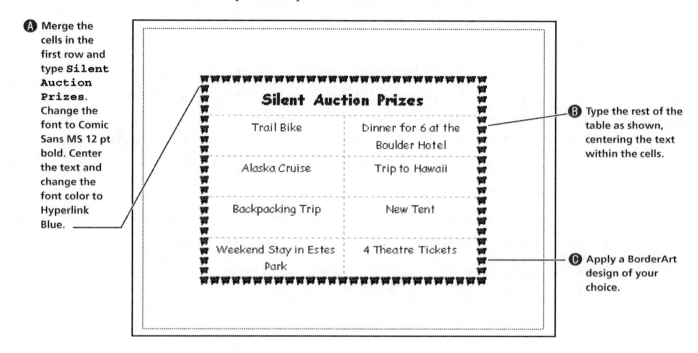

Silent Auction Prizes	
Trail Bike	Dinner for 6 at the Boulder Hotel
Alaska Cruise	Trip to Hawaii
Backpacking Trip	New Tent
Weekend Stay in Estes Park	4 Theatre Tickets

9. Preview your invitation card in Print Preview. *Do not delete the Boulder Park Business Information Set. You will use it in the following exercise to create an inventory list.*

10. Close the file and save your changes.

Assessment 9.2   **Create an Inventory List**

In this exercise, you will create an inventory list master form to be used by the staff to keep track of the park's athletic and playground equipment as well as miscellaneous items.

Before You Begin: *You should complete the Business Information Set in Assessment 9.1 before beginning this exercise.*

1. Create an Eclipse Inventory List business form.

2. Choose a Waterfall Color Scheme and Concourse Candara Font Scheme.

3. Choose the Boulder Park Business Information Set if necessary, make sure the Include Logo box is checked under Options, and click Create.

4. Close the Format Publication task pane and zoom the form so you can easily read it.

5. Save the inventory list **as-Boulder Park Inventory List** in the Lesson 09 folder.

6. Change the font in the first table row to 8 pt and center the text.

7. Delete any one of the table rows below the first row.

8. Insert a 1-inch tab after the text *Purpose:* and also after the text *Date:*.

9. Save your changes.

10. Make as-Boulder Park Inventory List a read-only file.

11. Delete the Boulder Park Business Information Set.

12. Close your inventory list.

Critical Thinking

Critical Thinking 9.1   Create a Thai Menu

In this exercise, you will create a daily specials menu for Richard's Northern Thai restaurant.

1. Open ct-Thai Daily Special Menu from the Lesson 09 folder.

2. Choose a different font and color scheme that you feel complement the menu.

3. Change the font size of the Daily Specials text to 9 pt.

4. Create a 2 x 9 table.

5. Resize and move the table until it fits in the middle of the menu.

6. Select the entire table and change the font size to 6 pt.

7. Type the following in your table:

Fried Rice with Shrimp	$9.00
Khanom Chun	$6.99
Tom Yum Kung	$8.50
Foi Thong	$6.50
Massaman Curry	$8.50
Noodles in Fish Curry	$9.00
Yellow Curry with Chicken	$8.50
Fish Cakes	$8.50
Papaya Salad	$7.50

8. Select the price column and center the prices.

9. Apply a border style of your choice.

10. Delete the row with the Fish Cakes entry.

11. Insert a row above the Foi Thong entry and type **Pad Baigrapao, $6.50**.

12. Print Preview the menu.

13. Close your menu and save your changes.

Critical Thinking 9.2   Create a Perfect Wedding Cakes Invoice

In this exercise, you will create a customer invoice master form for Chris, owner of Perfect Wedding Cakes.

1. Experiment with the various invoice design templates until you choose one that best fits the look for Perfect Wedding Cakes.

2. Experiment with different color schemes and fonts until you get the look you like.

3. Create a new Business Information Set. Use your imagination to complete the information. Create a tag line that best suits Perfect Wedding Cakes.

4. Find a picture of a wedding cake on the Internet; save it to the Lesson 09 folder and insert it as your logo.

5. Save your invoice as **ct-Perfect Wedding Cakes Invoice** in your Lesson 09 folder.

6. Delete the three lines in the Invoice # text box and replace each line with **Customer #**, **Invoice #**, and **Date**.

7. Experiment with adding tabs to each of the three lines you just typed so data entered by customers will be aligned.

8. Insert an additional row below the last row in the first table containing Your Order #.

9. Insert two blank rows in the Quantity table.

10. You've changed your mind about the additional row in the first table. Delete the extra row.

11. Practice changing the fill color in the first row of each of the two tables in the invoice to whatever fill color you think would look best.

12. Change the font color of these two first rows to a color that goes well with the fill color you chose.

13. Change whatever other formatting you think is needed for the invoice.

14. If you like, find an appropriate clip art or WordArt image and add it to your invoice.

15. Delete the Business Information Set.

16. Make the invoice template read-only.

17. Close the file and save your changes.

18. Exit Publisher.

LESSON 10

Creating a Web Site

In this lesson, you will use Publisher to plan, design, and create a company web site. You will add and delete web pages in your web site publication, and you will find that adding text, graphics, and hyperlinks on your web pages is just as easy as adding them in any other publication. You will also find that editing Navigation bars and adding backgrounds to your web pages is a snap. You will learn to create web forms, change form control properties, and set a data retrieval method for how a web site visitor's information is captured. You will then learn to preview your web pages and transfer your web content to a web server. Finally, you will learn to convert a brochure to a web page.

LESSON OBJECTIVES

After studying this lesson, you will be able to:

- Plan, design, and create a web site
- Add and delete web pages
- Edit text, graphics, and the Navigation bar
- Add a background to a web site
- Add hyperlinks and a hot spot
- Create a web form
- Change form control properties on a web form
- Set the data retrieval method for a web form
- Preview a web site
- Transfer and save web content to a web server
- Convert a publication to a web page

Case Study: Creating a Web Site

As an employee of Liam's Yellowstone Rafting and an old college buddy of the owner, Liam, you have been asked by Liam to create a web site for the company. Liam's whitewater rafting company has only been in business for one summer. Liam is conscious of the company's budget and realizes that creating a company web site using Publisher would be a cost-effective way to attract new customers.

You are comfortable using Publisher because you have had ample experience creating a variety of publications for the company, but you have never created a web site before.

You have done your homework by discussing the planning phase with Liam. You both decide that you will be the primary designer. Your target audience will include new and experienced whitewater rafting enthusiasts. Your web site visitors will see the benefits of becoming customers, and they will want to contact you for reservations.

This is the homepage, or first page, of a web site. ⎯

The Navigation bar contains links to the web pages in your web site. ⎯

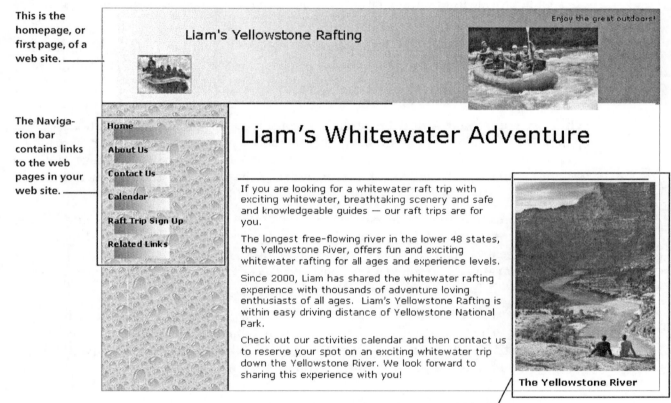

You can add pictures with captions to a web page.

Creating Web Sites

Publisher has web capabilities and graphic tools that make it easy to create multipage web sites for your business or personal use. You can create professional-looking web sites with attractive backgrounds, useful Navigation bars, and interesting links. You can test a finished web site with an Internet browser, and then publish the web site to the Internet so that your customers and friends can access it.

Planning a Web Site

The steps in planning a web site are similar to planning a publication, but with important differences. The following are questions to consider when planning a web site.

- **What is the goal of your web site?** Are you trying to sell a product, or persuade or inform your audience? Answers to these questions help a business decide whether its web site should provide information, be an electronic product catalog, or be another type of web site.

- **Who is your target audience?** The more you can define your ideal audience, the more you can tailor the design, content, and access to your web site so that it is appealing. This may influence the choice of design elements, the amount of text included on each page, and the degree of interactivity in the web site.

- **What are your constraints?** Constraints to consider include financial limitations, development staff (designers, programmers), maintenance staff (e-mail responses if used), privacy issues (guarding customers' personal information), security issues (preventing hacking), web site transactions (processing orders, using credit cards), customer service (customer support, warranties, returns, and so on), and foreign language services.

- **What customer/reader response do you want?** Will your web site provide information or do you want feedback? If you want visitors to interact with your site, what structure should the feedback take? Do you want e-mail inquiries for additional information such as a brochure or catalog? Do you want to collect credit card information? Answers to these questions will help you decide on the desired effect of your web site.

- **What will you do with the responses?** If you offer a product in exchange for money, you must be able to deliver. If you don't have enough merchandise for a timely response, you may risk alienating potential customers. You should decide on adequate resources to deal with potential responses your web site generates.

Designing a Web Site

The next step in creating a web site is the design phase. The following are steps you should include in the design of your web site.

- **Create a sketch of your web site.** The sketch should include a list of the key elements to appear on each web page. This information can include a title, an introductory paragraph, links to other sites, contact information, and graphics and pictures.

- **Decide on the number of web pages.** Will these pages be linked? It should be easy for your web site visitors to jump from one web page to another.

- **Add backgrounds, graphics and design elements.** Publisher provides more than 200 backgrounds you can use to make visually appealing web pages. Graphics can enhance your web site by breaking up blocks of text. You can use pictures, clip art, or any other type of graphic. You can also use the Design Gallery to add elements designed for your web pages. The Objects toolbar contains additional buttons to add web-related elements such as response forms and Navigation bars.

- **Add links to other web sites.** You can also add links to other web site locations that will be of interest to your web site visitors. You may want to list your customers and add links to their web sites after getting permission from them.

- **Preview your web pages.** Publisher shows you exactly how your web page will look by allowing you to view it in a browser (much like an e-mail letter) during its creation. It is a good idea to preview your work during the creation phase. Ask yourself, if you were a customer or web site visitor, would you find the web pages appealing, and easy to read and navigate?

- **Test the links.** If your web pages include links to other web sites, you want to make sure that the links are correct. You should periodically check the links to make sure they still work correctly.

Creating a Web Site Publication

Publisher has a special set of templates for creating web site publications. You can use the Easy Web Site Builder to help you create your web site. It allows you to choose the number and type of web pages to include in your web site. If you decide not to use the Easy Web Site Builder, you can always add new pages once you create the web site publication.

The first page is the homepage. The homepage is the top-level page for your web site. When you send customers or web site visitors the URL for your web site, you are sending them the address of this homepage.

A Web Tools toolbar displays when you are creating your web site publication. From this toolbar, you can easily edit, preview, and publish your web site. You can also add hyperlinks, online forms, and bookmarks.

You can redisplay the Easy Web Site Builder at any time to add more pages. This feature only adds pages; it does not remove them. You can also manually add pages and delete pages if you change your mind.

The Web Tools toolbar displays when your web site publication opens.

The homepage gives you helpful instructions on what data content and pictures to include.

The Navigation bar lists the various web pages in the web site.

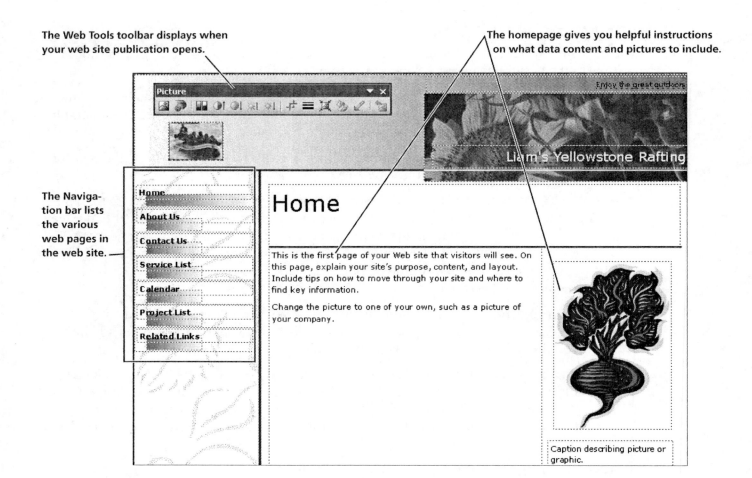

QR

QUICK REFERENCE: CREATING A WEB SITE

Task	Procedure
Create a web site	■ Select the Web Sites publication type.
	■ Select a design.
	■ Choose a Color Scheme and a Font Scheme.
	■ Create a Business Information Set.
	■ Choose a Navigation bar location and, if desired, check the Easy Web Site Builder.
Delete a web page	■ Display the page to delete.
	■ Choose Edit→Delete Page and click Yes.
Add a new web page manually	■ Display the page after which the new page should be inserted.
	■ Choose Insert→Page from the menu bar.
Add a new web page using the Format Publication task pane	■ On the Format Publication task pane, click the Insert a Page link under Web Site Options.
	■ Choose the type of page.

Hands-On 10.1   Create a Web Site Publication

In this exercise, you will create a web site publication for Liam's Yellowstone Rafting business using the Easy Web Site Builder. Then you will delete web pages.

Create a Web site Publication

1. Choose the Web Sites publication type.

2. Click the Classic Designs link, scroll down, and choose the Summer design.

3. Choose Waterfall Color Scheme and the Aspect Verdana Font Scheme.

4. Create the Business Information Set shown in the following illustration. Use the Logo Whitewater Raft file in the Lesson 10 folder for the logo.

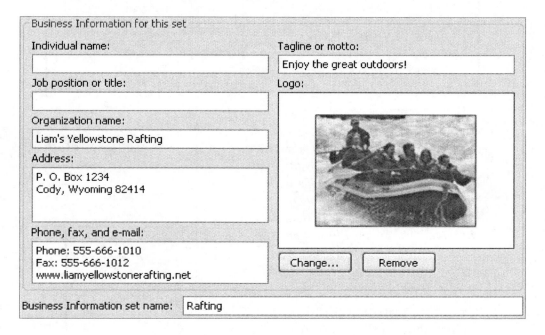

5. At the bottom of the right-hand pane under Navigation bar, choose Vertical Only. *This determines where the Navigation bar will appear on the web page.*

6. If needed, check Use Easy Web Wizard at the bottom of the pane and click the Create button.

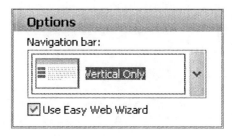

Publisher displays the Easy Web Site Builder dialog box.

Use the Easy Web Site Builder

7. Check the checkboxes for your web site as shown in the following illustration.

Notice that as you check each of the site goals, the design elements such as Home and About Us appear to the right of the goal. These elements will be included in your web site.

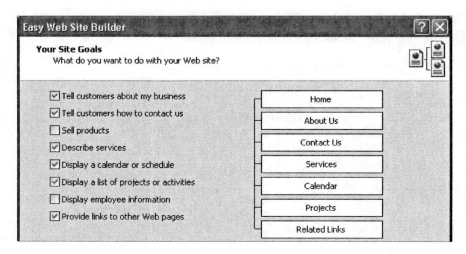

8. When finished, click OK.

A dialog box appears for a few seconds while your web site is being created, and then your web site opens together with the Web Tools toolbar. Your toolbar may be in a different location than that shown in the following illustration. Also notice that there are seven pages in your web site, with each page's topic reflected in the Navigation bar.

9. If need be, drag the Web Tools toolbar above the logo rafting picture so it is not covering anything on the homepage.

10. Take a minute and go to each page and view your initial web site publication.

Delete Web Pages

11. Go to page 6.

12. Choose Edit→Delete Page from the menu bar.

13. When the message appears verifying that you want to delete the page, click Yes.

14. Go to page 4.

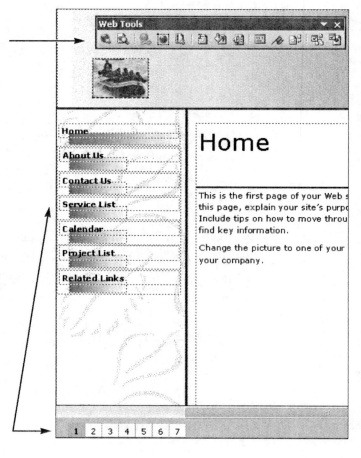

15. Choose Edit→Delete Page from the menu bar.

16. Click Yes when the message appears.
    There are now five pages in your web site publication.

17. Save your web site publication as **Rafting Web Site** in the Lesson 10 folder.
    Keep your publication open for the next exercise.

Editing the Web Site Publication

Once you create the web publication, you can replace the generic text and graphics with your own. You can customize each web page's layout in a manner similar to customizing a newsletter. Different types of pages have different layout choices. You can also change the background for your web site. The elements that are modified when you apply a background change vary based on the web site template chosen.

The Navigation bar contains hyperlinks to each of your web pages. It is important in multiple page web sites because it allows your customers and readers to move easily among the web pages.

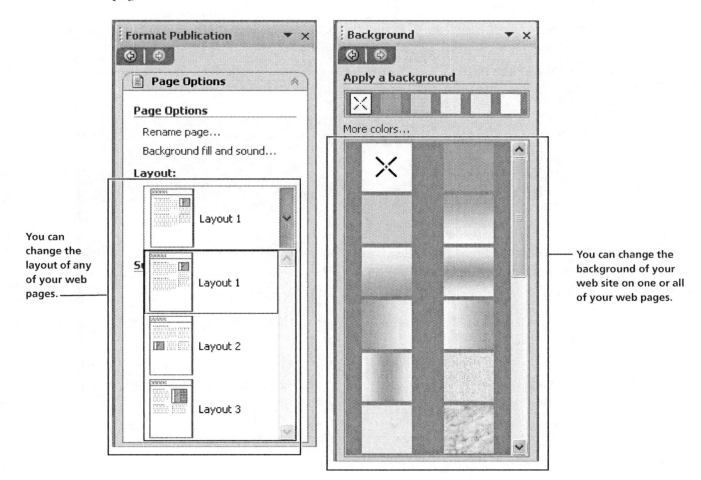

You can change the layout of any of your web pages.

You can change the background of your web site on one or all of your web pages.

QUICK REFERENCE: EDITING THE WEB SITE PUBLICATION	
Task	**Procedure**
Change a page layout	■ Display the page you want to change.
	■ On the Format Publication task pane, click the Page Options drop-down arrow.
	■ Choose a different layout.
Change the background of a Navigation bar	■ Click the Background button on the Web Tools toolbar.
	■ Choose a different background.

Hands-On 10.2   Edit the Web Site Publication

In this exercise, you will edit the homepage, change the background, edit the second and third pages, and change the page layout for the fourth page.

Edit the Home Page

1. Go to page 1.

2. Delete the graphic of a flower underneath the text box that says *Liam's Yellowstone Rafting*.

3. Move the *Liam's Yellowstone Rafting* text box above the logo picture in the upper-left corner of the page and change the font color to Accent 1.

4. Insert the Home Page Rafting picture file from your Lesson 10 folder. Resize and move the picture to this approximate location and size.

5. Click to select *Home* in the Home text box (not Home on the Navigation bar) and type **Liam's Whitewater Adventure**.

6. Click the text in the text box below *Liam's Whitewater Adventure* to select it.

7. Choose Insert→Text File from the menu bar and insert the Home Page Text file from the Lesson 10 folder.

8. Delete the graphic to the right of the text inserted in the step 7 and replace it with the Home Page Canyon file in the Lesson 10 folder. Resize and move the picture to the approximate size and location of the deleted graphic.

9. Replace the caption text below this graphic with **The Yellowstone River**. Change the font to 10 pt bold and centered.

The Yellowstone
River

Change the Background

10. Click the Background ⬛ button on the Web Tools toolbar.
The Background task pane displays to the left of your web site publication.

11. Follow these steps to choose a different background:

Ⓐ **Scroll down to display these backgrounds.**

Ⓑ **Click the drop-down arrow on Texture Fill (Water Droplets) and choose Apply to All Pages.**

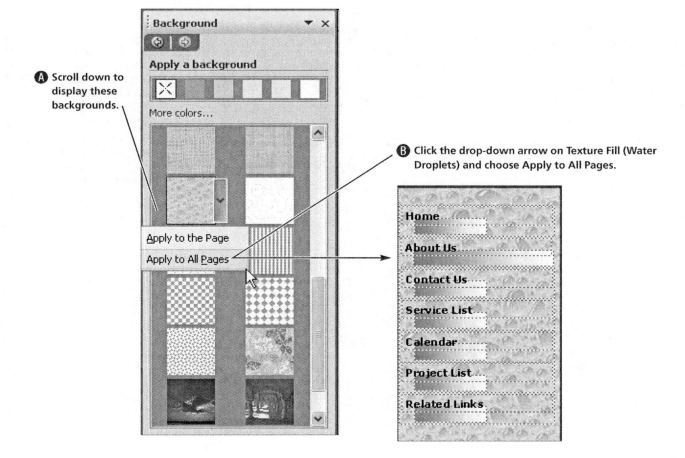

The new background now appears in each Navigation bar in your web site publication.

12. Follow these steps to switch to the Format Publication task pane:

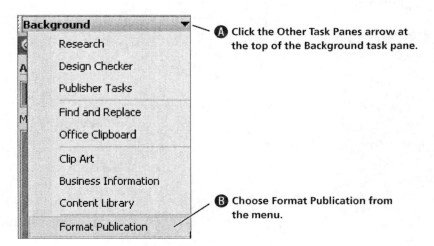

Ⓐ Click the Other Task Panes arrow at the top of the Background task pane.

Ⓑ Choose Format Publication from the menu.

Edit the Second Web Page

13. Go to page 2.

14. Delete the flower picture underneath *Liam's Yellowstone Rafting* text box.

15. Follow these steps to edit the page 2 web page:

Ⓐ Replace the default text with the About Us Text file from the Lesson 10 folder.

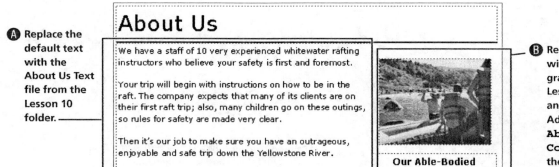

Ⓑ Replace the turnip image with the Rafting Staff graphic file from the Lesson 10 folder. Resize and move it as necessary. Add the caption, **Our Able-Bodied Conner**, then change the font to 10 pt bold and center the text.

Edit the Third Web Page

16. Go to page 3.

17. Delete the map picture underneath *Liam's Yellowstone Rafting* text box.

18. Follow these steps to edit page 3:

(A) Replace the default text with `Right Outside Yellowstone National Park`.

(B) Replace the default text with the Contact Us Text file in the Lesson 10 folder.

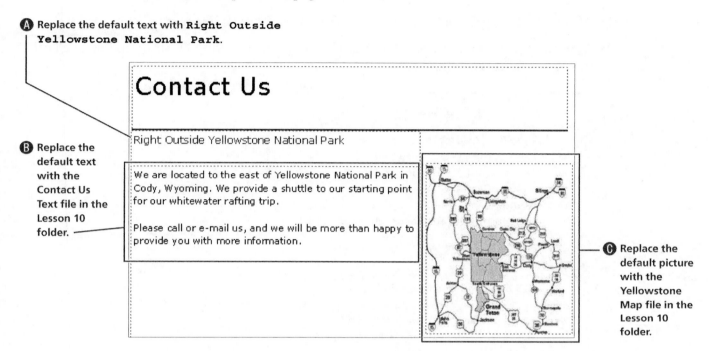

(C) Replace the default picture with the Yellowstone Map file in the Lesson 10 folder.

19. Scroll down and follow these steps to replace text shown in the following figure:

(A) Replace the default text with the text shown here.

(B) Replace the default text with the text shown here.

Change a Page Layout

20. Go to page 4 to display the Calendar Web page.

21. Click Page Options at the top of the task pane.

22. Click the Layout drop-down arrow and choose Layout 4.

23. Delete the flower graphic underneath *Liam's Yellowstone Rafting* text box.

24. Type the text in the three text boxes as shown in the following illustration. Delete all other text boxes in this column.

Schedule of Events

- **7/1-31/07**—Awesome 1-day whitewater rafting trips every day in July down the Yellowstone River. Meet at our Cody office at 6 am—shuttle to Yellowstone River. Call 555-666-1010 for more information and reservations.

- **7/15-31/07**—Incredible 1-day hikes through Yellowstone National Park. Meet at the Gardiner Entrance at 8 am each morning. Call 555-666-1010 for more information and reservations.

- **7/2-30/07**—Fishing schools include a morning of classroom instruction covering equipment, fly selection, entomology and reading river currents. Call 555-666-1010 for more information and reservations.

25. Save your changes.
Keep your web site publication open for the next exercise.

Adding Hyperlinks

Each time you click an area on a web page and jump to another location, such as another web site or a different location within your web site, you are using a hyperlink, which is an electronic connection to those locations. You can also create links to e-mail addresses and to documents on a specific computer. You learned to create text hyperlinks in e-mails in Lesson 7, Designing a Newsletter, so you already have some experience in this area. Publisher automatically places hyperlinks in the Navigation bar.

Adding a Hot Spot

A *hot spot* is a picture or graphic that contains a hyperlink. Your web site visitors can click the hot spot in the same way they click text hyperlinks. Alternative text is displayed for web site visitors who have turned off graphics or for those who use text-only browsers.

The mouse pointer changes to a hand when positioned on a text or picture hyperlink. The change in the mouse pointer icon is called a mouse-over event. *Event* is a term used in web technology. Clicking a hyperlink or button is considered an event.

The hand pointer indicates a picture hot spot.

This picture hot spot launches an e-mail.

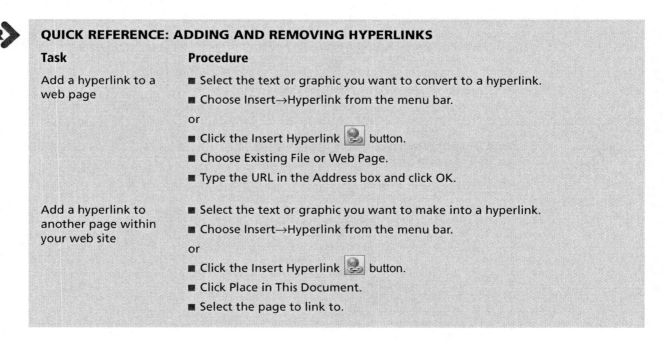

QUICK REFERENCE: ADDING AND REMOVING HYPERLINKS

Task	Procedure
Add a hyperlink to a web page	■ Select the text or graphic you want to convert to a hyperlink. ■ Choose Insert→Hyperlink from the menu bar. or ■ Click the Insert Hyperlink 🔲 button. ■ Choose Existing File or Web Page. ■ Type the URL in the Address box and click OK.
Add a hyperlink to another page within your web site	■ Select the text or graphic you want to make into a hyperlink. ■ Choose Insert→Hyperlink from the menu bar. or ■ Click the Insert Hyperlink 🔲 button. ■ Click Place in This Document. ■ Select the page to link to.

QUICK REFERENCE: ADDING AND REMOVING HYPERLINKS (CONTINUED)

Task	Procedure
Remove a hyperlink	■ Select the text or graphic that is hyperlinked. ■ Choose Insert→Hyperlink and click Remove Link.
Create a hot spot in a publication	■ Right-click on the graphic and choose Hyperlink on the shortcut menu. ■ Click where to link to, such as E-mail Address or Existing File or Web Page.
Create a hot spot in a web page	■ Select the graphic you will use as the hot spot. ■ Click the Hot Spot ▣ button on the Objects toolbar. ■ Drag to create a hot spot over a section of the graphic. ■ The Insert Hyperlink dialog box appears when you release the mouse button. ■ Insert at hyperlink for the hot spot.

Hands-On 10.3   Add Hyperlinks

In this exercise, you will add a hyperlink to an external web site. Then you will create a hyperlink to another page within your web site publication.

1. Go to page 5, the Related Links web page.

2. Select and delete the graphic in the upper-right corner of the page.

Create a Hyperlink to a Web Site

3. Click on the text *Web Site or Page Name 1* to select it and replace it with **Yellowstone National Park.**

4. Select the text you just typed.

5. Click the Insert Hyperlink 🌐 button on the Standard toolbar.
   The Insert Hyperlink dialog box appears.

6. Follow these steps to create the hyperlink:

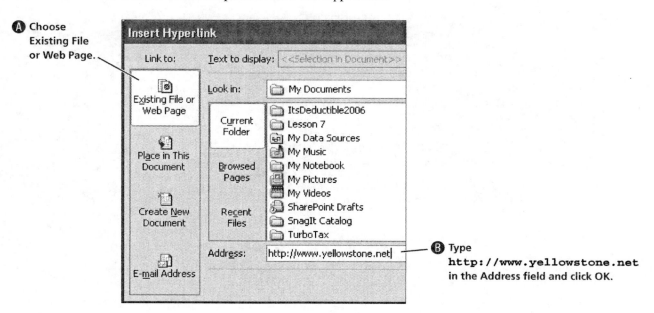

Ⓐ Choose Existing File or Web Page.

Ⓑ Type **http://www.yellowstone.net** in the Address field and click OK.

7. Select the default text and replace with the text shown in the following illustration.

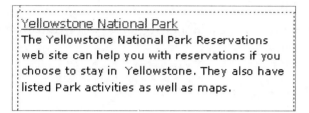

Yellowstone National Park
The Yellowstone National Park Reservations web site can help you with reservations if you choose to stay in Yellowstone. They also have listed Park activities as well as maps.

Create a Hyperlink to a Page on Your Web Site

8. Click the text *Web Site or Page Name 2* in the text box to the right of the Yellowstone National Park hyperlink and type **Map of the Yellowstone Area**.

9. Select the text and click the Insert Hyperlink button on the Standard toolbar.

10. Follow these steps to create the hyperlink to page 3 of your web site:

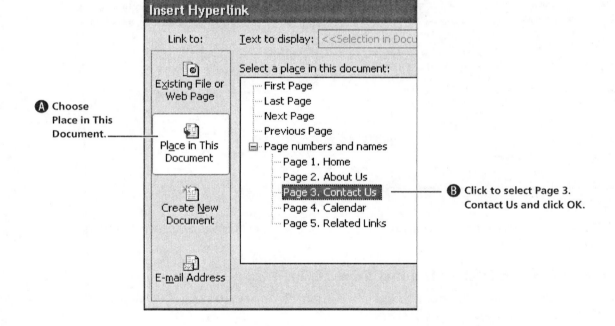

Ⓐ Choose Place in This Document.

Ⓑ Click to select Page 3. Contact Us and click OK.

11. Select the default text and replace it with the text shown in the following figure.

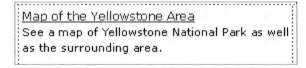

Map of the Yellowstone Area
See a map of Yellowstone National Park as well as the surrounding area.

12. Delete any remaining unused text boxes on this page.

Add a Hot Spot

13. Go to your Home page on page 1.

14. Right-click the picture of the rafters in the upper-right corner of your Home page and click Hyperlink on the shortcut menu.
The Insert Hyperlink dialog box displays.

15. Follow these steps to finish creating the hot spot:

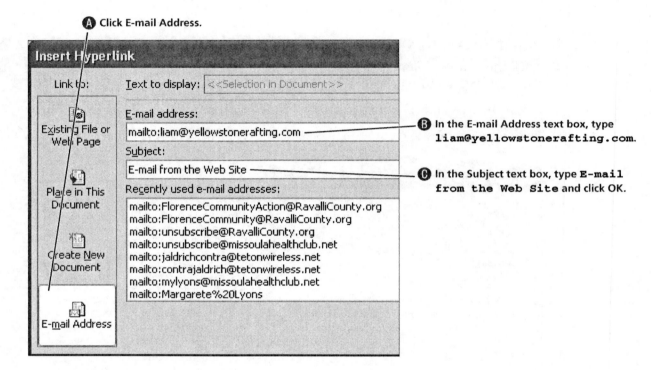

Ⓐ Click E-mail Address.

Ⓑ In the E-mail Address text box, type **liam@yellowstonerafting.com.**

Ⓒ In the Subject text box, type **E-mail from the Web Site** and click OK.

This picture is now a hot spot or picture hyperlink that, when clicked, opens the user's e-mail message window.

Add Alternative Text to the Hot Spot

16. Right-click the same picture and choose Format Picture on the shortcut menu.
The Format Picture dialog box displays.

17. Click the Web tab.

18. In the Alternative Text box type **Click the picture of the fun-loving rafters to e-mail Liam's Yellowstone Rafting.**

!TIP! *Alternative text appears to a web site visitor who has turned off graphics or who uses a text-only browser.*

19. Click OK.

20. Save your changes.
Keep your web site publication open for the next exercise.

Adding a Web Form

In the early days of designing web pages, adding a web form to a web page was not easy. Publisher, however, now makes it easy for anyone to add a web form.

A web form allows web site visitors to fill out information online on your web site. The information is then collected and stored on a web server or e-mailed to you, depending on your preference. A web server is a computer that stores your web site and makes it available on the Internet.

The easiest way to create a web form in Publisher is to add a page to the site that uses one of the form layouts. You can choose from one of three forms: Sign-up form, Response form, or Order form. You can then customize your form to your needs. Publisher also allows you to insert a web form on an existing page.

Customizing a Web Form

Web forms contain form controls that are individual boxes and buttons used by web site visitors to enter data. This data is then transmitted to your web site via a submit button.

Using Form Controls

Form controls can include a checkbox, which is a square box that presents a yes/no choice, and an option button, which is a round button that presents one choice. A text area allows the user to enter multiple lines, such as an address.

You can add new form controls or delete or move existing ones. You can also change their properties. For example, you may want to include a text box that allows your customers to type in their comments and then specify the maximum number of characters they can type.

Set the Data Retrieval Method

Every web form must have a *Submit* command button to send the information that your web site visitor enters in your form. You set properties for the Submit button that determine what happens to the form information when the Submit button is clicked. The submitted information can be saved in a data file on your web server, sent to you in an e-mail, or saved using a special program from your Internet Service Provider (ISP).

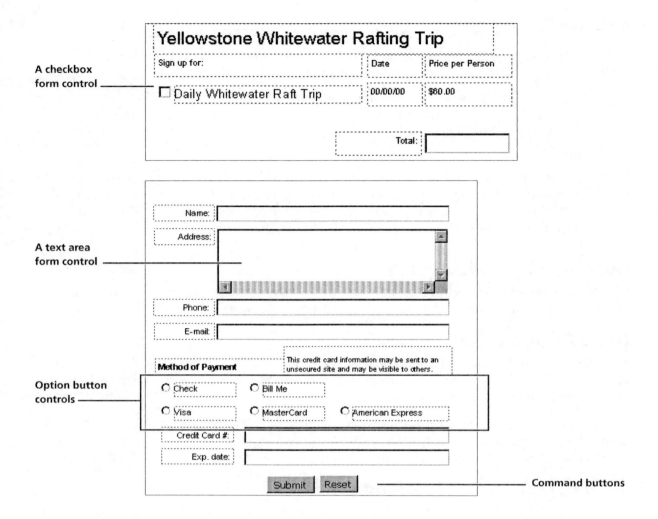

A checkbox form control

A text area form control

Option button controls

Command buttons

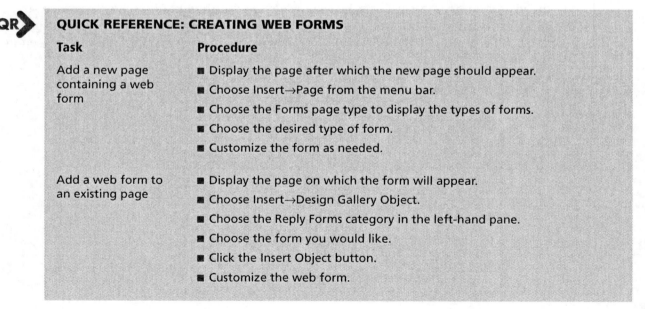

QUICK REFERENCE: CREATING WEB FORMS

Task	Procedure
Add a new page containing a web form	■ Display the page after which the new page should appear. ■ Choose Insert→Page from the menu bar. ■ Choose the Forms page type to display the types of forms. ■ Choose the desired type of form. ■ Customize the form as needed.
Add a web form to an existing page	■ Display the page on which the form will appear. ■ Choose Insert→Design Gallery Object. ■ Choose the Reply Forms category in the left-hand pane. ■ Choose the form you would like. ■ Click the Insert Object button. ■ Customize the web form.

QR

QUICK REFERENCE: CREATING WEB FORMS (CONTINUED)

Task	Procedure
Delete a form control	■ If the control is grouped with others that you do not want to delete, click the Ungroup button. ■ Click the form control to select it. ■ Press the ⌈Delete⌉ key.
Change a form control's properties	■ Click an individual control to select it. ■ Right-click the form control. ■ Choose Format Form Properties from the menu. ■ Set the properties for that control.
Set the data retrieval method	■ Click any control to select it. ■ Right-click the control. ■ Choose Format Form Properties from the menu. ■ Click the Form Properties button. ■ Choose one of the data retrieval methods. ■ Set the properties for the chosen method.

 ## Hands-On 10.4   Add a Web Form

In this exercise, you will add a Web Sign-up Form as a new web page, delete and move form controls, change a form control text box's properties, and set the data retrieval method.

Add a Web Form

1. Go to page 5.

2. Choose Insert→Page from the menu bar.

3. Choose the Forms page type, choose the form type Sign-up Form, and click OK.

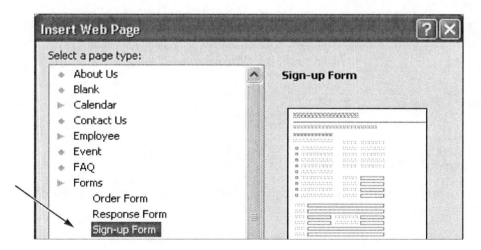

A dialog box briefly appears saying that the publication is being changed. When finished, a new Sign-up Form page appears as page 6 of your web site.

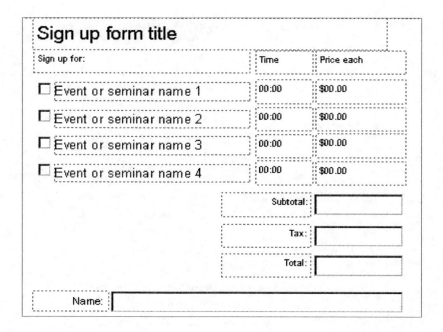

4. Select and delete the graphic in the upper-right corner of page 6.

Edit the Forms Link on the Navigation Bar

In this part of the exercise, you will rearrange the order of the links on the Navigation bar and modify the text in a link.

5. Click anywhere on the Navigation bar to select it.

6. Right-click on a text box in the Navigation bar and choose Navigation Bar Properties on the shortcut menu.

7. The Navigation Bar Properties dialog box displays.

8. Under Links, choose Form and click the Move Up button.
Form should now be located above Related Links.

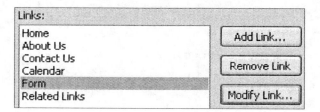

9. Click the Modify Link button.

10. In the Text to Display box, select the text and type **Raft Trip Sign Up**.

11. Click OK twice.
The link on the Navigation bar changes to Raft Trip Sign Up.

Delete Form Controls

12. Follow these steps to select multiple form controls:

Ⓐ Place your mouse pointer to the left of this sold blue line directly to the left of *Event or seminar name 2*. Be careful not to place your mouse on the right side, which will move the sign-up form's white background instead of selecting the text boxes.

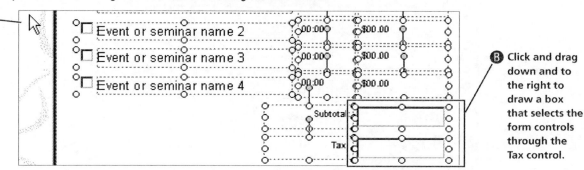

Ⓑ Click and drag down and to the right to draw a box that selects the form controls through the Tax control.

13. Press the ⌦ Delete ⌫ key.
This deletes the selected form controls.

Move Form Controls

14. Follow these steps to move the Total form control:

Ⓐ Place your mouse pointer to the left of the solid blue line, directly to the left of Total, and click and drag down and to the right far enough to select the Total text box and the form control box to the right of it. ⎯⎯⎯

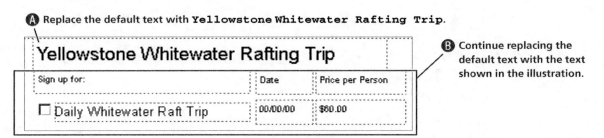

Ⓑ With the two items selected, place your mouse pointer anywhere on the controls until your mouse turns to a move pointer and drag *up* to approximately this location. Click in the scratch area to deselect the controls. ⎯⎯⎯

Edit Form Controls

15. Follow these steps to edit the text:

Ⓐ Replace the default text with `Yellowstone Whitewater Rafting Trip`.

Ⓑ Continue replacing the default text with the text shown in the illustration.

Yellowstone Whitewater Rafting Trip		
Sign up for:	Date	Price per Person
☐ Daily Whitewater Raft Trip	00/00/00	$60.00

Change the Total Form Text Box Properties

16. Double-click in the blank text box to the right of the text box labeled Total.
The Text Box Properties dialog box displays.

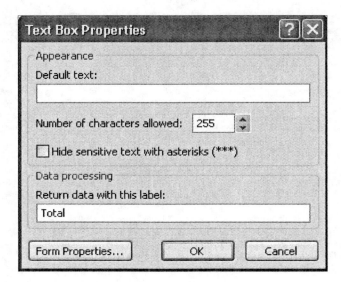

17. In the Number of characters allowed, select 255, type **10**, and click OK.

Set the Data Retrieval Method

18. Scroll down until the Submit button appears.

19. Double-click on the Submit button.
The Command Button Properties dialog box displays.

20. Click the Form Properties button.

21. Follow these steps to fill out the form properties.

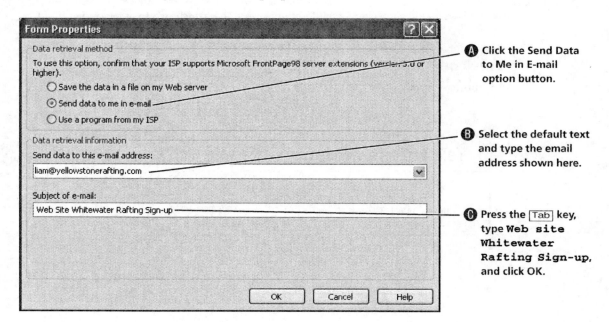

A Click the Send Data to Me in E-mail option button.

B Select the default text and type the email address shown here.

C Press the ⟦Tab⟧ key, type **Web site Whitewater Rafting Sign-up**, and click OK.

22. Click OK again to close the Command Button Properties dialog box.

23. Save your changes.

    Keep your web site publication open for the next exercise.

Previewing and Publishing a Web Site

It is important to preview and examine your web site before publishing it to the Internet. You can preview your web site using Publisher's Web Page Preview feature and correct any errors before your web site becomes public on the Internet.

Publishing a Web Site

Once you preview the web site, you can publish it to the Internet, which means transferring the publication files to a web server. The actual publishing of a web site is beyond the scope of this book; however, the following instructions are included to make you aware of the steps involved.

Saving a Web Site Publication as a Web Page

The first step in transferring your files to a web server is to contact your Internet Service Provider (ISP) and obtain a Uniform Resource Location (URL) address for your files. Once you have done this, you are ready to create a network place in Publisher. A network place is a shortcut to a location on the web server where your pages reside. The Publisher steps to transfer your files are the following:

■ Choose File→Publish to the Web from the menu bar.

■ Click OK to close the Publish to the Web warning box, if necessary.

■ In the Publish to the Web dialog box, click My Network Places.

■ Type the URL of your web site as the File Name and press Enter to connect to the server.

■ At this point you will be prompted for a username and password. You must have a username and password that is valid for this specific server.

■ The contents of your web server will appear in the window. Save your web pages and they will be saved directly to the server.

 TIP! *Some versions of Windows include a Web Publishing Wizard that you can use to transfer a single file or a single folder to a web server. Also, if you are familiar with file transfer programs (FTP), you can download free or shareware FTP programs from most large file archives on the Internet, such as http://shareware.cnet.com.*

Publishing to the Web Incrementally

After you publish your web site, you will probably make changes to your files. As you make these changes, you can publish them incrementally to your web site. This means that you only need to republish the files that you have made changes to. You will want to make sure your Publisher web options are set to publish incrementally.

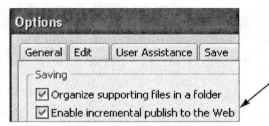

- Choose Tools→Options from the menu bar.

- Click the Web and choose Enable Incremental Publish to the Web.

QUICK REFERENCE: PREVIEWING AND PUBLISHING A WEB SITE

Task	Procedure
Preview a web site	■ Click the Web Page Preview 🔍 button. ■ Click the links on the Navigation bar to go to each web page.
Publish a new web site	■ Click the Publish to the Web 🔍 button on the Web Tools toolbar. ■ Click My Network Places. ■ Type the web address in the File Name box and press Enter. ■ If prompted, enter your user name and password and click OK. ■ Navigate to the folder on the web server where you want to save your publication files. ■ Type a file name in the File Name box and click Save.

Hands-On 10.5   Preview a Web Site

In this exercise, you will preview your web site and check your links.

1. Go to page 1.

2. Click the Web Page Preview 🔍 button on the Web Tools toolbar.
   A dialog box appears briefly. Then the first page of your web site displays in your browser window.

Checking Links

3. On page 1, hover your mouse pointer over the rafting picture until it turns into a hand and click.
   An e-mail should open addressed to liam@yellowstonerafting.com.

4. Close this e-mail without sending and return to your browser window.

5. Click each link on the Navigation bar to preview each web page.
   Your web pages may look different than they do in Publisher, depending upon which browser is installed on your computer.

6. Close your browser window.

7. Close and save your web site publication.

Converting a Print Publication to a Web Page

You can convert existing business publications to web pages. Publisher makes it easy to convert a publication such as a brochure. First, you need to convert your publication to web format. In this format, you can then change web page titles and preview the web page. When you change a web page title, the title will appear in the title bar of your browser when the page is displayed on your web site. At this point, though, the web page still needs to be saved in a web format.

Publisher allows saving the web page in two different formats. A web page can be saved as a Single File Web Page in a special format called MIME HTML (MHTML, often shortened as MHT) that contains the entire publication in a single file. No folder for supporting files such as graphics is needed. The second format is Web Page, Filtered. This format creates a version in HTML format that does not have any Publisher codes. It is a smaller file, and it creates a folder for any support files such as graphics.

QR>

QUICK REFERENCE: CONVERTING A PUBLICATION TO A WEB PAGE

Task	Procedure
Convert a publication to a web page	■ Open the publication. ■ Choose File→Convert to Web Publication from the menu bar. ■ Click the Yes or No option button to save the publication again or not. ■ Click Next. ■ Click Yes or No to add a Navigation bar or not. In a multipage publication choose Yes; in a single-page publication choose No. ■ Click Finish.
Change a web page title	■ Click the Web Page Options button on the Web Tools toolbar. ■ Type a new title in the Page Title box.
Save a publication as a web page	■ Click File→Save As from the menu bar. ■ Click the drop-down arrow to open the Save As Type list. ■ Choose Web Page. Depending on your Windows file management settings, either *.htm or *html may appear. ■ If desired, type a different filename in the File Name box, and click Save.

Hands-On 10.6   Convert a Brochure to a Web Page

In this exercise, you will start creating a brochure for Liam's Yellowstone Rafting. Then you will use the draft to test the conversion process.

Create a Brochure

1. Create a Bounce Brochure.

2. Save the brochure as **Web Site Conversion Brochure** in the Lesson 10 folder.

Convert a Print Publication to Web Format

3. Choose File→Convert to a Web Publication from the menu bar.
   The Convert to Web Publication dialog box displays.

4. Click the Yes, Save My Print Publication... option button, and click Next.

5. Click the Yes Add a Navigation Bar option button because there are two pages in the brochure, and then click Finish.
   Notice that the Web Tools toolbar appears with your web page.

Change the Web Page Titles

6. Click the Web Page Options button on the Web Tools toolbar.

7. In the Web Page Options Page Title box, type **Liam's Yellowstone Rafting** and click OK.

8. Go to page 2 and again click the Web Page Options button, type **Join Us for Whitewater Rafting** in the Page Title box, and click OK.

9. Go back to page 1 and click the Web Page Preview button on the Web Tools toolbar.
   The two Page Title buttons in the middle of the preview page will not appear when your web pages appear on your web site. Notice that the page title, Liam's Yellowstone Rafting, *appears in the title bar along with the name of your browser.*

   Liam's Yellowstone Rafting - Mozilla

10. Click the Page Title buttons to switch from one web page to another to preview and close the browser window.

Save the Publication as a Single File Web Page

The brochure is now formatted for web use, but it is still a standard publication. You will need to save it in web format to become a real web page

11. Choose File→Save As from the menu bar.

12. Navigate to the Lesson 10 folder.

13. Click the Save As Type drop-down arrow to open the list.

14. Choose Single File Web Page and click Save.

15. Delete the Rafting Business Information Set.

16. Close your web page to return to the main Publisher screen.

 # Concepts Review

True/False Questions

1. The more you can define your ideal audience for your web site, the more you can tailor the design and content so that your web site is appealing.   TRUE   FALSE

2. You can add elements designed for your web pages from the Design Gallery.   TRUE   FALSE

3. The Easy Web Site Builder allows you to choose the number and type of web pages to include in your web site.   TRUE   FALSE

4. The Navigation bar can contain hyperlinks to other web sites.   TRUE   FALSE

5. You can customize each web page's layout.   TRUE   FALSE

6. You can only create hyperlinks to your own web pages and documents located on a specific computer.   TRUE   FALSE

7. A picture or graphic that contains a hyperlink is known as a jump link.   TRUE   FALSE

8. Every web form must have a submit command button to send the information that your web site visitor enters into your form.   TRUE   FALSE

9. After you save your publication in a web format, you can then change web page titles and preview the web page.   TRUE   FALSE

10. When converting an existing publication to a web page, you can only save your file in a Web page, Filtered file format.   TRUE   FALSE

Multiple Choice Questions

1. The first page of a web site is known as the _____.
   a. related links page
   b. homepage
   c. contact us page
   d. web form page

2. Which of the following is not included in web site design?
   a. Decide on the number of pages.
   b. Add links to other web sites.
   c. Preview your web pages.
   d. Determine the constraints.

3. What can you not do from the Web Tools toolbar?
   a. Add a new web page.
   b. Add hyperlinks.
   c. Publish your web site.
   d. Change the background.

4. Which of the following is not a Web Form?
   a. Response form
   b. Order form
   c. Maintenance form
   d. Sign-up form

 # Skill Builders

Skill Builder 10.1   Create Your Personal Web site

You are seeking a job as an elementary or middle school principal. In this exercise, you will create your own personal web site that contains your résumé and includes a Business Information Set.

1. Choose the Kid Stuff Classic Design web site from the main Publisher screen.

2. Choose the Cranberry Color Scheme and Binary Verdana Font Scheme.

3. Choose a Vertical Only Navigation bar and uncheck the Easy Web Wizard.

Create a Business Information Set

4. Create a Business Information Set with your contact information. The logo is located in the Lesson 10 folder as sb-School Picture.

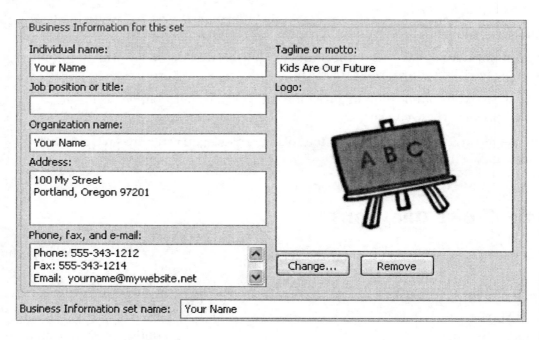

5. Save your Business Information Set and click Create.
   Your one-page web site publication opens to your homepage.

Edit the Text

6. Select the text in the text box below Home and replace with the text shown in the following illustration. Also replace the caption text below the owl.

As both an Elementary and Middle-School Principal as well as a math and science teacher for the last 17 years, I have had an ongoing passion. And that passion is to see your school children discover their love of learning.

I am currently looking for my next Elementary or Middle-School principal opportunity on the West Coast where I can make a contribution to your school children and your community.

Please call or e-mail me directly.

Everyone Loves a Bookworm!

7. Save your web site publication as **sb-My Web Site** in the Lesson 10 folder.

Add a Page to the Web site

8. Click the Insert a Page link on the Web Site Options section of the Format Publication task pane.

9. Click Project List/Resume in the Insert Web Page dialog box and choose Project List.

10. Click OK.

Edit the Text

11. Replace the Project List heading with **Résumé**.

12. Delete the text box below *Résumé*.

13. Replace the default text with the text shown in the following illustration; delete the More Details text boxes and the Project Name 5 text boxes.

Westport Middle School Principal

2000-2007 created innovative school programs; Principal of the Year

Evanston Elementary Principal

1995-2000 redesigned school curriculum; Illinois School of the Year

San Francisco 8th Grade Teacher

1990-1995 taught math and science; 1995 Teacher of the Year.

Stanford University

1987 B.S. Mathematics; 1989 Masters in Education

14. Delete the Business Information Set.

15. Save your changes.
Keep your web site publication open for the next exercise.

Skill Builder 10.2   Add a Hyperlink

In this exercise, you will add an e-mail button to make it easy for visitors to your web site to contact you.

Before You Begin: *You must complete Skill Builder 10.1 before beginning this exercise. The sb-My Web Site file should be open on your screen.*

1. Go to page 1.

2. Click the Design Gallery Object  button on the Objects toolbar.

3. Click the Buttons category, choose the Half Capsule E-mail, and click Insert Object.
   The e-mail object appears in the center of your web page.

4. Drag the e-mail object below the last line in the main text box.

Add a Hyperlink to the Object

5. Select the E-mail text in the object.

6. Right-click and choose Hyperlink from the shortcut menu.

7. Click E-mail Address under Link To at the left side of the dialog box.

8. Type **yourname@mywebsite.net** in the E-mail Address box and click OK.

9. Save your changes.
   Keep your web site publication open for the next exercise.

Skill Builder 10.3   Add a Web Form

In this exercise, you will add a response form so visitors can contact you.

Before You Begin: You must complete Skill Builder 10.2 before beginning this exercise. The sb-My Web Site file should be open on your screen.

1. Go to page 2 of the web site publication.

2. Click the Insert a Page link in the Format Publication task pane under Web Site Options.

3. Choose Forms, choose Response Form from the Select a Page Type list, and click OK.

Modify Navigation Bar Properties

4. Right-click on the perimeter of the Navigation bar and choose Navigation Bar Properties from the menu.

5. Choose the Project List link and click the Modify Link button.

6. Replace the default text in the Text to Display box with **Résumé** and click OK twice.

7. Select the Form link and click the Modify Link button.

8. Replace the default text in the Text to Display box with **Response Form** and click OK twice.

9. Replace the default response form text with the text shown in the following illustration.

Modify Submit Button Properties

10. Scroll down and right-click on the Submit button.

11. Choose Format Form Properties from the shortcut menu and click the Form Properties button.
The Form Properties dialog box appears.

12. Choose Send Data to Me in E-mail and type **yourname@mywebsite.net** in the Send Data to This E-mail Address box.

13. Click OK twice.

14. On the Web Tools toolbar, click the Web Page Preview button to preview your web site publication.

15. Close and save your changes.

Skill Builder 10.4 Convert a Newsletter to Web Format

In this exercise, you will open a newsletter and convert it to a web page. Then you will preview the web page.

1. Open sb-Convert Newsletter from your Lesson 10 folder.

2. Choose File→Convert to a Web Publication from the menu bar.

3. Choose the Yes option to save your print publication and click Next.

4. Choose the Yes, Add a Navigation Bar option and click Finish.

5. Make sure you are on page 1.

Modify the Page Titles

6. Click the Web Page Options 🖳 button on the Web Tools toolbar.

7. Replace the default Page Title text with **Holiday Employee Thank You** and click OK.

8. Go to page 2 and, again, click the Web Page Options 🖳 button.

9. Replace the default Page Title text with **Happy Holidays!** and click OK.

Preview the Web Page

10. Go back to page 1 and click the Web Page Preview 🔍 button on the Web Tools toolbar.
   Notice there are two Page Title buttons in the middle of the preview page. These will not be visible when your web pages appear on your web site. Also notice that the page title, Holiday Employee Thank You, *appears in the title bar along with the name of your browser.*

   > 📺 **Holiday Employee Thank You - Mozilla**

11. Click the bottom Page Title button to see the other page title in the browser.

12. Close the browser.

13. Save the file as **sb-Newsletter Filtered Web Page**.

14. Close your newsletter and return to the main Publisher screen.

 # Assessments

Assessment 10.1   Customize a Vacation Web Site

In this exercise, you will open a web site and customize it.

1. Open as-Vacations Web Site from your Lesson 10 folder.

2. Change the Color Scheme to Lagoon and the Font Scheme to Opulent Trebuchet.

3. On page 1, change the background to one you think would look best.

4. Go to page 2, open Design Gallery and add a Framed Oval E-mail button.

5. Drag it down and to the right of the To Contact Us text.

6. Add a hyperlink to the following e-mail address: **vawter@vawtervacations.net**

7. Go to page 4 and delete the Project List page.

8. Edit the Navigation Bar Properties to replace the default Text to Display with **Vacation Sign Up Form**.

9. On page 4, change the background to one you feel would look best.

10. Save your publication.
    Keep your web site publication open for the next exercise.

e-mails

xyz @ micosoft.com

Assessment 10.2   Customize a Web Form

In this exercise you will customize your web site by adding formatting, deleting form controls, changing form control properties and setting the data retrieval method. You will then preview and test your web pages.

Before You Begin: *You must complete Assessment 10.1 before beginning this exercise. The as-Vacations Web file should be open on the screen.*

1. On page 4, search for appropriate clip art and add it to this page.

2. Bold the font and change it to a color of your choice for all four trip names.

3. Change the form control properties for Name form box, to allow 40 characters.

4. Delete all of the form boxes and text boxes from the bottom of the page, starting with Method of Payment, excluding Submit and Reset.

5. Set the Submit button properties retrieval method to Send Data to Me in an E-mail. Use your e-mail address.

6. Preview each of your web pages in your web browser.

7. Test the e-mail link on page 2 to make sure it opens an e-mail addressed to your e-mail account.

8. Go to page 4 and check to make sure you can place check marks in the choice of vacations.

9. Close your browser window.

10. Save and close your web site publication.

Assessment 10.3   Convert a Résumé to a Web Page

In this exercise, you will open a résumé, convert it to a web page, and save it as a single file web page.

1. Open as-Resume in your Lesson 10 folder.

2. Convert it to a web publication, saving it as a print publication.

3. Do not add a Navigation bar.

4. Change the Page Title to **My Résumé**.

5. Preview your web page then close your browser window.

6. Save the résumé as a Single File Web Page.

7. Name the file **as-Resume Web Page**.

8. Close your résumé.

Critical Thinking

Critical Thinking 10.1 Create Eleni's Delectable Pastries Web Site

Your friend, Eleni Ford, has started her own business baking and selling all sorts of delectable dessert pastries. She would like you to set up a web site for her business. In this exercise, you will create a web site for Eleni's Delectable Pastries.

1. Create a web site based on the Gingham design.

2. Choose a font and color scheme that you feel complement Eleni's web site as well as your choice of type of Navigation bar.

3. Create a Business Information Set for Eleni. Use fictional information and make up a catchy tagline. Use the ct-Pastry Chef graphic file in the Lesson 10 folder for the logo.

4. Add one page that informs visitors about Eleni's business.

5. Add two more pages: one to contact Eleni and one for a special offer.

6. Choose a font scheme and background that complements your design.

7. On the homepage and special offer page, use clip art and pictures you find on your own that enhance these pages. Be sure to add captions underneath the clip art or pictures.

8. On the homepage, make up the text in the main text box about Eleni's Pastries.

9. Add a hot spot to the clip art or picture you added to the homepage and link it to Eleni's e-mail address.

10. On the contact page, delete the heading text box and make up contact information below the Contact Us text box. Eleni would like visitors to phone, fax, or e-mail her.

11. On the contact page enter Eleni's contact information. Add whatever formatting you like.

12. Also on the contact page, type in Eleni's address underneath the map and format it so it stands out.

13. On the special offer page, make up the text for the text boxes and the special offer Design Gallery object.

14. Preview your web pages.

15. Save the file as **ct-Pastries Web Site** in the Lesson 10 folder.

16. Close your web site publication.

Critical Thinking 10.2   Create a Family Web Site

You have wanted to create a family web site for several years. You have also volunteered to research places for the family reunion next year and would like to put this information on the web site. In this exercise, you will create a web site about your family.

1. Think about the planning the design of your web site. Create a sketch or outline of what you would like to include.

2. Experiment with the various web site designs until you choose one that best fits the look of your family.

3. Experiment with different color schemes, fonts, and Navigation bar options.

4. Create a Business Information Set with your immediate family's contact information.

5. Your family will be sending you lots of photos in the near future to add to the family web site. Experiment with adding a photo web page.

6. Add a Calendar page and experiment with changing the page layout. Add some fun family events that are coming up that you would like to notify your family about. Experiment with adding different backgrounds.

7. Find some clip art or pictures and add to your web site. Be sure to add captions.

8. Add a hot spot to a clip art image or picture and link it to your e-mail address.

9. Add a new page with Related Links.

10. Change the name of Related Links on the Navigation bar to **Family Reunion.**

11. Research various vacation spots for the family reunion on the Internet, noting down web site links to include on the family web site.

12. On the related links page, create links to these vacation spots and add descriptions to each link.

13. Preview your web page.

14. Test the various links you created.

15. Ask your fellow classmates to review your web site and give you feedback.

16. Delete your Business Information Set.

17. Save your web site as **ct-Family Web Site** in the Lesson 10 folder.

18. Close your web site publication and exit Publisher.

APPENDIX A

Storing Your Exercise Files

This appendix contains an overview for using this book with various file storage media, such as a USB flash drive or hard drive. Detailed instructions for downloading and unzipping the exercise files used with this book appear in exercies for each type of media.

The following topics are addressed in this appendix:

Topic	Description	See Page
Downloading the Student Exercise Files	Retrieving the exercise files and copying them to your file storage location.	332
Using a USB Flash Drive	Storing your work on a USB flash memory drive.	333
Using the Documents Folder	Storing your work in the My Documents folder.	337
Using a Network Folder	Storing your work in a custom folder on a network.	339
Using a Floppy Disk with This Book	Using a floppy disk with this book is not recommended. This topic covers how you can use a floppy with most of the lessons.	340

Downloading the Student Exercise Files

The files needed to complete certain Hands-On, Skill Builder, Assessment, and Critical Thinking exercises are available for download at the Labyrinth website. At the end of each media type topic is an exercise with instructions to copy the files to your computer and prepare them for use with this book.

 NOTE! *It is not possible to store all of the unzipped student exercise files on a floppy disk. See the Using a Floppy Disk with This Book section in this appendix for instructions on using a floppy disk to work with student exercise files.*

Using a USB Flash Drive

NOTE!

Most students using this book store their files on a USB flash drive.

A USB flash drive stores your data on a flash memory chip. You simply plug it in to a USB port on any computer and Windows immediately recognizes it as an additional disk drive. USB flash drives typically can store 256 megabytes (MB) or more. Large capacity USB flash drives can store 1 gigabyte (GB) or more. Flash drive versatility, capacity, and reliability have made them a popular replacement for the role once filled by the ancient (in computer terms) floppy disk.

Win XP

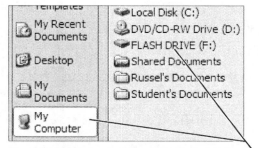

The Word 2007 Open dialog box displays a flash drive in the My Computer view in Windows XP.

Win Vista

The Word 2007 Open dialog box displays a flash drive in the Computer view in Windows Vista.

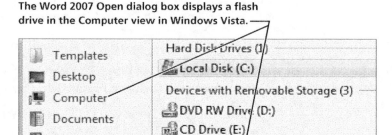

USB Flash Drive Letter

When you plug in a USB flash drive to a Windows computer, Windows automatically assigns it the next available drive letter. Windows uses drive letters to identify each drive connected to the computer. For example, the primary part of the hard drive is always identified as the C drive. A CD/DVD drive is typically the D or E drive. Windows assigns a drive letter to your flash drive when you plug it in. The drive may receive a different drive letter on each computer you use it with.

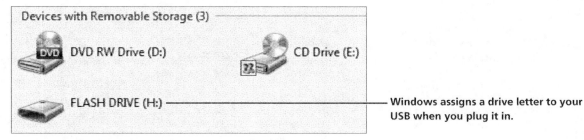

Windows assigns a drive letter to your USB when you plug it in.

Windows lists a USB flash drive as a removable storage device.

TIP! *Your USB flash drive may receive a different drive letter on different computers. This does not affect any files stored on the drive.*

Hands-On A.1 Download and Unzip the Exercise Files—USB Flash Drive

Follow these steps to download a copy of the student files necessary for this book.

1. Launch Internet Explorer.

2. Enter **labpub.com/learn/pub07** in the browser's address bar and tap ⌈Enter⌉.

3. Click the Student Exercise Files link below the Downloads heading.
   A prompt to run or save the student exercise files appears.

4. Click the Save button.
   Internet Explorer asks where you wish to save the downloaded file.

5. Carefully plug your USB flash drive into a USB port on the computer.

6. Click the Close ⌈×⌉ (Win XP) / 🞩 (Win Vista) button if a window appears asking what you want to do with the plugged-in flash drive.

7. Follow these steps for your version of Windows to choose the flash drive as the save destination:

Win XP

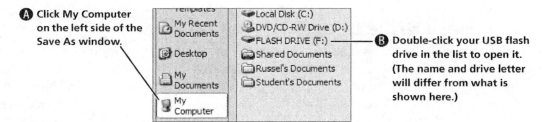

Ⓐ Click My Computer on the left side of the Save As window.

Ⓑ Double-click your USB flash drive in the list to open it. (The name and drive letter will differ from what is shown here.)

Win Vista

Ⓐ Click the Browse Folders button on the lower-left side of the dialog box if it does not display the computer option like the figure for steps B and C.

Browse Folders

Ⓑ Click Computer on the left side of the Save As window.

Ⓒ If necessary, scroll down the drive list until the flash drive is visible, and then double-click your USB flash drive in the list to open it. (The name and drive letter will differ from what is shown here.)

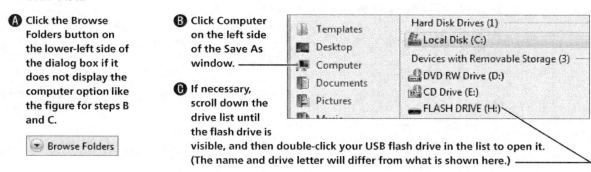

Now that you've shown Windows where to save the file, you are ready to download it.

The rest of the instructions for this exercise apply to both Win XP and Vista.

8. Click the Save button.

After a pause, the exercise file will begin downloading to your computer. Continue with the next step after the download is complete.

!NOTE! *If you are downloading the files via a dial-up modem connection, it will take several minutes or more for the download to be completed.*

Unzip the Files

9. Click the Open Folder button on the Download Complete dialog box.

If the Download Complete dialog box closes after the download is completed, you will need to open a folder window to the USB flash drive you used in step 7:

- **Win XP**: Choose Start→My Computer. Double-click to open your USB flash drive.
- **Win Vista**: Choose Start→Computer. Double-click to open your USB flash drive.

10. Double-click the pub07_student_files icon, as shown at right. *Windows may ask if you wish to run the software. This confirmation helps protect your computer from viruses. In this case, you know the file is safe.*

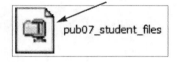

11. Choose Run if Windows asks you if you are sure you want to run this software, otherwise continue with step 14.

A prompt appears, telling you where the student exercise files will be unzipped.

12. Click the Unzip button.

The self-extracting archive unzips all of the student exercise files for this book into the new folder. This should take less than one minute to complete.

13. Click OK to acknowledge the successful unzip process.

14. Click the Close button to close the self-extractor window.

All of the files necessary to use this book are now unzipped to your file storage location. They are located in a new folder named Publisher 2007.

Since the zip file is no longer needed, you will delete it in the next step. (You can always download it again if you need fresh copies of the exercise files in the future.)

15. (Optional) Make sure that the pub07_student_files zip file is chosen, and then tap the Delete key on the keyboard. Click OK if you are asked to confirm the deletion.

Renaming Your Flash Drive

It may be easier to identify your flash drive on various computer systems if you give it a custom name. For example, you can use your first name, or a generic name such as Flash Drive or Pen Drive. The next exercise shows how you can rename your flash drive on most computer systems.

 NOTE! *Some Windows systems may not give you renaming privileges for drives. This depends on privileges associated with your login name.*

Hands-On A.2　Rename Your USB Flash Drive

You may find it convenient to rename your USB flash drive to make it easier to recognize when you save or open files.

 TIP! *Some Windows systems may not give you renaming privileges for drives.*

1. Plug in the USB flash drive to an available USB port.

2. Click the Close ⌧ / ⌧ button if a window appears asking what you want to do with the plugged-in flash drive.

3. Follow the step for your version of Windows:
   - **Win XP**: Choose Start→My Computer.
   - **Win Vista**: Choose Start→Computer.

4. Right-click your USB flash drive and choose Rename from the context menu.

 NOTE! *In the next step, Windows may display a prompt indicating that you cannot rename this flash drive. You have not done anything wrong! You can use the drive with its current name. You may also want to try renaming it later using a different login.*

   If you have renaming rights, Windows highlights the existing name.

5. Type **Flash Drive** (or any other custom name you wish to use) as the new drive name and tap ⌷Enter⌷, or click OK if you receive a prompt that you do not have sufficient rights to perform this operation.
   If you were unable to rename the flash drive, don't worry. Renaming the flash drive is a convenience for recognition and has no other effect.

Using the Documents Folder

Many computer labs do not allow students to use this folder.

Windows creates a unique Documents folder for each login ID. This folder resides on the main system drive (usually the C drive). The Office 2007 application programs provide a Documents navigation link in their Open and Save As dialog boxes for quick navigation to this folder.

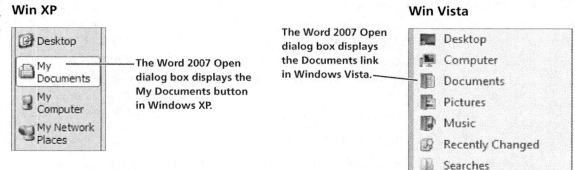

Win XP

The Word 2007 Open dialog box displays the My Documents button in Windows XP.

Win Vista

The Word 2007 Open dialog box displays the Documents link in Windows Vista.

Hands-On A.3   Download and Unzip the Exercise Files— Documents Folder

Follow these steps to download a copy of the student files necessary for this book.

1. Launch Internet Explorer.

2. Enter **labpub.com/learn/pub07** in the browser's address bar and tap Enter.

3. Click the Student Exercise Files link below the Downloads heading.
   A prompt to run or save the student exercise files appears.

4. Click the Save button.

5. Follow the steps for your version of Windows:
   - **Win XP:** Choose My Documents on the left side of the Save As window.
   - **Win Vista:** If necessary, click the Browse Folders button, and then choose Documents on the left side of the Save As window.

   Now that you've shown Windows where to save the file, you are ready to download it.

6. Click the Save button.

   After a pause, the exercise file will begin downloading to your computer. Continue with the next step after the download is complete.

!NOTE! *If you are downloading the files via a dial-up modem connection, it will take several minutes or more for the download to be completed.*

7. Click the Open Folder button on the Download Complete dialog box.

   If the Download Complete dialog box closes after the download is completed, follow the step for your version of Windows to open a folder window to the Documents folder you used in step 5.

   ■ **Win XP**: Choose Start→My Documents.
   ■ **Win Vista**: Choose Start→Documents.

8. Double-click the pub07_student_files icon, as shown at right. *Windows may ask if you wish to run the software. This confirmation helps protect your computer from viruses. In this case, you know the file is safe.*

9. Choose Run if Windows asks you if you are sure you want to run this software, otherwise continue with step 10.

   A prompt appears, telling you where the student exercise files will be unzipped.

10. Click the Unzip button.

    The self-extracting archive unzips all of the student exercise files for this book into the new folder. This should take less than one minute to complete.

11. Click OK to acknowledge the successful unzip process.

12. Click the Close button to close the self-extractor window.

    All of the files necessary to use this book are now unzipped to your file storage location. They are located in a new folder named Publisher 2007.

    Since the zip file is no longer needed, you will delete it in the next step. (You can always download it again if you need fresh copies of the exercise files in the future.)

13. (Optional) Make sure that the pub07_student_files zip file is chosen, and then tap the [Delete] key on the keyboard. Click OK if you are asked to confirm the deletion.

Using a Network Folder

NOTE!

Your instructor or a computer lab assistant can tell you how to locate a network drive if this is where you are to store your files.

You may use a system connected to a network. There may be a folder on a network server computer in another location that is dedicated to storing your work. Usually, you will find this folder within the (Win XP) *My Network Places* or (Win Vista) *Network* folder of your computer. The Office 2007 application programs provide a Network link in their Open and Save As dialog boxes for quick navigation to this folder. You may have to navigate deeper into the folder to locate your personal network drive folder.

Win XP

In Windows XP, the Word 2007 Open dialog box displays the My Network Places button.

Win Vista

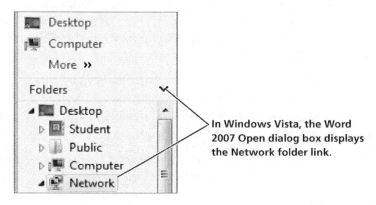

In Windows Vista, the Word 2007 Open dialog box displays the Network folder link.

Hands-On A.4 Download and Unzip the Exercise Files—Network Drive Folder

Follow these steps to download a copy of the student files necessary for this book.

1. Launch Internet Explorer.

2. Enter **labpub.com/learn/pub07** in the browser's address bar and tap [Enter].

3. Click the Student Exercise Files link below the Downloads heading.
   A prompt to run or save the student exercise files appears.

4. Click the Save button.

5. Follow the steps for your version of Windows:

   ■ **Win XP:** Choose My Network Places on the left side of the Save As window, and then navigate to your network folder.

   ■ **Win Vista**: Click the menu button as shown at right, and then choose Network. Navigate to your network folder.

   Now that you've shown Windows where to save the file, you are ready to download it.

6. Click the Save button.
The download begins. Continue with the next step after it is complete.

!NOTE! *Downloading the files via a dial-up modem connection will take several minutes.*

7. Click the Open Folder button on the Download Complete dialog box.

If the Download Complete dialog box closes after the download is completed, you will need to open a folder window to the file storage location you used in step 5.

8. Double-click the pub07_student_files icon, as shown at right. *Windows may ask if you wish to run the software. This confirmation helps protect your computer from viruses. In this case, you know the file is safe.*

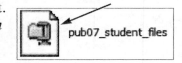

9. Choose Run if Windows asks you if you are sure you want to run this software, otherwise continue with step 10.
A prompt appears, telling you where the student exercise files will be unzipped.

10. Click the Unzip button.
The self-extracting archive unzips all of the student exercise files for this book into the new folder. This should take less than one minute to complete.

11. Click OK to acknowledge the successful unzip process.

12. Click the Close button to close the self-extractor window.
All of the files necessary to use this book are now unzipped to your file storage location. They are located in a new folder named Publisher 2007.

Since the zip file is no longer needed, you will delete it in the next step. (You can always download it again if you need fresh copies of the exercise files in the future.)

13. (Optional) Make sure that the pub07_student_files zip file is chosen, and then tap the Delete key on the keyboard. Click OK if you are asked to confirm the deletion.

Using a Floppy Disk with This Book

It is not recommended that students use floppy disks with this textbook. There are two primary reasons for this:

■ Due to the increasing sophistication of files you can create with programs in the Microsoft Office 2007 Suite, it is no longer practical to store all of the exercise files for this book on a floppy disk.

■ Many computers no longer feature a floppy drive, and this trend should continue as USB flash drives take over the portable file storage role once filled by floppies.

This section describes how to work around the space limitations of floppy disks for most of the lessons in this book.

Storage Limitations of Floppy Disks

As you work through the exercises in this book, you will create numerous new files that must be saved. A floppy disk will not have enough storage capacity to hold all files created during the course. Thus, you must store your exercise files on a hard drive, and then copy and paste (copy) individual lesson folders between this hard drive and the floppy disk. Use the following instructions to work with this book using a floppy disk.

Hands-On A.5   Using a Floppy Disk with This Book

If you have no choice to use the recommended USB flash drive or other file storage location with this book, use the following procedure to work with the lessons using a floppy disk.

1. Following the instructions in Hands-On A.3, download and unzip the student exercise files for this book to a folder on a computer hard drive or other storage location.

2. Open a folder window to the location where you unzipped the files.

3. Select the folder for the next lesson you will study, and then give the Copy command.

4. Open a window to your floppy disk, and then use the Paste command to paste (move) the folder and its files to the floppy disk.

5. Study the lesson, choosing the $3\frac{1}{2}$ Floppy (A) drive then the lesson folder to open and save files as directed in the exercises.

6. After you complete the lesson, *cut* and paste (do not copy and paste) the lesson folder from the floppy disk back to the same location from which you copied it originally.

   Choose Yes to All if Windows asks if you wish to replace any files with the same name in the destination folder.

7. Repeat steps 2–6 for each lesson.

   If Windows tells you the floppy disk is full, check to make sure that you moved (cut and pasted) the folder in step 6. (The previous folder should no longer be on the floppy disk.)

Glossary

Align To arrange two or more items along an edge

Aspect Ratio Ratio of width to height; if you resize one dimension more than another, the picture can become distorted

Attention-getter Predesigned graphic accent that includes a few words of art

AutoCorrect Program feature that automatically corrects misspellings and grammar errors as you type

Margins White space between the edge of design element and the edge of a page

AutoFit Feature that automatically resizes type and manipulates text to fit within a text box

Booklet Multipage publication that is folded or bound

Border Line around the outside of an object—such as a text box, a picture or, a drawing—that is visible when the publication is printed

BorderArt Small graphic that is repeated around the edge of an object, forming a border

Bring to Front Command that places the currently selected object in front or on top of other objects

Bullet Character that appears to the left of the first line of a paragraph to call attention to that paragraph's beginning point

Bulleted List Used to illustrate items that can occur in any order or that are of equal importance

Business Forms Specialized forms such as invoices, inventory lists, order forms, purchase orders, expense reports, time cards, and so on

Business Information Set Stored information about your business and how to contact you

Calendar Specialized table that Publisher can format with any month and year

Caption Text placed below a graphic that describes the image

Catalog Graphic representation that presents a list or display of items

Cell Intersection of a row and column in a table

Clipboard Temporary holding area used by Windows programs to move or copy text

Color Schemes Coordinated sets of matched and complementary colors that may be applied to a publication

Crop To conceal portions of an image

Data Source Files Files containing names, addresses, and other information used in a mail merge

Design Layout and choice of colors, fonts, and artwork that enhance a publication

Design Checker Feature that proofreads your layout to help you find layout problems that might prevent the publication from looking good in print

Design Gallery Objects Objects created by the Design Gallery that contain text or graphic images that can be edited for size, shape, and content

Design Sets Groups of matching elements in the Design Gallery that contain common themes, colors, or objects

Desktop Publishing Program Program that allows you to combine text and graphics as well as tables and charts from other programs to produce typeset-quality documents that can be printed commercially or on a desktop printer

Drag and Drop Moving or copying technique in which an object such as a text box or picture is dragged to a new location

Drawing Tools Toolbox buttons that let you create geometric designs

Drop Cap Ornamental capital letter at the beginning of a paragraph that is much larger than surrounding letters; drops into the lines beneath it or rests on the baseline

Embedded Graphic Graphic stored inside the Publisher file rather than as a separate image

Field Type of information from the data source in a mail merge, such as Last Name

Field Code Code that indicates the place in a publication where the Mail and Catalog Merge feature should insert a field from a data source record

Fill To add a color, pattern, or texture to a design element

Fill Color Hue added to shade a design element

Filtered HTML File HTML file created in Microsoft Office (Publisher) that contains only true HTML codes with no codes for formatting in its original application

Font Typeface; a style of lettering

Fixed Color Color not included in a template's color scheme; does not change when the color scheme changes

Font Schemes Coordinated sets of matched and complementary fonts that can be applied to a publication

Form Control Individual field on a form such as a text box, option button, or checkbox

Formatting Toolbar Buttons on a toolbar that change the appearance of objects with a publication

GIF Graphics Interchange Format; commonly used file format for graphics used in web pages because of its small size

Graphic Image Piece of artwork in electronic form

Group To link multiple objects together so they can be selected, moved, and/or resized as a single entity

Grouping To turn several objects into one, which allows an easy way to move multiple items

Handles Small hollow circles displayed around the perimeter of a selected object, such as a text box or a picture

Home Page First page in a web site

Horizontal Ruler Measuring guide that appears above the publication window

Hot Spot One of multiple hyperlinks on a single graphic, such as multiple city hot spots on a map of a state

Measuring guide that appears above the publication window HTML HyperText Markup Language; text encoding used to create web pages

Hyperlink Text or a graphic object that does something when clicked, such as opening a web page or starting a new e-mail message

JPEG Popular file format for storing photos

Label Sheet Page of peel-off labels that can be printed on a desktop printer

Logo Distinctive symbol, shape, or color that visibly identifies a company or product

Mail Merge Process of combining a list of names and addresses with a publication such as a postcard or a certificate containing placeholder fields so a personalized copy of that publication is created for each name

Mailing and Catalog Merge Task Pane Publisher task pane feature that steps you through the merging process and allows you to customize the data source and publication

Margins White space between the edge of design element and the edge of a page

Margin Guides Lines that repeat on each page separating the margins from the other design elements

Masthead Box or section printed in each issue of a newsletter publication that lists information such as the name, publisher, location, volume, and date

Menu Bar   Contains menus from which you choose Publisher commands

Microsoft Office Online   Microsoft web site that continually offers new download resources for creating publications

Navigation Bar   Collection of hyperlinks to other related pages in the same web site; typically consistent across all pages in the web site

Nudge   To move a selected object a certain precise distance by pressing an arrow key

Object   Generic term for any text box, picture, drawing, or other piece of data in a publication that can be resized, moved, joined, or layered

Object Shadow   Gives an object the illusion of depth by adding a shadow behind it

Objects Toolbar   Contains buttons used to create and enhance publication objects

Orientation   Direction in which paper is printed

Page Navigation Icons   Page icons that display for each page in a publication; located at the bottom of the workspace

Picture   Generic term for artwork, including photographs, line drawings, cartoons, and other graphic creations

Point Size   Font-size measurement; one point is $\frac{1}{72}$ of an inch

Print   Create output from a publication into paper form

Print Preview   Feature that lets you see exactly how the publication will look when printed

Publication   Document created in Publisher

Publication Gallery   Collection of often-used publication types that help you visualize and create designs

Publisher Address List   Simple database stored in a Publisher format; contains contact information about people you want to correspond with

Pull Quote   Short statement taken from a story and set aside from the body of text

Range   Rectangular block of cells selected as a group

Record   Group of related fields in the data source for a single person, place, or thing

Redo   To reverse an Undo action

Rulers   Horizontal and vertical measurement guides located beneath the toolbars and to the left of the workspace

Rotate   To change the position of an object in degrees from a horizontal plane

Rotation   An object's position measured in degrees from horizontal plane

Scheme Color   Color placeholder defined by the chosen color scheme for the publication; changes if you change the color scheme

Scratch   Area surrounding the publication page that can be used to store design elements

Select   To highlight something (usually text or an object border) so that whatever command you issue applies to it

Sidebar   Small piece of text set off with a box or graphic and placed beside an article

Spelling Checker   Used to check a story or publication for spelling errors

Story   Text in a text box plus any text boxes linked to it; a single story can span several text boxes on several pages, as in a newspaper or magazine

Status Bar   Located at the bottom of the Publisher window; provides information relevant to the current task

Table   Information arranged in a grid of rows and columns

Task Pane   Area of the Publisher window used to organize design templates, color schemes, font schemes, and other layout tools in a visual gallery that appears alongside the publication

Template   Specially formatted publication with placeholder text

Text Box   Object in which text is typed

Text Overflow Text that does not fit within a single text box

Text Wrapping Automatic placement of text around design elements

Toolbars Contains buttons for frequently used Publisher commands; organized by subject, such as formatting or objects

Two-page Spread View that enables you to see two pages at once

Undo To reverse an action or command

Ungroup To reverse a group operation so that objects that were formerly grouped are once again separate

URL Uniform Resource Location; the full address of a web site, such as http://www.microsoft.com

Vertical Ruler Measuring guide that displays to the left of the page

Web Browser Program designed to display web pages, such as Internet Explorer

Web Form Form that a web site visitor can fill in and submit to the web site owner

Web Page Document designed to be viewed in a web browser

Web Server Computer that stores your web site and provides it on the Internet

Web Site Related collection of web pages with hyperlinks between them

White Space Blank space in a publication

WMF Windows Metafile; format in which Publisher provides its clip art

Workspace Area where a new or existing publication appears and its surrounding scratch area

Wrapping Process of reshaping text so that it fits in the shape of a text box or image

WordArt Object containing curved or wavy text

Zoom To make a page scale larger or smaller so that you can move in or away from page objects

Index